The Writer's Resource

The Writer's Resource

The Watson-Guptill Guide to

- Workshops
- Conferences
- Artists' Colonies
- Academic Programs

David Emblidge and Barbara Zheutlin

Getting Your Act Together™

Produced for Watson-Guptill Publications by
David Emblidge — Book Producer

Watson-Guptill Publications
New York

Getting Your Act Together™

Series Concept: David Emblidge

Series Editor: David Emblidge

Researchers: Keren Weiner, Barbara Zheutlin

Database design: Chris Blair, Stuart Cohen, David Emblidge

Copy Editor: Katherine Ness

Book design & icons: Bill Cooke

Page makeup: Robin O'Herin

Bill Cooke + Company

Illustrations: Roy Germon

Photographs: See credits with each image.

Indexer: Letitia Mutter

The text of this book was created in Microsoft Word and Q&A for Windows, and pages were subsequently designed in Quark XPress. Program descriptions were imported from the database using the X-Data extension. Display typefaces used include Frutiger and Officina Sans. Veljovic is used for the main text.

Library of Congress Catalog Card Number: 97-60099

©1997 David Emblidge, Book Producer
10 9 8 7 6 5 4 3 2 1
Printed in the United States

Getting Your Act Together™ is a registered trademark
of David Emblidge — Book Producer.

Contents

Foreword

WHETHER YOU SEE YOUR LOVE of writing as a potential source of income or simply as a means of reflecting the world around you, writing is a passion that can enrich and reward you for the rest of your life. Your goal may be to capture a poem on paper or to write a children's story, a full length novel, or a "how-to" in your field of expertise. You may want to record your family history or to compile a volume of inspirational thoughts and observations. Regardless of the scope of your ambition, the capacity for expressing your ideas in a well-structured, engaging manner will take time to perfect. Clear, graceful writing is not as simple as it first appears, and the hard work required is sometimes daunting at the outset. Yet where can you turn for the necessary guidance and feedback?

In the days of the craft guilds, an artist would be apprenticed to a master, acquiring skills and techniques only after years of rigorous on-site training. Today, a writer interested in comparable tutelage has an incredible array of writing programs to choose from. I began my own lengthy apprenticeship as a young pup of twenty when I attended a writers' workshop in Yellow Springs, Ohio — a conference I returned to as a teacher some thirty years later.

A writer is always learning, and a *good* writer is always seeking ways to extend the range of his or her talent. *The Writer's Resource* offers comprehensive information about the variety of writing programs available. *The Writer's Resource* not only offers an overview of writers' conferences — advising you whom to contact and what to expect — but also includes up-to-date fax numbers and e-mail addresses to maximize your chances of finding an affordable workshop in a location that's close enough to serve your purposes.

Sue Grafton
past president, Mystery Writers of America,
and author of the Kinsey Millhone alphabet mysteries

Introduction

WELCOME TO *The Writer's Resource,* a compendium of information and ideas for the writer—professional or amateur or anywhere in between. Whether you want to develop new skills, schmooze with editors and publishers, or network with fellow writers, in this book you will find scores of opportunities. Before you get down to particulars, cruise the aisles as though this were a department store, and have fun dreaming about programs you might someday attend and what the written results might be. We wish you all the best.

How to Use This Book

USE THIS BOOK as you would the counsel of a wise friend. Absorb the information that seems noteworthy to you; take heed of opinionated statements; consider the logic behind suggested strategies for getting into, and through, the kind of creative writing program you want. But remember that your own personal preferences for type of program, location, cost and schedule will be just as important or even more so than any information you may find in these pages. Creative writing, like all the arts, is intensely personal; so too are education and training in the craft of writing. What works well for Writer A will be a disaster for Writer B. Wallace Stevens gave us a poem called "Sixteen Ways of Looking at a Blackbird." This book should indicate that there are at least that many ways to further your development as a writer.

In Part One, "Living to Write, Writing to Live," we talk about the need to think of writing as a *vocation* before plunging into the struggle of making writing your *business.* There's a certain chemistry, perhaps alchemy, that needs to be achieved to make a go of it as a writer, whether you are financially self-sustaining or not. A mix of determination, confidence, vulnerability, openness and practical savvy all must come into focus in you, the writer, whether you're producing a novel or a corporate report.

Part Two, "Creative Writing Programs in the U.S. Today," forms the bulk of the book. After listing associations and organizations you may want to join, we switch to a gazetteer format and move state by state through descriptions of Residential Programs (aka artists' colonies or retreats), Workshops and Conferences. At the end of each state we list a selection of Academic Programs in creative writing.

Part Three, "The Business of Writing," covers the numbers game from soup to nuts: financial aid, marketing your work, negotiating deals, and setting yourself up in the writing business.

Definitions

 Residential Program

A program devoted to housing writers and/or other artists for periods of a week, several months or even a year; and providing anything from total seclusion to scheduled daily confabs and critiques of residents' work, or at least a high degree of literary camaraderie. "Colony" and "retreat" are synonymous here.

 Workshop

You say potayto, I say potahto. What's a workshop to you may be a conference to me. The terms are used casually in the creative writing field, and we have done our best to balance two goals here. One, to honor the terminology used by the programs themselves; two, to distinguish workshops and conferences by a simple rule when conditions permit. To wit: A Workshop is generally a small group of writers, meeting once or regularly over a period of days, weeks or months, for the clear purpose of sharing and critiquing their own work. In a Workshop, actual writing often takes place, or assignments are made for the upcoming meeting. Here the writer-participants do most of the talking, although often there is a workshop leader or facilitator who is a more experienced and perhaps more widely published writer.

 Conference

A Conference is generally a larger gathering of writers (larger than a Workshop), meeting for a day, a weekend, or a week, perhaps annually or, for special topics, one time only. Within a Conference there may be smaller group sessions that operate like Workshops (hence the confusion of terminology). More typical, however, are plenary sessions in which experts hold forth on topics of practical usefulness (literary skill development, making a buck) or give readings from their own work. Some Conferences offer interaction between the experts and attendees; many do not. A few offer, and often charge extra for, manuscript reviews.

 Academic Program

If the program leads to a degree (MFA or MA) or a genuine academic certificate, it's listed as an Academic Program in this book. We do not cover PhD programs with creative writing components.

Yet even this simple definition fails to cover all cases. Many universities have extension programs (or continuing education programs) providing classes and special events that are sometimes called simply "courses" or, more confusingly, "workshops" or even "conferences." We have done our best to weed out these programs, transplanting them to our Workshops or Conferences categories per se. Some of these are genuinely excellent programs, and some are the best bargains in this book. Often such programs grant CEUs (Continuing Education Units) or another kind of academic credit.

We mean to cast no aspersions on any academic creative writing program when we say that many of them are nearly clones of many others, hard to distinguish without a level of detail (particularly a description of faculty) that is beyond the scope of this book. Of course there are vast differences in quality. Podunk Junior College for the Artistically Challenged is not the same as the Iowa Writers' Workshop.

We list Academic Programs for a given state at the end of that state's section in the gazetteer. And we provide in Part Two some advice about choosing and following the academic track as a writer. But unlike Residential Programs, Workshops and Conferences, Academic Programs are not described in detail.

How the Information Is Displayed

Think "Upstairs" and "Downstairs." Upstairs is the information block that looks like this example.

Downstairs you'll find one or more paragraphs of description.

In the Upstairs section, most items are self-explanatory, but a few categories bear explanation.

Icons:

 = Residential Program

 = Workshop

 = Conference

 = Academic Program

92nd St. Y

  For Fiction and nonfiction writers, poets Upper East Side, Manhattan — *1395 Lexington Ave., New York, NY 10128* **Voice:** 212-415-5760 **Contact:** Melissa Hammerle, Karl Kirchway, Co-Dirs. **Founded:** 1939 **Open:** Fall and spring **Admission:** Sample manuscripts, permission of the instructor required; request catalogue **Deadlines:** Fall, mid-Sept.; Spring, late Jan. **Cost:** Varies from $60 to $220 for seminars and workshops **Financial Aid:** Scholarship **Size-Class:** Under 25 **Handicapped Access**

Addresses: The on-site mailing address where, usually, the program takes place. If a second address is given, typically it's for the off-season or for applications only. When mailing an application, make sure you put the program name first, because many are small projects under the umbrellas of large universities.

Country: Always the U.S. or its territories unless otherwise stated.

Contact person: The one to ask for if you want well-informed, up-to-date information. The bigger the program, the harder it will be for would-be applicants to get through to the director, but go ahead and ask. Many programs have coordinators, secretaries or administrative assistants who are helpful and informative.

Open: Most program dates shift a bit annually. We give the likely time period.

Admission: Almost all programs require an application form, but after that the road divides into many paths, with some asking for everything just short of an FBI clearance. Rule of thumb: programs requiring manuscript submission, statement of purpose, resume, and references are by far the more selective and more rigorous of the lot. The converse is generally true, too.

Concerning application fees: Sometimes they're broken out, sometimes they're folded into general tuition. If the fee seems egregious relative to overall quality, then *caveat emptor.* Most programs require a modest fee with the application, to be applied to the tuition if you attend.

Deadlines: Can't live with 'em, can't live without 'em. Some programs are sticklers for deadlines, like certain editors we know; others are open until the room fills (presumably to permit good last-minute applicants to sneak through the door). The best advice is to apply early, increasing your chances of connecting with specific teachers you may want. Financial aid applicants often must apply earlier than others. Read the fine print. Concerning deadlines, we tell you what the programs told us. In the absence of information here, be sure to inquire.

Cost: We have done our best to untangle a confusing web here. We give program fee (or tuition), followed by room and board, then materials fee if applicable. Sometimes there are discounts for early registration. Often there are discounts for members of relevant professional organizations. If attendees arrange their own housing, we say nothing here about housing cost (but check for advice in the Description). Some programs have cost schedules too complicated to display here. Call for the details.

Financial Aid: Potayto and potahto, again. A "Scholarship" in one program is a "Fellowship" in another. Often a "Work/Study" grant is linked to a "scholarship." The bigger and older programs may have various endowed scholarships, not necessarily mentioned in the program's general brochure. Be sure to request a financial aid application at the outset if you're in need (as noted above, watch out for early deadlines, different from those for general applications). Often a financial aid application requires additional supporting documents (reference letters, manuscript). Because of the welter of confusing data, we do not list the amount of financial aid available in specific programs.

Size — Attendees and Size — Class: Some programs give the total number of attendees; some give typical "class" or workshop size. We report what seems most representative.

Handicapped Access: Programs at institutions receiving federal tax dollars are likely to have handicapped-accessible facilities, but still the specific rooms used for the writing program may be difficult to reach. We report "Handicapped Accessible" only when the program itself makes this claim. Many programs that do not claim to be handicapped accessible actually are because the meetings take place in convenient hotels or on campuses with appropriate facilities. We suggest you ask the contact person, being sure to review access to classrooms, dining facilities, sleeping quarters, etc., especially if the program takes place in a rustic setting.

How the Information Was Gathered

It would have been fun to visit every program, but that would have taken a lifetime, and then you would not have this book in your hand. We called program directors and chatted with them about the history and direction of their programs; we read brochures, catalogues and application forms; we spoke to participants in some programs; we contacted arts administrators in some state agencies and private foundations. And we kept our ear to the ground. In the world of creative writing workshops, conferences and residencies, rumor is rampant, and while sometimes a hint worth following emerges, more often it's about as reliable as the weather in New England (where Mark Twain said, if you don't like it, wait five minutes).

The upshot is that this book makes a serious effort to be objective and accurate about facts and information while also indulging itself, and you, in opinionated descriptions of the programs.

Bear in mind our research time frame: We started research in '95, wrote and edited in '96, and published in spring '97. The world of non-profit arts programs is always in flux, and costs (almost) never go down. Make your own inquiry for current information. We plan to update this book every two years.

How You Can Participate

READERS ARE INVITED to respond. Please correct our mistakes, offer your perspectives, and let us know what else you'd like to see in the next edition. Please tell us where you bought or borrowed this book.

Use the postcard that was bound into this book or write to: Editors, Getting Your Act Together™, C/o Watson-Guptill Publications, 1515 Broadway, New York, NY 10036.

Acknowledgments

INFORMATION AND HELP on this project came from all quarters. We especially want to thank the many program directors and administrative assistants who sent us their program information and answered our detailed questions. As Series Editor I am grateful to Candace Raney and Glenn Heffernan at Watson-Guptill for having recognized the potential of the Getting Your Act Together™ Series, and to editors Bob Nirkind and Liz Harvey for having shepherded this book toward publication. For dogged research with good humor, I salute Keren Weiner and Barbara Zheutlin. Barbara is also co-author of this book, having written well and with great care. For patient and imaginative database design, thanks to Chris Blair and Stuart Cohen (Stuart wrote *The Photographer's Resource* in this series). Kathie Ness provided sensible copy editing with a manuscript in a thousand pieces. Bill Cooke's patient work and clean book design are a model for those who, against such odds, might otherwise surrender to hysteria. The same kudos go to Robin O'Herin for her work on page makeup. Artist Roy Germon provided a lively variety of evocative images, and indexer Letitia Mutter gets the award for precision and persistence.

David Emblidge
January 1997

PART ONE

Living to Write,
Writing to Live

On Becoming a Writer

F OR MANY WRITERS, there was a moment in childhood when they recognized for the first time that they had a story to tell or a feeling to
share, and someone really wanted to listen. The seeds of a great
oak had been sown.

For some, the beginning is the first blank book or diary received as a
gift, its stark white pages calling out for words to make them come alive.
As the pages fill, perhaps with private thoughts or a record of events at
summer camp, the mundane and ephemeral are transformed, magically,
merely by being written down, into the significant and permanent.

From that moment onward, a budding writer's eyes are open for the
telling detail, the shade of meaning, the nuance in speech or gesture
that can reveal a character, or as Emily Dickinson put it, "a certain slant
of light" that is the essence of a moment in a specific place.

Once the floodgates of self-expression are opened, there's usually no
shutting them. From that time on, a writer-to-be seeks opportunities
and outlets, or at least stores the accumulating words in diaries, in manuscript notebooks or, these days, in a web of computer files for projects
that may or may not see the light of day.

This book is meant for writers who take themselves seriously, who
want to grow and expand, to make contact with others practicing the
same craft, to build a network of professional contacts who can provide
help along the often meandering road toward publication. And it's meant
for those who take delight in words well spoken, lyrics gracefully
rhymed, tales well plotted and told, reportage and other nonfiction work
tailored appropriately for the subject and polished to a shine.

In an age heavily dominated by images from the electronic media,
from television and the film world, one might naturally ask, Is writing a
dead horse, no longer worth even a modest bet? On the contrary, for
book sales keep rising, though there is a great deal of schlock in the
market. And certainly not so according to the evidence in this very
book, where the liveliness of the creative writing scene in the U.S. is
abundantly clear. Despite the laments about the death of literary culture
one sees on op-ed pages or hears from the neo-conservative movement,
which seems to fear pop culture more than it understands its restless
origins, there are arguably more people in the U.S. today in creative
writing programs, and practicing the craft of writing at some level of
seriousness or professionalism, than ever before. Are we who love the
written word up against the wall, defending ourselves from the
onslaughts of "a confederacy of dunces"? Some days it seems to be so.
But thumb through this book, and your courage and confidence in the
vitality of American literary culture will revive.

What brings people to the craft and the business of writing? Some are
attracted to what they perceive to be the writer's life. Having arrived at
this fork in the road, you need to ask some serious questions.

If you have the skills of a competent writer, what do you want to do
with them? How big a part of your life do you want writing to be? What

do you want to accomplish with your words, and for whose benefit? Perhaps you want your words to tell personal stories or to express your deepest emotions. You want your writing to be all about you. Or you might prefer to focus your attention on recording facts, illustrating themes and ideas. You want to be the documentarian.

The key question is: What will satisfy you? Will you be content just writing poems to be saved for a rainy day, stored in a desk drawer with a ribbon around them? Or do you want to make a living from your craft, as a technical writer, an historian, a children's book author? There's a world of difference.

If the professional track is for you, you will need a lot more than just the hunger to write. You need to know how writers work and what it is like to be a professional, facing deadlines, adapting to styles you may or may not fully endorse, negotiating for (and chasing after) money. It's not at all just a matter of sipping sherry with literary friends and discussing the latest books of your favorite authors. Indeed, it's more a matter of brewing that extra cup of coffee and staying up late to push yourself to produce, produce, produce. A decision of this importance—turning professional—requires the very best information you can get and a sensitive ear to the murmurings of your heart.

The best way to find out what writers do and how they live is to talk to experienced pros about all aspects of their work. Talk to people at different levels in their careers and in different specialties to get the most complete view. Ask all the questions you can think of. At the very least, you should know what options you face in stepping up to the ranks of the professional and be able to imagine yourself living and working that way.

A Career in Writing

Choosing a career in writing is a bold step. As a profession, writing is alluring but also fraught with perils. It can yield great personal and professional rewards, but the demands are high. For every glamorous, expenses-paid assignment, there are a dozen cranky clients, research that leads to a dead end, and technical problems with computers and editing. Along with every perfectly composed, beautifully phrased line or paragraph come ten or a hundred that are not quite right or are just plain awful.

What follows here is a partial list of the avenues a writer might choose, and a brief description of what each type of writing entails.

To locate publishers of certain types of books or magazines, consult the following standard reference books or ask a reference librarian for other similar tools.

Literary Marketplace, often called "LMP," for book publishers.

Writer's Market, for book and magazine publishers.

Magazines for Libraries, for consumer magazines and some professional journals.

International Directory of Little Magazines and Small Presses, for small presses producing books and literary magazines.

Academic Books, Textbooks

You might have hated them in school, but you can learn to love them now: textbooks can be a gold mine for a writer. Competition for these jobs is tough, usually requiring specialized, relevant academic training (for instance, a natural science degree for biology text authors). An academic or textbook publisher (or department of a larger general house) hires writers in this category more often on its own initiative than in response to proposals from the writers themselves. With multiculturalism sweeping the nation's school curriculum reform efforts, many humanities and social science textbooks are undergoing massive revisions. Bilingual writers, especially those who know Spanish and who have a broad liberal arts background, can find challenging work here. Getting the assignments is the trick, and you'll often find that doing piece work as a junior staffer on a big project is the way to get your foot in the door.

Children's and Young Adult Books

Nine writers out of ten believe with a passion, at some point in their careers, that they have a children's or young adult (YA) book in them. Almost all of them are wrong. Editors' desks at children's and YA book publishers are swamped with unsolicited proposals. Only a tiny fraction ever make it into print. Of course this is true in other genres, too.

These sobering facts shouldn't discourage you if you have that passion about a children's or YA book and if you try out your material not just on friends but on (a) disinterested, well-read kids and (b) disinterested contacts in the book business (booksellers, manuscript reviewers, book reviewers). Remember that for children's books, the illustrations are key. It's better to submit none than something that falls short of the best. Study the publisher's other recent books to see what the editors like. In this intensely competitive market, workshops and conferences for aspiring children's and YA book writers can be especially valuable, particularly for mingling with open-minded editors.

Corporate and Industrial

It's a big world out there, and words are important everywhere, not just in traditional literary circles. Technical writing demands clear expression, immersion in the technical field itself, and a liking for the corporate culture, where physical products and technical services are king and queen. This is as true for computer books for laypeople as it is for instructions for astronauts about setting up a space telescope.

There's more. Corporate reports, newsletters and, these days, Web sites all demand both colorful expression and the ability to think as the corporation itself does, to speak in the company's collective voice. The same is true with writing for marketing and advertising, which is harder than it looks. The ability to be persuasive, truthful and eye-catching all at once takes some learning. Here, though courses are available, nothing beats an apprenticeship under a real master.

Where are the jobs in corporate and industrial writing? Think "marketing" and "corporate communications." Usually the writers can be found in, or at least attached to, these departments.

Drama

Many successful playwrights have passed through drama school at some stage of their careers, and most have spent some years down in the trenches, usually in New York or Los Angeles or another big town, scrabbling for the chance to have their work produced. The sad joke is that 90 percent of the waiters and waitresses in New York are out-of-work actors and 50 percent of the cab drivers are playwrights (many with advanced degrees) who would love to put those actors to work ... on stage. If this is your intended métier, check your personality profile for a high perseverance rating.

You can also go the television drama route, and this can be enormously rewarding if you win a spot as the sole or a collaborative writer on a TV series. In this area not only are the dramatist's writing skills important, but the schmooze factor is critical. It's almost certain that to be read by the producers at the networks or the cable companies, you'll need an introduction from someone who knows so-and-so. One tip, perhaps obvious: Any job in the industry is better than any job outside the industry if a TV writer is what you want to be.

Playwrights are almost always on their own; rarely is a play commissioned. That's why working in or near an academic institution is so appealing to playwrights. It provides a venue. Otherwise, the writer must rely on a network of theater friends to find the producers or directors who want to read new scripts. Beginners should check out the local theaters (amateur and professional) to see whether there are open readings of new works. Getting published as a playwright almost always follows being (successfully) produced, and even a box office success does not automatically mean a publisher will print the play. The fact is, there is a very small market for plays as reading literature.

Essays

Do you fantasize about being born again as the next E. B. White, blessed beyond all counting with a regular column in *The New Yorker* and assigned to the best beat of all, human nature? We have yet to see this job posted in the want ads. If it's an essayist you want to be, abundant knowledge on a limited subject and a good fit in the right publishing niche are two essential elements for building your career. If you love birds, try writing for birding and natural history publications. If it's fashion, try for a gig with *Women's Wear Daily* or *GQ*. If it's politics, before you aim for the *New York Times* Op-Ed page, cut your teeth at the local rag.

Remember, too, that almost all the great essayists, from Addison and Steele to Joan Didion, have been diarists, too. Write for yourself as though you were writing for posterity.

Freelance

"Handyman: No Job Too Small." This is not a bad attitude to start out with, but anyone wanting to become a freelancer with a real income will soon find that the all-purpose, all-subjects approach does not work in today's highly specialized job market. Find your niche. If it's sports biographies, or knitting books, or auto repair manuals, then so be it.

Most successful freelancers have learned to be good businesspeople, too. Unsalaried, without benefits, improvising from month to month, it's a good way to end up on the unemployment lines, except that you can't qualify because no employer has paid in benefits for you. If the freedom of the freelance route appeals to you, don't be naive. Attend workshops about being in business for yourself, and if you're not a natural-born hustler, then concentrate on building a few close relationships with people who can send you paying work, and often. Read Part Three of this book, on the business of writing.

Journalism

Which kind of journalist would you be? Magazine, newspaper, television/radio, electronic media? As a rank beginner, try your hand at many things. Right after college, a writer we know worked for the Associated Press, covering everything from hog futures to airplane crashes to an interview with Nelson Rockefeller. A boozy-breathed editor hovered over his desk, sharpened blue pencil ready in the holster behind her ear, with a sharpened tongue, too. The deadline was always right now. He learned to write a clear sentence—with attribution, mind you—on the first pass. An invaluable experience.

Despite the plethora of magazines in the U.S. today, there are far fewer staff positions for journalists than you might think. And newspapers are a shrinking, endangered species. Freelancers, or stringers (the newspaper equivalent), provide most of the copy. Making a career of journalism depends less on a series of exciting one-time-only deals than on developing long-term relationships with a few editors who want you back again and again. Workshops and conferences that help you learn to write a good proposal are worth the tuition for sure.

Mystery

Like the romance novel (see below), the mystery has huge commercial potential. This widely known fact naturally attracts hordes of mystery writer wanna-be's, and so the marketplace is busy with competition. If you enjoy reading a good mystery for its technical features (plot and character development, etc.), and if you can network among the editors who acquire mystery material, then you have a chance here. Mystery writers' clubs and conferences provide valuable training in the skills part of the job. Writers with a legal background or a knowledge of forensics may have a leg up. If you invent the next Hercule Poirot, a publisher will love you. Paying your dues in this genre may require some writing done to suit a publisher's mystery formula.

Nonfiction

We think the term "nonfiction" is unfortunate to begin with. How good can it be when it's actually a label for something that it's not? But we're stuck with this catch-all category, in which you could become anything from Daniel Boorstin, the historian, to Click and Clack, the hosts of the country's most popular automobile repair show on radio (who also became authors). In this book there are many listings for workshops and conferences offering "nonfiction" training, and usually here this means serious literary writing or high-level journalism. Among today's nonfiction heavyweights, Annie Dillard and John McPhee are examples. Dillard, a natural history cum spirituality writer, stays generally within one niche. McPhee specializes in being a generalist. One never knows what he will cover next—basketball, cooking or geology? There are more nonfiction writers like Dillard than like McPhee, a lot more. If nonfiction is your path, check the index carefully for those programs meant to produce the next Click and Clack or McPhee.

Novels and Short Stories

It is still hard to grasp the fact that before the 18th century, these job categories for writers did not exist. A raconteur you could be, a troubadour, an epic or lyric poet, a dramatist, but not a novelist. We have the advent of cheaper printing and binding (the unholy paperback did it) and the skills of the Dickenses and James Fenimore Coopers and their lookalikes to thank for starting the booming industry that fiction writing is today.

There is a large market for the short story, but there are few ways to make much money in it. The truly savvy big (and small) publishing houses are always on the lookout for first novels from as yet undiscovered talent. Developing the skills and finishing several highly polished manuscripts are vital first steps. To these ends, you'll find a host of workshop and conference opportunities described in this book.

If you are seriously determined to go down this path, and if your work has advanced to the point where it's beginning to win some applause, then you may qualify for a residency at a writers' colony, or you might want to investigate an academic program.

Poetry

If, as Shelley said, "poets are the unacknowledged legislators of the world," then why is it so hard to make a living through poetry? Any Tom, Dick, Harry or Jane can run for political office, but try supporting a family on your sonnets. Of all the genres and possible writing career paths, this one is best left to those who choose it because they are simply compelled to by an inner expressive urge. A reliable day job or a trust fund in the background doesn't hurt.

As an avocation, pursuing poetry is another story, and a happier one. There is no reason for any writer to avoid poetry on this nonprofessional level, and indeed poetry workshops abound and are often well worth the time and money, whether they concern publication or not.

Some would argue, in fact, that the strict discipline of metrical rhymed poetry is healthy for writers in all other genres, too. Journalists and technical writers: sign up for the sonnet workshop today!

Romance

At the circus, the juggler tosses the rings into the air and you say to yourself, Hey, with a little practice I could do that! Then, at home, with a can or two of old tennis balls, you give it a try. The balls spill unforgivingly across the floor, and you don't even have a musical beat to follow or spotlights in your eyes or a crowd yearning for a perfectly astounding performance. Anybody can write a romance, you say?

Think again. Yes, it's a formulaic genre, but it takes a knack and a heck of a lot of practice. And then it takes effective networking to make the right editors notice that you're out there with skills and plot ideas. For all these reasons, the romance writers' associations and the various romance writing workshops and conferences are worthy investments for the aspiring writer in this genre. Only a few fiction publishers publish in the romance genre. Choose your (would-be) publishers carefully. The good news: If you hit it at all, you'll probably hit it big. Mass-market paperback sales in the romance genre can be huge. Hold out for royalties!

Scholarly

First become a scholar; then become a scholarly writer. If this seems obvious, you'd be surprised how many unsolicited, inappropriate submissions editors at scholarly presses (mostly university presses, though some are commercial) receive month after month. There are precious few self-styled uncredentialed scholars. Most writers in this genre have advanced degrees and hold or have held university teaching or think-tank research positions. The world of scholarly books is colorful and important, and on the reference book side of it there is good money to be made. Scholarly writing is usually a by-product of an academic career rather than of a writing career in itself.

Scholarly writers, do your readers a favor. Take a fiction or poetry or nonfiction writing workshop and deepen your skills in the areas of description, character portrayal and the like. It can only help.

Screenplays

A world apart, shot through with vast commercial potential and fraught with difficulties. We recommend another volume in the *Getting Your Act Together*™ series, *The Filmmaker's Resource* by Julie Mackaman, in which you'll find academic and other programs where screenwriting is the main course. These programs are excluded here.

Travel

Fantasy time. A plane ticket, a rented Range Rover, a string of reservations made for you in charming B&Bs and a fistful of travelers' checks. You're being paid to "do" the Scottish highlands for a travel publisher. Such publishers are likely to be book, magazine, newspaper or cable TV documentary people.

There are terrific gigs to be had, if you can persuade the right editors to assign you, and travel writing is indeed a great way to see the world. But don't be naive. It's hard to get the good jobs, you may put on weight from excesses of restaurant food, and you may spend a lot more time in airports than you bargained for. The skills you'll need can be polished through many of the specific travel writing workshops described in this book, and in many of the nonfiction workshops as well. We think the best travel writers are the most well-informed ones, which is to say they are intrepid interviewers and voracious readers. They can do as the Romans do when they're in Rome; they have a catholicity of taste (aquavit in Finland, roasted grasshoppers in the Kalahari). They are often also expected to be skilled with a camera.

If truth be told, a lot of "travel" writing is done from home, or at best from the library (or nowadays off the Internet). We know an editor who once edited and rewrote the chapters for three southern states in a Fodor's guide without ever having set foot in any of them and without venturing beyond the New York Public Library.

Nonetheless, it's a venerable tradition. If motoring and writing his way through southwestern France was legit for the highbrow novelist Henry James, then surely a cruise to Tahiti—with paddle tennis in the afternoon, stargazing at night and gourmet meals in between—is okay for high- or lowbrow you.

Western

Everything said above about mystery and romance writing applies here as well. Big money can be made. Certain formulas for plot and character development are often followed. Only certain fiction publishers have western lists. The social network for writers of westerns may be different, but the skills you'll need are much the same. Add to the mix the fact that you must know your history exceedingly well. Our editor friend once labored to salvage a western in which the author had trains leaving New York for the territories by way of a tunnel under the Hudson: a little hard to do, even for a tough cowpoke, when the tunnel had yet to be built.

Religious and Spiritual

This a booming publishing market, with serious and beautiful books and articles, and useful ones, and a great deal of flimflam and sentimentality. Often what passes for "spirituality" is actually "self-help" with a denominational spin on it. The upsurge of interest in both traditional evangelical religion and the new forms of spirituality has had an impact on the world of writing programs, too. There's a conference or workshop for people of every religious persuasion, from Baptists to Buddhists. With few exceptions all are excluded here because their emphasis tends to be as much on their own brand of spirituality (or even more so) than on writing per se. The programs included here generally do not have a religious slant.

The Decision to Become a Professional

Many writers never make a formal decision to specialize in one kind of writing versus another. The process just happens. They start writing because they enjoy it or feel they have something to say, and their personal styles evolve. In time, they find themselves gravitating toward one type of writing or another. This form of self-selection is a healthy way to discover one's own best path. Each person ends up doing the kind of writing to which he or she is best suited by dint of skill, preference and personality.

In choosing to become a professional writer, you elevate your commitment to the medium. It is no longer an infatuation but more like a marriage, complete with responsibilities and sacrifices. It begins to shape the way your life unfolds. In exchange for that heightened commitment, you expect to reap rewards in terms of financial gain, social benefits and personal satisfaction. All these are possible. But in writing, as in many professions and all marriages, the good stuff does not always come easily.

Writing is competitive. For many of the same reasons you might want to make a career out of being a writer, plenty of other people do, too. And while demand for clearly written copy and gripping story lines is growing in these information- and entertainment-hungry times, there will always be more people who want to make a living at writing than there will be paying markets to support them. In time, the less talented, less passionate, less highly motivated writers will eventually drop away and take up other work. The desire of every new professional is to be one of those who can weather the competition and build a successful career.

The demands on professional writers are quite different from those on even the most gifted amateurs. Professionals need to be able to produce manuscripts that fulfill the demands of the clients who pay for them. In the best of situations, that means writers finding clients who love the way they see and then put that vision and those observations into words, and are happy to pay them to do what they love. Many times, though, it is not that simple.

Professionals must produce top-quality work on every assignment, no matter how they feel or what logistical limitations they face. It does not matter if the client's editor breathes fire or if the subject is tough to research or if the sources of information are reticent. Professionals produce professional-grade writing. No publisher or client, upon reading a manuscript that exceeds expectations, will ever ask you how you did it. A fine restaurant's reputation is based not on a few fabulous meals but on a consistent string of excellent ones. The same holds true for professional writers.

Writing is one of those fields that calls so strongly to some people that they never actually work through the process of making the decision to become professionals. They know right from the beginning that they are and always will be writers. They have a love affair with words that leaves them no other choice. Establishing a career is a manifestation of the inevitable.

For most of us, though, the decision to become a professional needs to be carefully considered.

Do not become a writer by accident or default. Do not take up professional writing just because you find scribbling enjoyable and cannot think of anything else to do. It is too challenging a career. If the well-documented minimal income of most would-be writers isn't enough to scare you off, then the likelihood of a long string of rejections may be. Before novelist F. Scott Fitzgerald hit the big time with *This Side of Paradise,* he had received and suffered enough rejection letters to wallpaper his shabby one-room apartment. You simply have to want it with everything you've got, and then you have to build your career in writing as carefully, and strategically, as you would in any other field. The decisions you make deliberately and carefully, rather than just fall into, will ultimately yield greater satisfaction.

The Decision to Remain an Amateur

The root meaning of the word "amateur" is "lover." The amateur gets to do what he or she loves, without having to answer to anyone else. Many of the most passionate writers prefer to remain amateurs all their lives rather than sacrifice their deep personal relationship with the medium of words to the exigencies of earning a living.

They have a career, an occupation elsewhere, and spend their evenings, weekends and vacations pursuing their truest love, putting words on paper. Amateur writing has many opportunities, including the chance to have work published in minor or even major publications on a freelance basis. Occasionally there is the happy surprise of earning real money.

Serious amateur writers may be as skilled as professionals. They may have the technical expertise and personal vision for which editors and clients would gladly pay. Instead, they remain amateurs to preserve their harmonious relationship with their own work. They simply don't want to objectify their work, turn it into a commodity and put it on the auction block. Anyone who loves writing should think carefully about what will be lost by becoming a professional, as well as what will be gained. It would be a shame to have one's love affair with writing ground down by the need to turn words into cash.

Getting Your Act Together

Whether writing is a career or an avocation for you, your desire to use this book shows that you take it seriously. You recognize the need to hone your skills and to learn new ways of developing your work. You see how shifting market forces, technological advances (the computer especially) and the never-before-so-important game of networking have changed the way writing is done and sold.

In picking up this book, you seek to expand your knowledge about writing, to acquire specific skills or to advance your vision.

This book has been created to help you. It catalogs hundreds of different ways in which to advance your writing life, whether you choose to make writing your profession or to pursue it as an amateur. You will find descriptions of workshops and training facilities for all types of writing, plus organizations of and for writers, art colonies, specialized writing schools and academic institutions that have strong writing programs.

All writers thrive on the satisfaction of crafting the unforgettable sentence or paragraph or stanza or dialogue. It is our wish that the information offered here will help you to become the writer you want to be.

PART TWO

Creative Writing Programs in the U.S. Today

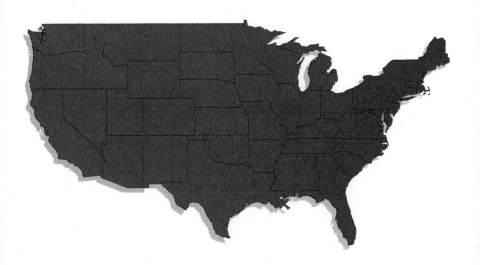

Only Connect

Associations, Organizations and Unions for Writers

Immediately below you'll find a listing of national associations, organizations and unions (or other labor organizations) that you may want to join. For similar state, regional and local organizations, ask your reference librarian or call your state arts council. In the gazetteer of program descriptions that follows, you will see certain programs (workshops, conferences . . .) sponsored by regional associations for writers and other artists. If noteworthy, we give some information about the association at that point.

Writing is usually a solitary act. But the yin and yang of it mean that the solitude needs to be balanced by association, fraternity and sorority, and sometimes by going to the barricades together. Hence this section's title, "Only Connect," borrowed shamelessly from E. M. Forster.

There is much to be said for joining appropriate professional or amateur writers' organizations. We all learn from one another, both on the writing side and on the business side. Especially for people who live and work in far-flung places, away from the hub of publishing and literary activity in major cities like New York, Boston, Chicago and San Francisco, an organization's newsletter and annual meeting may the best and only places to hear what peers and colleagues are doing about the same opportunities or problems you may be facing. The better organizations emphasize service: insurance plans, job networking, how-to skills workshops, etc. We advise spending your membership dollars only for these real benefits.

We have seen too many resumes listing memberships in shell organizations that provide no real services and offer no warmth, camaraderie or collegial networking to their members. Writers are no more immune than other workers to the American penchant for "joining up," what Garrison Keillor pokes fun at when he says his *Prairie Home Companion* is brought to us by the "American Federation of Associations."

You'll do better if you choose the one or two associations that actually serve your purposes as a specific kind of writer. Certainly if you are a poet, then the poetry associations are for you. If you are a journalist, find your specialty group of reporters. And so on.

The one overarching organization all writers may want to consider is the relatively young National Writers Union (NWU), founded in 1983. NWU, now an affiliate of the AFL-CIO, works hard to provide the services we associate with traditional labor organizations: contract and payment advice, legal counsel, and a clearinghouse of work-related business information. One NWU bonus is access to a health insurance plan.

Because most writers have to negotiate on their own behalf rather than collectively, negotiations can be dicey if the person on the opposite side of the table is the "hit man" for a giant corporation. Enter the NWU with model contracts, precedents you can review, and moral support (which was part of the winning formula when David negotiated with Goliath).

NWU is in the forefront of the struggle to protect writers' copyright interests in electronically published and distributed material. In the brave new world of electronic rights—a kind of lawless Wild West of publishing—it's nice to have a friend riding shotgun. And there are the educational seminars sponsored by NWU, as well as the occasional social get-together. If you are not yet a member, take the plunge, declare yourself a latter-day Wobbly, dig out the old Pete Seeger records and join the movement. The presence of an "NWU" line on your resume sends a signal to all employers that you are awake to the labor-management issues of the day.

Associations and Organizations

Academy of American Poets
Who: Individual and institutional members **What:** Largest organization committed to supporting poets and poetry. Sponsors a national series of readings, residencies and publications. Offers awards, prizes and fellowships. Founded 1934. **Contact:** Academy of American Poets, 584 Broadway, Suite 1208, New York, NY 10012; 212-274-0343; http://www.tmn.com/Artswire/ poets/page.html **Membership:** Open to all. Annual dues.

American Society of Journalists and Authors
Who: More than 1,000 independent nonfiction writers **What:** Offers members discount services, meetings with editors, an exclusive referral service, publications and a monthly newsletter. Has sponsored conferences, symposia and workshops. Access to health insurance. **Contact:** ASJA, 1501 Broadway, Suite 302, New York, NY 10036; 212-997-0947 **Membership:** Eligibility requirements.

Associated Writing Programs
Who: 3,300 members, including writers, teachers and students affiliated and unaffiliated with academic institutions. **What:** Advocacy and services for its members, including an annual conference (see listing), a bimonthly publication, job listings and a job placement service. Sponsors contests leading to $2,000 award and publication by a university press. See its *AWP Guide to Writing Programs* for descriptions of over 300 writing programs. **Contact:** AWP, Tallwood House, Mailstop 1E3, George Mason University, Fairfax, VA, 22030, 703-993-4301, e-mail: awp@gmu.edu **Membership:** Open to all. Annual dues.

Editorial Freelancers Association
Who: Self-employed editors, writers, indexers, proofreaders, researchers, desktop publishers, translators **What:** Publishes annual membership directory, newsletter and the "Business Practices Survey," which includes a detailed analysis of actual payments for copyediting, proofreading, editing, rewriting and indexing. Sponsors meetings, guest speakers, courses and social events. Provides Job Phone, a job listing service, for an additional fee. Access to health insurance. **Contact:** EFA, 77 W. 23rd St., New York, NY 10010; 212-929-5400 **Membership:** Open to all freelancers. Annual dues.

Independent Writers of Chicago

Who: More than 200 professional writers **What:** Publishes the *IWOC Directory*, a detailed guide to its members, referenced by specialty. Offers a job referral service and a legal referral service, as well as access to health insurance and a credit union. Publishes a newsletter; provides sample contracts, seminars and a payment rate survey. **Contact:** IWOC, 7855 Grosspoint Rd., #M, Skokie, IL 60077; 847-676-3784 **Membership:** Professional membership has eligibility requirements. Associate membership is open to all. Annual dues.

International Association of Crime Writers (North American Branch)

Who: Professional writers **What:** Promotes crime writing as a significant art form, translates crime writing into other languages, defends authors against censorship and other forms of tyranny. Sponsors conferences, including an annual celebration in Spain. Publishes a quarterly newsletter and anthologies. Sponsors social events; awards the Hammett prize for literary excellence. **Contact:** IACW, JAF Box 1500, New York, NY 10116; 212-243-8966; e-mail mfrisque@igc.apc.org **Membership:** Eligibility requirements. Annual dues.

International Women's Writing Guild

Who: An international network of women writers **What:** Sponsors summer conference, workshops and two "Open House/Meet the Agents" events (see program listing). Offers access to health insurance. Publishes newsletter and a list of literary agents and other writing services. **Contact:** IWWG, P.O. Box 810, Gracie Station, New York, NY 10028; 212-737-7536, http://www.iwwg.com **Membership:** Open to all. Annual dues.

Mystery Writers of America

Who: Mystery and crime writers **What:** Promotes equitable contracts for its members; monitors tax and other legislation affecting writers. National office in NY houses reference library. Regional chapters in Boston, Chicago, Denver, Houston, Seattle, San Francisco and Los Angeles sponsor monthly meetings. Publishes a newsletter and an annual anthology; awards "Edgars" (named for Edgar Allan Poe) for distinguished works (see conference listing in *Illinois*). **Contact:** MWA, 17 E. 47th St., 6th floor, New York, NY 10017; 212-888-8171 **Membership:** Eligibility requirements. Annual dues.

National Association of Science Writers, Inc.

Who: Half of the 1,800 members are "active"—writers editors, broadcasters, filmmakers. Half are "associates"—individuals who work for government agencies, universities, corporations, hospitals, foundations, museums, research labs and public relations firms. **What:** Publishes a quarterly journal with news and job listings. Holds a meeting during the annual meeting of the American Association for the Advancement of Science. Presents annual awards. Regional groups sponsor dinners, lectures, workshops and field trips to improve science reporting. Access to health and disability insurance. **Contact:** NASW, P.O. Box 294, Greenlawn, NY 11740; 516-757-0069. **Membership:** Five categories with eligibility requirements. Annual dues.

National League of American Pen Women
Who: More than 5,000 women in more than 200 branches throughout the U.S. **What:** Founded in 1897 as an alternative to the all-male Press Club, the League sponsors workshops, discussions, lectures, contests, a magazine and a biennial convention. **Contact:** NLAPW, Pen Arts Bldg., 1300 17th St. NW, Washington, DC 20036; 202-785-1997 **Membership:** By invitation. Eligibility requirements for each of the three types of membership—art, letters and music.

Novelists, Inc.
Who: Published popular-fiction authors **What:** Sponsors a monthly newsletter and a national conference (see program listing). **Contact:** Novelists, Inc., P.O. Box 1166, Mission, KS 66222; 816-561-4524; e-mail: muttering@ juno.com **Membership:** Eligibility requirements.

Pen American Center
Who: More than 14,000 poets, playwrights, essayists, editors and novelists (hence the acronym PEN) throughout the world **What:** The New York office is the largest of the 124 centers affiliated with International Pen. Promotes freedom of expression through international and domestic human rights campaigns on behalf of writers, editors and journalists censored, persecuted or imprisoned because of their writing. Sponsors public literary events, awards and outreach projects. Publications include *Grants and Awards Available to American Writers, 19th ed., 1996–1997.* **Contact:** PEN American Center, 568 Broadway, New York, NY 10012; 212-334-1660 **Membership:** By election. Elgibility requirements. A related organization, Friends of Pen, supports Pen activities and is open to all.

Poetry Society of America
Who: Poets and readers **What:** Founded in 1910, PSA is a nonprofit organization that sponsors a variety of projects designed to encourage people to read, listen to and write poetry. Activities include poetry seminars, peer workshops, a Web page, brief poetry "spots" on TV and on posters in subways and buses, and an extensive annual awards program. Publishes a biannual journal and books of poetry selections. **Contact:** PSA, 15 Gramercy Park, New York, NY 10003; 212-254-9628; http://www.poetrysociety.com **Membership:** Open to all. Annual dues.

Poets & Writers
Who: A nonprofit organization, not a membership organization; its services are available to all. **What:** Sponsors readings and workshops. Publishes the bimonthy magazine *Poets & Writers*, as well as *Writers Conferences: An Annual Guide to Literary Conferences* and *Into Print: Guides to the Writing Life.* Distributes guides to copyright laws, literary agents, artists colonies, grants and awards, in addition to books on getting published and the craft of writing. The Information Center answers inquiries and publishes *A Directory of American Poets and Fiction Writers*, listing more than 7,000 poets and fiction writers. **Contact:** Poets & Writers, 72 Spring St., New York, NY 10012; 212-226-3586; e-mail: infocenter@wonline.com, or for the magazine: PWSubs@ aol.com

Society of Children's Book Writers and Illustrators

Who: Over 10,000 writers, illustrators, editors, publishers, agents, librarians, bookstore personnel and educators interested in children's literature **What:** Founded in 1968, a professional guild that lobbies for equitable treatment for authors and artists. Publishes a bimonthly bulletin. Promotes an exchange of information among its members. Sponsors awards, grants, meetings, workshops and a national conference (see program listing). **Contact:** SCBWI, 22736 Vanowen St., Suite 106, West Hills, CA 91307; 818-888-8760 **Membership:** Eligibility requirements for full membership. Associate membership is open to all. Annual dues.

Teachers and Writers Collaborative

Who: Writers and educators **What:** Founded in 1967, T & W publishes a magazine and distributes books on numerous subjects related to the teaching of writing. Opened the Center for Imaginative Writing in 1992, which houses books, videos, films, autdiotapes, software and periodicals on teaching writing and the writing process. Sponsors a writer-in-residence program within schools, special events, workshops, seminars and receptions. **Contact:** T & W, 5 Union Square West, New York, NY 10003; 212-691-6590 **Membership:** Open to all. Annual dues.

Western Writers of America

Who: Writers dedicated to preserving and celebrating the heritage of the American West **What:** Sponsors an annual conference; publishes a magazine and a membership directory. Founded in 1955. Concerned with both the past and present-day American West. **Contact:** James Crutchfield, 1012 Fair St., Franklin, TN 37064; 615-791-1444; http:// www.imt.net/~gedison/wwa.html **Membership:** Eligibility requirements. Annual dues. Subscription to the magazine is open to all.

Women's National Book Association

Who: Publishers, librarians, booksellers, writers, editors, agents, designers, illustrators, and book and magazine producers—women and men. **What:** Local chapters sponsor speakers, workshops and discussion groups. WNBA, an umbrella organization, sponsors educational programs at the American Booksellers Association, American Library Association and Modern Language Association annual meetings. Publishes a newsletter. Founded in 1917 to promote recognition of women's achievements in the book industry. **Contact:** WNBA, 160 Fifth Ave., New York, NY 10010; 212-675-7805; e-mail: 4164812@MCIMAIL.COM; http://www.he.net/susannah/wnba.htm **Membership:** Open to all through chapters. Annual dues. In areas where there is no chapter, corresponding membership is available.

Unions & Other Labor Organizations

The Authors Guild

Who: 6,500 professional writers, in all genres **What:** Focus on legal and business issues (copyright, freedom of expression, electronic rights, royalties, taxes). Lobbies on national and local levels. Provides access to health and life insurance. Sponsors seminars on the latest developments in publishing.

Publishes a quarterly. Provides legal reviews and legal counsel regarding contracts. Founded 1921. **Contact:** Paul Aiken, Exec. Dir., Authors Guild, 330 W. 42nd St., New York, NY 10036; 212-563-5904 **Membership:** Eligibility requirements.

Dramatists Guild
Who: 6,300 playwrights, composers and lyricists **What:** Founded in 1920. Fights for fair royalties, protection of subsidiary rights, artistic control and copyright ownership. Maintains contracts for all levels of theatrical procution; provides a toll-free number for advice on all theater-related business matters. Gives information on agents, producers, contests, theaters, conferences. Publishes a literary quarterly, a newsletter and an annual resource directory. Sponsors symposia nationwide. Access to health insurance. **Contact:** Dramatists Guild, 234 West 44th St., 11th fl., New York, NY 10036; 212-398-9366 **Membership:** Eligibility requirements for active members. Associate membership open to all theater writers without preconditions.

National Writers Union
Who: 4,200 freelance writers, including journalists, novelists, biographers, historians, poets, textbook authors, commercial writers, technical writers and cartoonists. **What:** A labor union, the NWU is an affiliate of the United Auto Workers, with 13 locals nationwide. Offers group health insurance; helps resolve disputes with publishers. Develops and publishes numerous resources for its members, including guidelines for negotiating electronic rights, the *NWU Guide to Freelance Rates and Standard Practice*, a *Preferred Literary Agent Agreement* and the *NWU Guide to Book Contracts*. Publishes a quarterly magazine. Negotiates contracts with newspapers and magazines. The local chapters sponsor readings, workshops, job banks, local media guides, newsletters, speaker's bureaus and computer bulletin boards. **Contact:** NWU East Coast Office, 113 University Place, 6th Floor, New York, NY 10003; 212-254-0279; NWU West Coast Office, 337 17th St., Suite 101, Oakland, CA 94612; 510-839-0110; e-mail: nwu@nwu.org; http://www.nwu.org/nwu/ **Membership:** Eligibility requirements. Annual dues. The NWU Supporters Circle is open to all who wish to support the union.

Writers Guild of America
Who: Professional writers in motion pictures, television and radio **What:** A labor union, the WGA provides protection for its members under various Minimum Basic Agreements concerning fees, payments, rights, credits, arbitration of disputes. Provides for employer contributions into pension and health funds. Provides a registration service for literary materials. **Contact:** East Coast, WGAE, 555 W. 57th St., New York, NY 10019; 212-767-7800; West Coast, WGAW, 8955 Beverly Blvd., West Hollywood, CA 90048; 310-550-1000 **Membership:** Eligibility requirements. Initiation fee and annual dues.

Selecting a Program

YOU'RE SHOPPING FOR SHOES. Your feet tell you they need new ones in order to do well what they were born to do. In the shoe store there is an overwhelming array of possibilities. Loafers and sandals, wing tips and high heels, Wellingtons and Aqua-mocs, Reeboks and Nikes and Converse. What you need is a shoe-shopping consultant!

In the writing programs department, the array of possibilities can also be dizzying. Until, that is, you take inventory of what you really want or need. We suggest a process that goes, loosely, like this:

Imagine the best place to do your writing work. Is it urban or rural? Busy with artistic compatriots or far way from everybody? Does working in the presence of famous or highly successful writers inspire or intimidate you?

Do you work best with structured time (structured for you by a teacher) or in a free-floating atmosphere where work, meals, sleep, indeed night and day, blend into one another while you're in the writing mode?

Do you want to write while in a workshop, or do you want to listen to others talk about writing, or do you want a mix of both?

Are you hungry for skill development instruction or is it hard-nosed business management advice you need?

How do you feel about exposing your work to peers, or to a mentor? Are you looking for private one-on-one manuscript critiques of your work, or are you not yet ready to bring your work out into the (sometimes harsh) light of day?

Do you like events with hundreds of people scurrying about to this seminar or that, or are you looking rather for six good folks with whom you can meet for quiet, sustained dialogue about your writing?

Is it your own current writing project you want to push forward, or are you looking for a workshop teacher who will coach you through a series of writing aerobics classes with exercises and guided discussion, perhaps in a genre that's new to you?

Do you want to travel to the workshop (can you afford to?), or do you need something near home with little or no added expense beyond the program itself?

Do you want to meet editors and publishers and press the flesh as a networker? Are you willing to pay to schmooze with those who may buy your writing, or does the mere thought of it make you vaguely seasick?

The list will expand a bit as you pose your own useful questions. If you sort out these entirely personal issues first, the process of sorting through the array of writers' workshops and conferences will be easier and more fun.

If this is the first time you've considered a workshop or conference experience, read randomly through the entries for a half hour; then go back to the self-inventory suggested above; then read again, using the index to find programs suited to your needs. It won't be long before you have a substantial list, then a winnowed list, of programs to contact for brochures and application forms. Start a few months in advance if possible. In your local community, read the bulletin boards at the coffee shop or the YMCA or the college or university. Sometimes a great one-time-only workshop opportunity shows up on your doorstep—no need to fly to Montana! If you want to enter an ongoing program, ask the program director for names of a few recent participants whom you might query. Be sure you understand all the costs and whether the application fee is refundable. We believe this book is the most extensive guide of its kind, but we know we haven't captured the entire universe of writing programs in these pages, so keep a sharp lookout yourself.

And don't let the potentially endless job of searching for the ideal writing workshop become a substitute for writing itself. Your most important workshop will always be your own desk and whatever time you can devote to your own creative work.

Special Advice on Artists' Colonies

It's a dream most writers entertain at one time or another: a week, a month, a whole season or even a year away from other mundane responsibilities and frivolous distractions. Nothing but open time and a a clean sheet of paper between you and the completion of your next great work. The artists' colony is a venerable tradition in America, and for serious writers who can disconnect temporarily from the everyday world, such programs can be paradise regained.

Most, but not all, colonies are situated in beautiful rural settings. Most, but not all, serve a variety of artists in addition to writers. Most, in fact almost all, require of attendees some kind of track record of publications or at least substantially completed manuscripts (which the colony will pass through a review committee). All colonies require serious recommendations and references from the applicant. The message is clear: artists' colonies are for the more experienced writer and only very rarely for the beginning amateur.

Some artists' colonies are Cadillacs, some are Chevrolets and some, frankly, are donkey carts. Some will cost you a fortune; others will pay you a stipend just to be there whether you finish your novel or not. Some ask you to make a virtue out of the Spartan life (be alert to the brochure that says "rustic yet comfortable"), while others, like the MacDowell Colony, offer private cottages designed by top-rank architects (can you write a convincing postmodern play while summering in a faux Tudor house?). Some have prestige that will advance your career, and others are a distraction from career and work as well.

Remember, we live in an age of advertising hype. Anyone with a desktop publishing program can whip up a handsome brochure. If you are contemplating the expense (in dollars or time, or both) of a residential writing program at an artists' colony, look below the surface before you quit your day job or write any checks.

At most colonies the writers and other artists are very much on their own, some to the point where strict rules are enforced to keep the distractions of conversation and visitors to a minimum. If you're not used to extended isolation or total independence and unstructured time, you might try it in small doses first. You can't expect to turn yourself into a monk overnight. Other colonies are lively social communities where evening meals and after-dinner readings and discussions are de rigueur. The scuttlebutt on a few colonies says that not much work gets done but the schmooze factor is high and, for the adventurous, the likelihood of a romantic or sexual romp is equally high. (Don't bother checking the index; we did not sort on the latter category.)

Most serious artists' colonies expect applicants to have a substantial project underway, a project whose own momentum insists upon time and space to grow toward completion. For a writer who has yet to find his or her niche or next subject, a residential program is a bad bet. Don't go in order to find out what you might want to write. Go because you can't help but go, and because everything else in your life is falling by the wayside anyway.

And if you apply and are accepted, be wary of the extremes. You may think you'll love the isolation, but make a plan to check in periodically with family at home. You may think you'll write the entire novel in your month at the colony, but keep the emphasis where it should be, on quality. You'll write as much as you can, and it will get finished when it gets finished, not a day or a draft before.

Most of all, if you go, be sure to leave some time to be grateful. A stint at a writers' colony should be decidedly hard work, but it is also a rare privilege. You may never see much remuneration for your craft but at the colony, you are free to indulge your imagination quietly. That's a freedom you simply cannot buy back home in a kitchen full of caterwauling kids or at your business where the highest literary form is acronym soup on an interoffice memo.

Special Advice on Academic Programs

There are statistics, we're told, that show that a college degree raises your likely lifetime earnings by a substantial amount over what you could expect if you stopped after high school. But the difference between the lifetime earnings of those with an undergraduate degree compared to those with a graduate degree presents a cloudier picture. Sure, an astrophysicist with a PhD will do better than someone who majored in rocks for jocks at Podunk Junior College. The question here is: What if you're a writer? Is a graduate degree worth the trouble and expense?

For writers, we believe the statistics are generally useless. In fact we wouldn't even approach the question of getting an academic degree in writing from the angle of its likely impact on our earnings. Why? Because for most creative writers, income from writing is a crapshoot. A first novel can earn nothing or a fat advance. It can earn a measly advance and yet take off because of a favorable review in the right place. Or it can be a dud as a book but sell big to Hollywood as a film option. Poetry, like philosophy, bakes no bread, and to be published at all, many poets spend their own money rather than earn anything for their labors. And so forth. Economically speaking, writing is an irrational adventure.

If you want to teach writing, that's a different story. In most schools (secondary and college level), a graduate degree is necessary, if not to get the job then certainly to advance. But this isn't a book about how to become a teacher of writing. If that's your goal, we suggest talking to the English or creative writing department chairperson at the largest university near you. We are far less enthusiastic about education departments, where the emphasis is more on process and quantification than on quality, content and imagination. Ask the English (or literature) department about not only the content of the program, but also the job placements of recent graduates, and try to query some of those graduates about the actual usefulness of the degree program. If you go for it, and if you become a good teacher of writing—no matter how humble, and trust us, a few years of teaching freshman composition will humble anyone—you will have our applause for sure.

Our concern here is the graduate degree in creative writing per se, for those who want to be writers, full- or part-time. Often this is the Master of Fine Arts in Writing (MFA) degree, though in many places it's simply a Master of Arts with a concentration in writing (MA). Some PhD programs have a creative writing track; the emphasis, however, is more likely to be on scholarship and literary criticism. There are some exceptions, and writers headed for the groves of academe should read the catalogue fine print carefully. If you want writing only, don't sign up for a degree requiring that you spend half your time and money on the abstractions of literary criticism (which these days ranges from highly politicized multiculturalism studies to arcane psycholinguistic theories). For further reference, see the Associated Writing Programs' *Official Guide to Writing Programs,* 7th edition.

The good and bad news is that there are scores of academic creative writing programs all across the country. Good news because you can probably find an appropriate program close to home if that's necessary; bad news because deciding which one will serve you best isn't easy. Our advice follows.

We think the best graduate creative writing programs tend to be the smaller ones, where a close, dynamic relationship between teacher and student is possible or even required. So the first suggestion is: Think small. Next, we believe that the best creative writing teachers—with some exceptions, of course—tend to be creative writers themselves, people who teach as a form of service (and no doubt to pay the bills) to younger writers coming along. Look for a program staffed by writers who are actively publishing (whether in small journals or with big publishers isn't the point). The best student-teacher relationships in creative writing are essentially protégé-mentor relationships, which means that new students ought to know or have reason to believe that the faculty in their chosen program has good candidates for this invaluable and highly sensitive role.

An interesting option in graduate-level creative writing programs is the "low residency" arrangement, where students spend only a few days or weeks per year on campus and otherwise work via mail, telephone and (at the trendier, wired places) by modem with their tutors. If a full-time job or family commitments tie you down at home, a low-residency program may be your ticket. The required personality trait for success here is solid self-discipline. Without the peer pressure all on-campus students feel naturally from their surroundings, the at-home writing student has to make arrangements to produce the same results. The presence of a well-stocked (and quiet) university library can make all the difference to a writer. At home, without this resource, progress may be limited. Baksheesh paid regularly to your spouse or doting uncle to take the kids off your hands for a few hours a week is probably a frequent part of the recipe for success, too.

Then there is the content of the program. There are numerous curricular approaches to the teaching of creative writing (including the one that says it can't be taught at all). Our preference (you might not share this view) would be for programs that require (yes, we said require) the student to write extensively in several genres while concentrating on one. Fiction might be your specialty, but we'd argue that your fiction writing will improve if you have to produce sonnets and dialogue for the stage as well. Second, although studies in literary criticism might be useful for the intellectual development of some creative writers, we think that far more important is wide reading in the primary creative works and major authors of the genres where you expect to do most of your own writing. If you mean to be a contemporary poet with environmental themes, find a school and courses that will let you (better yet, make you) read eclogues and pastoral verse in the classical tradition, in the Romantic period, and in nonwestern literary cultures. Catullus, Wordsworth and Basho should become your mentors just as much as Professor So-and-So at the university. Don't pretend you're becoming a playwright while systematically avoiding the work and the joy of closely reading Shakespeare.

Last, inquire about the final project required for graduation. Go for a program that will push you to do something better and bigger than ever before and then will reward you with concrete help in getting your work published or performed. Again, talk to students currently in the program or recently graduated from it. It's a common scandal that graduate school is for many people an excuse not to finish anything, a time in limbo. If you turn up evidence that a creative writing program has a lot of hangers-on who have spent years "finding themselves" on campus while eking out a living as clerks in the local used-book shop… , well, as your mama told you long ago, "You better shop around."

At the end of each state's coverage of Workshops, Conferences and Artists' Colonies we list Academic Programs, a selection of graduate-level creative writing programs. We believe these to be among the noteworthy ones. If there is another one near you that seems convenient to your plans, apply the criteria discussed above, and if the answers are good, open the door and walk through.

Writing Programs

Residential
Program

Workshop

Conference

Academic
Program

Alabama

Alabama Writers' Conclave

🔄 **For fiction and nonfiction writers, poets** *Central Alabama, about 30 mi. S of Birmingham — Univ. of Montevallo, Montevallo, AL 35209; 117 Hanover Rd., Homewood, AL 35209,* **Voice:** 205-871-6855 **Contact:** Harriette Dawkins, Dir. **Founded:** 1923 **Open:** 3 days in midsummer **Admission:** Registration form only **Cost:** $45 for 3 days; single room $32.25 per day **Size-Attendees:** About 400 **Handicapped Access**

DEEP IN THE HEART of Dixie, and deep in the dog days of summer, a long-standing writers' conference with workshops, lectures and readings for writers in several genres — including the short story, often given short shrift elsewhere. The 1996 program included a "publishers panel." AWC members receive a newsletter and can even purchase a history of their own organization. This conclave is open to writers at all levels, and you can attend for 1, 2, or 3 days.

Writing Today Writers' Conference

✏️🔄 **For all writers** *Birmingham-Southern College, Box 549003, Birmingham, AL 35254* **Voice:** 205-226-4921 **Founded:** 1980 **Open:** 1 weekend in mid-Apr. **Admission:** Registration form only **Deadlines:** Late Mar. **Cost:** $85 for 2 days; luncheon $20 per day **Financial Aid:** Scholarship **Size-Attendees:** Up to 600 **Degree or Certification:** CEUs available

AN IMPRESSIVE CAST, efficient planning and plenty of imagination make this one of the better conferences outside the major East and West Coast cities. With support from arts and humanities councils, bookstores, other businesses, foundations and private individuals, WTWC is by now a long-standing success story. Writers at all levels in a host of genres can find something stimulating here.

Featured speakers in 1996 included essayist–music commentator Albert Murray, *New Yorker* film critic Terrence Rafferty, poet James Tate, and novelist-historian Shelby Foote. And these are only the featured faculty. Specialists in religious writing, children's books, book collecting and selling your work effectively fill out the program. A particularly interesting conference for Southern writers.

🏠 Alabama Academic Programs

University of Alabama, English Dept., Box 870244, Tuscaloosa, AL 35487; 205-348-5065; MFA Creative Writing

Alaska

Sitka Symposium on Human Values and the Written Word

✏️🔄 **For writers, teachers** *Coastal SE Alaska — Island Institute, P.O. Box 2420, Sitka, AK 99835* **Voice:** 907-747-3794 **Contact:** Carolyn Servid, Dir. **Founded:** 1984 **Open:** 1 week in June **Admission:** Registration form only **Cost:** $250; housing $39–$49 per night **Size-Attendees:** 55

MORE AMBITIOUS than programs focused solely on writing, this weeklong conference is concerned with the relationship between culture and landscape, the role stories play in helping people understand the world, and the notion of community. The Sitka Symposium draws a unique combination of individuals together—writers and anthropologists, naturalists, linguists, folklorists and biologists—to explore such themes as "Earth Household: Community and the Natural Common Wealth." Past symposiums have focused on "Stories We Live By: Our Habit, Our Heritage, Our Hope" and "The Spirit of Human Work."

The symposium takes place in downtown Sitka, on Baranof Island—still home to Tlingit Indians and once home to Russians. Accessible only by ferry or plane, Baranof Island is part of a mountainous (rain forest) chain along Alaska's southeastern coast. Nationally prominent naturalists and writers read from their work and wrestle with finding responses to our global dilemmas. There are panels, group discussions and readings by leaders as well as participants. Critiques of manuscripts are available if the work is submitted by the May deadline (inquire for details).

In addition to the symposium, the Island Institute sponsors a Resident Fellows Program, which offers 3 single residencies in January, April and November. Residents receive a stipend for food and live in a small apartment; they are expected to participate in at least 1 community activity a week, such as a public presentation about their work in a workshop or school. The Institute also sponsors a Visiting Writers Series in cooperation with the University of Alaska. The Institute's interests include "the nature of communities; the purpose and practice of education; the cultures of Alaska's Native peoples and their relationship to the Western world; the foundations and evolution of cultural perspective; and human relationships to the rest of the natural world."

"This is that ideal thing: home grown, community-based, sustained for a decade now by mostly voluntary and always inspired work, national in reputation, global in its concerns," writes faculty member Robert Hass, U.S. poet laureate.

Alaska
Academic Programs

University of Alaska Anchorage, English Dept., 3211 Providence Dr., Anchorage, AK 99508; 907-786-4355; MFA Creative Writing
University of Alaska Fairbanks, English Dept., P.O. Box 755720, Fairbanks, AK 99775; 907-474-7193; MFA Creative Writing

Arizona

Pima Writers' Workshop

For fiction and nonfiction writers, screenwriters, poets Pima Community College — 2202 W. Anklam Rd., Tucson, AZ 85709 **Voice:** 520-884-6974 **Fax:** 602-884-6975 **Contact:** Meg Files **Founded:** 1987 **Open:** 1 weekend in May **Admission:** Registration form only **Deadlines:** Manuscript by early May **Cost:** $65 (additional for credit) **Size-Attendees:** 200 **Handicapped Access**

THE EMPHASIS IS ON encouragement at this event sponsored by Pima Community College. The workshops are not run simultaneously; rather, they follow one after another over the 2 days. In 1996 they included "Enough Talk About Me: Taking the Self Out of Self-History," "It Don't Mean A Thing If You Ain't Marketing," as well as sessions on practicalities, such as getting an agent to return your calls. There are optional manuscript conferences with an agent or published author on a first-come, first-served basis. The special guest reading in 1996 was given by Nancy Mairs [*Waist-High in the World: (Re) Constructing (Dis) Ability*].

Reader's Digest Writers' Workshop

For nonfiction writers *Varies —*
Northern Arizona University, P.O. Box 6024,
Flagstaff, AZ 86011 **Voice:** 520-541-9625
Fax: 520-541-9625 **Founded:** 1974 **Open:**
Varies **Admission:** Registration form only
Cost: $125–$150 (some meals incl.) **Size-
Attendees:** 250 **Handicapped Access**

THIS IS A PRACTICAL workshop for nonfiction writers, with a focus on writing for the marketplace. Generally *Reader's Digest* co-sponsors the event with a university, which hosts the workshops. Past events have met on campuses in Arizona, Oklahoma, Oregon, Nebraska and Nevada, with faculty members from host campuses serving as some of the instructors, along with published authors and editors from magazines such as *National Geographic Traveler, Woman's Day* and *Field & Stream* in addition to the *Digest*.

Particularly useful to writers who want to enter the commercial magazine marketplace, this workshop provides sessions on practical matters, from writing a query letter to generating multiple sales of a story idea.

There are 2 contacts for these workshops: Ray Newton, listed above, coordinates the conferences in the West. Pat McNeeley coordinates the conferences that take place in the East. She can be reached at the School of Journalism, University of Southern Carolina, Columbia, SC 29208 (803-777-5166).

University of Arizona Poetry Center Residency Program

For poets *Near downtown — 1216 N.*
Cherry Ave., Tucson, AZ 85719 **Voice:** 602-
321-7760 **Open:** June–Aug. **Admission:**
Application, manuscript **Deadlines:** Postmarked Feb. 15–Mar. 15 **Cost:** Transportation, meals

POETS WHO LOVE the southwestern desert environment would probably most appreciate this opportunity. Participants live for 1 month during the summer in an historic adobe guest cottage in a quiet neighborhood in Tucson, 2 houses from the nationally acclaimed University of Arizona Poetry Center, which houses a spectacular collection. Resident poets may immerse themselves in days and evenings of reading and writing poetry—no schedule, no other residents.

Only those who have *not* published more than one full-length work may apply (chapbooks and self-published books excepted).

Arizona Academic Programs

Arizona State University, English
  Dept., Tempe, AZ 85287; 602-965-
  7454; MFA Creative Writing
University of Arizona, English
  Dept., P.O. Box 210067, Tucson, AZ
  85721; 602-621-3880; MFA Creative
  Writing

Arkansas

Arkansas Writers' Conference

For *fiction and nonfiction writers,
poets* Hotel in Little Rock — 6817
Gingerbread La., Little Rock, AR 72204
Voice: 501-565-8889 **Contact:** Peggy
Vining, Dir. **Founded:** 1944 **Open:** 1st
weekend in June **Admission:** Registration
form only **Cost:** $10; awards luncheons $12
each; awards banquet $13 **Size-Attendees:**
225 **Handicapped Access**

ITERARY CONTESTS are the emphasis
at this conference. Over 30 awards
are given out at this annual event,
some at an awards luncheon the first
day, more at the awards banquet on the
second day. The workshops focus on
writing romance, mysteries and humor.
The featured speaker is usually a best-
selling author; in 1996 Leonard Bishop
gave 2 presentations: "The techniques,
not the art of writing" and "Dare to be
a great writer." As if in counterpoint, art
was the focus for Andrea Hollander
Budy, Lyon College artist-in-residence,
who spoke on "The Music of Language:
Why It's Important in Both Poetry and
Prose."

Lucidity Poets' Ozark Retreat

For *poets* Off the beaten track
in NW Arkansas — Rt 2, Box 94, Eureka
Springs, AR 72632 **Voice:** 501-253-9351
Contact: Ted Badger **Founded:** 1992 **Open:**
3 days in Apr. **Admission:** Registration form
only **Cost:** $20

UCIDITY, THE INITIATOR of this retreat, is a quarterly journal of verse
of a very specific nature: "No poems about birds, bees, butterflies, sunrise, sunset, politics, philosophy or your
religious persuasion. We seek poetry

dealing with daily human encounters
and relationships." Take a look at the
journal to determine whether this is the
conference for you. You can order
copies from Bear House Publishing at
the same address listed for the retreat.

The conference offers poets an opportunity to read, listen to and discuss
poetry in Eureka Springs, a small, colorful town in the Ozarks. There are
workshops for critiquing poems, prizes
given out at an awards banquet, as well
as "read-around" sessions. Bring your poems—they are what count at this event.

Southern Autobiography Conference

For *fiction and nonfiction writers,
poets* Central Arkansas — UCA, Administration Bldg. 120, Conway, AR 72035
Voice: 501-450-5073 **Fax:** 501-450-5066
E-mail: carold@ecom.uca.edu **Contact:**
Carol Daves **Open:** 2 days in Apr. **Admission:** Registration form only **Cost:** $25
(includes lunches, snacks)

OU WILL NOT FIND workshops on
the craft of writing or on finding
an agent here; the emphasis is on
readings and discussions centered
around a theme. This conference, supported by the Arkansas Humanities
Council and NEH, brings a variety of
writers to the UCA campus to explore
a subject relevant to the region. In 1996
writers focused on "Separate Pasts: Diversity & Community." Workshops included "Lies That Last," "Southern
Views," "Mixing in the Mountains," "Of
the Mulberry Family: An Arkansas Epi-
logue" and "And I Only Am Escaped
Alone to Tell Thee."

Writers from Alabama, Arkansas,
Mississippi, North and South Carolina,
and Tennessee have participated, reading from their work. Each conference
explores the South through personal
narratives written and read by natives.

White River Writers' Workshop

For poets Lyon College campus — Lyon College, P.O. Box 2317, Batesville, AR 72503 **Voice:** 501-793-1766 **Fax:** 501-698-4622 **E-mail:** ahbudy@aol.com **Contact:** Andrea Hollander Budy, Dir. **Founded:** 1995 **Open:** 1 week in June **Admission:** Application ($15), writing sample, personal statement **Deadlines:** May 15 (Apr. 1 for financial aid) **Cost:** $425; $325 meals and lodging **Financial Aid:** Loans; Scholarships; Fellowships* **Size-Attendees:** 12 maximum

WHITE RIVER WRITERS' Workshop offers serious poets an opportunity to spend a week with nationally acclaimed poets and 50 other selected participants. Mornings are devoted to workshops, individual conferences on writing, presenting poetry and time for writing. Afternoons include lectures, panels, participant readings. Evenings offer rare treats as the faculty of prize-winning poets and participants give readings.

A few of the noteworthy aspects of this workshop: it is small, it is poetry-centered, it focuses on writing as process, it is a gathering of equals (a significant statement given the impressive caliber of the faculty), it encourages discourse … and it takes place in Arkansas. The setting is the foothills of the Ozark Mts. Batesville (population 10,000) is near the Ozark Folk Center State Park and Blanchard Springs Caverns. Lyon College, an established, well-endowed liberal arts college, sits on the banks of the White River.

Arkansas Academic Programs

University of Arkansas, English Dept., Fayetteville, AR 72701; 501-575-4301; MFA Creative Writing

California

Art of the Wild

For fiction and nonfiction writers, poets Near the N shore of Lake Tahoe — Dept. of English, UC Davis, Davis, CA 95616 **Voice:** 916-752-1658 **Founded:** 1992 **Open:** 1 week in July **Admission:** Manuscript, letter **Deadlines:** Early May **Cost:** $565 (evening meals incl.) **Financial Aid:** Loans **Size-Attendees:** 96.

MOUNTAINS, TREES, streams and lakes provide the backdrop for a week of workshops that brings a stellar group of writer-teachers together at a Squaw Valley ski resort to explore the wilderness, nature and the environment. Fiction, nonfiction and poetry programs convene simultaneously (you can apply to more than one). There are sunrise nature walks, field trips, evening readings and seminars that feature scientists and naturalists as well as literary agents, editors, publishers and writers. Past staff has included poet Gary Snyder and Rick Bass (*The Lost Grizzlies*).

Co-sponsored by the Squaw Valley Community of Writers and the UC Davis Department of English, this intensive workshop distinguishes itself from many others by the caliber of its staff, its mountain locale and its deep concern for both the natural world and the craft of writing. Mornings are devoted to workshops led by writers. Afternoons feature lectures and panels with literary agents, editors and publishers, and evenings highlight the writing staff with readings from their works.

"The world outside the window offers rugged beauty (and a glimpse of the toll of development); we use it as a living laboratory: via daily daybreak nature walks, seminars with scientists and Sierra researchers, and Tuesday mountain-and-lake field studies."

45

Beyond Baroque Literary/Arts Center

For poets, fiction writers In Venice, famous LA beach town — *681 Venice Blvd., Venice, CA 90291* **Voice:** 310-822-3006 **Fax:** 310-827-7432 **Founded:** 1968 **Open:** Year-round **Cost:** $30 annual membership; some workshops extra

HOME TO INNOVATIVE poets, Beyond Baroque is a literary center that offers free as well as tuition-based poetry and writing workshops. Some meet for 2 sessions; others weekly for 6 weeks; the times and subjects vary. Beyond Baroque's lively weekly readings feature original, intense, wild, experimental, witty, punk, postmodern writers. Some inhabit the disenchanted fringe of the LA culture scene; others established it.

Contributing to the hip energy and community here are film screenings, musical events, performance art and publisher co-sponsored events—Incommunicado Press, Poetry Flash, Amok Books, among others. Also on site: a small-press library and writers resource center, and an active small-press bookstore. Attend one of the readings and pick up a monthly schedule; that's probably the best introduction to Beyond Baroque.

Book Passage Writers' Conferences: Mystery Writing, Travel Writing

For mystery writers, travel writers Marin County, 10 min. N of Golden Gate Bridge — *51 Tamal Vista Blvd., Corte Madera, CA 94925* **Voice:** 415-927-0960; 800-999-7909 **Fax:** 415-924-3838 **E-mail:** messages@bookpassage.com **Founded:** 1992 **Open:** Mystery: 4 days in July; Travel: 4 days in Aug. **Admission:** Registration form only **Cost:** $450–$485; $65 for manuscript evaluation **Size-Attendees:** 100 **Handicapped Access**

WHAT MAKES these conferences unique is their sponsor: Book Passage, an independent bookseller. Where would writers be if there were not booksellers to distribute their efforts? Bay Area writers demonstrate their support for Book Passage by actively participating in these 2 distinct events, which take place in the bookstore and at a nearby hotel.

It may be a mystery why this is so, but the San Francisco Bay Area has more than its share of mystery writers, which makes the annual Book Passage Mystery Writers' Conference a true feast for mystery lovers. Homicide detectives, private eyes, and crime scene investigators mix it up with authors, agents, publishers and editors.

The faculty of mystery writers guides the new and professional writer through a variety of "Craft of Crime" workshops—practical workshops on how to pace suspense fiction, bury clues, build a plot, create atmosphere, craft dialogue, create a series character.

Intriguing question-and-answer sessions might feature a detective, a police dispatcher, a cop and a bounty hunter. Each evening, a well-known writer addresses the group (Elizabeth George and Martin Cruz Smith appeared in 1996).

The Book Passage Travel Writers' Conference draws journalists, newspaper and magazine editors, publishers, book authors, agents and photographers. Mornings are devoted to intensive 3-hour writing workshops. Afternoons offer a choice of workshops, including "Guidebook Roundtable: What Publishers Want," "The Ethics of Travel Writing" and "Adventure Travel Writing: Going Out on a Limb." Evening readings feature well-known authors (Isabel Allende and Jan Morris in 1996).

Before or after the conference, there are opportunities to pursue one's interest in travel by exploring the area—San Francisco, Point Reyes, John Muir State Park and the wine country are a few of the nearby highlights.

For both conferences, the fee covers the opening dinner, lunches and the closing reception.

California Writers' Club Conference

For fiction and nonfiction writers, poets, screenwriters Conference center near Monterey — California Writers' Club, 2214 Derby St., Berkeley, CA 94705 **Open:** 2½ days in June or July, odd-numbered years **Admission:** Registration form only **Cost:** $250 (meals incl.); housing $65–$200; manuscript critique extra **Size-Attendees:** 450

WHAT A JUXTAPOSITION: a peaceful setting—the Asilomar Conference Center, where sand dunes and pines coexist on the edge of the Pacific—for a jam-packed conference with an emphasis on selling and mingling.

The Stanford Creative Writing Program

This unique program, founded 50 years ago by Wallace Stegner, is one of the most prized in the country. While it is based at Stanford University, it offers no degree. Instead, if you are lucky enough to become one of the 10 individuals selected, you receive a fully funded 2-year fellowship, which includes tuition and a living stipend. To be accepted, you must describe your "writing plans and what the fellowship would contribute to them." You are not required to have a BA, and there is no age consideration.

The only requirement is that you participate in a workshop, where you are considered a "working writer" rather than a student. In the workshop you receive close attention from the faculty and your peers so that you can perfect your efforts. The faculty is excellent, and your peers are as skilled as you are.

If you are highly motivated, already well accomplished, and seeking 2 years of support—financial and critical—this is a program to consider. Stanford is a major university, which means there are resources galore. San Francisco and Berkeley are nearby, if you seek the stimulation of an urban environment. Just over the rolling hills, an hour or so away, lie the Pacific Ocean, Santa Cruz and Half Moon Bay.

Speakers and faculty are drawn from *Writer's Digest, Arizona Highways, Publishers Weekly, Parent's Magazine, California Highway Patrolman, Field and Stream, National Geographic Traveler,* Capra Press, Silhouette Books and various (mostly small) presses and literary agencies in California.

Sponsored by the California Writers' Club, which has several branches (see also the Jack London Writers' Conference), this conference offers a chance to meet with agents and editors and to attend a variety of workshops plus a trade show. "Scanning the Desktop Publishing Industry," "Insider Tricks to Getting Books Published" and "Forecasts and Current Trends in Publishing" were among the 1996 topics.

Cruise Conferences for Writers

For fiction and nonfiction writers *Varies* — P.O. Box 10, Orangevale, CA 95662 **Voice:** 916-987-9489; 800-979-3548 **Contact:** Carol O'Hara **Founded:** 1994 **Open:** Varies **Admission:** Registration form only **Cost:** $1,000 up **Size-Attendees:** 60–80

HERE'S ONE OF THE latest novelties in writers' conferences: the cruise conference. How about sailing from San Francisco to Florida aboard a first-class luxury liner, studying writing in one-on-one workshops as you pass through the Panama Canal? *Writer's Digest* and NEO-CON (3 entrepreneurial writers/conference directors with a hot idea) are co-sponsors of cruise conferences for writers in exotic locales. Just imagine: days full of workshops on how to write a query letter, or how to sell your travel stories, or recalling your family history—mixed in with adventures on sea and land.

You disembark at various beautiful locations and then return to the ship to study, write and continue on the cruise. The workshops are led by a mix of professional magazine and book writers. Sessions focus on practical issues, the craft and business of writing. Past cruises have explored the Caribbean

and the Inside Passage from Anchorage to Vancouver, with scenic trips along the way to see fjords, to tour Valdez, Juneau, Sitka, Ketchikan. Conference directors design flexible programs, and for those with less time there may be options to attend part of a conference. A special cruise around New Zealand and Australia was in the works for 1997. Prices begin at $1,000 and vary depending on the kind of cabin reserved, when the reservation is made (discounts for early sign-up), and the length of the flight to join the trip (discounted airline tickets are available).

Djerassi Resident Artists Program

For all writers 45 mi. S of San Francisco — 2325 Bear Gulch Rd., Woodside, CA 94062 **Voice:** 415-747-1250 **Fax:** 415-747-0105 **Founded:** 1979 **Open:** Apr.–Oct. **Admission:** Application ($25), writing sample, project proposal **Deadlines:** Mid-Feb. **Cost:** None **Size-Attendees:** 8–12 per month

BREATHTAKING VIEWS, wide-open pastures, woods, and free room, board and studio space—what more can an artist ask for? Residents include artists in music, visual arts, choreography and media arts, as well as writers. Interdisciplinary exchange is part of the plan at Djerassi.

Writers live in a comfortable 2-story redwood Artists' House with a fireplace in the library/living room. Each writer's room has a large desk, work space and outdoor deck. Along the trails on the 600 acres of land you will see sculptures created by former resident artists for the site. Emerging and mid-career artists are encouraged to apply. There is time for solitude (no visiting between 8 a.m. and 5 p.m.) as well as time for social interaction, when everyone gathers around 1 big table for dinner. A chef cooks dinner during the week; the residents collaborate at cooking parties on the weekends.

Djerassi encourages the avant-garde, reflecting the interests of its executive director, text/sound composer Charles Amirkanian, and his wife, visual artist Carol Law, who acts as general manager. The Resident Artists Program was created by Dr. Carl Djerassi (an inventor of the birth-control pill), in memory of his daughter, a poet and painter, to provide "the gift of time" to established and emerging artists.

ROBIN CLARK

A playful welcome to Djerassi Resident Artists Program.

Dorland Mountain Arts Colony

For all writers *Between San Diego and Riverside* — *P.O. Box 6, Temecula, CA 92593* **Voice:** 909-676-5039 **Open:** Year-round **Admission:** Application, writing sample **Deadlines:** Sept. 1, Mar. 1 **Cost:** $50 processing fee; $5 a day **Financial Aid:** Loans; Fellowship

DORLAND MOUNTAIN Arts Colony offers a primitive retreat with individual cottages for its residents on a 300-acre nature preserve. "Primitive" can have a dozen meanings. At Dorland it means that there is no electricity. Instead, residents use kerosene lamps, wood stoves for heat, and propane for the cooking stove, water

heater and refrigerator. The notion is that without electricity an artist will discover a different rhythm, one that will nourish creativity.

The point is privacy, and time to create. Communication with other residents is primarily through notes left in each other's mailboxes. There is 1 pay phone. Occasional voluntary potluck dinners may be the sole opportunity for social interaction, and even these are optional.

Dorland is for those who want to be left alone. There are miles of trails, a spring-fed pond and scenic overlooks with views of the Temecula Valley, an area of vineyards, horsefarms, oak trees, rolling hills and bedroom communities for San Diego and Riverside. Most residents stay for a month.

Dorland began as a private retreat, founded by Ellen Babcock Dorland, a world-famous concert pianist and music teacher who teamed with an environmentalist friend to set up the colony for visual artists, writers and composers. For more than a decade the land was owned by the Nature Conservancy; in 1988 the Conservancy turned the land back over to Dorland with the agreement that it will be left undeveloped forever.

Earth Writers Workshop

For nature writers, poets, fiction and nonfiction writers *80 mi. N of LA* — *International Center for Earth Concerns, 2162 Baldwin Rd., Ojai, CA 93023* **Voice:** 805-649-3535 **Contact:** Karen Collins **Founded:** 1996 **Open:** 1 weekend in May **Admission:** Registration form only **Deadlines:** Month prior to workshop **Cost:** Workshop $250; Intensive $100 **Financial Aid:** Loans; Scholarship **Size-Attendees:** 15

THE INTERNATIONAL CENTER for Earth Concerns, a small environmental education center, launched a new workshop in 1996 to give writers an opportunity to explore the natural world and our relationship to it. The writing component of the event focuses on

49

helping participants develop their skills in a variety of forms—from essays, journal writing and literary journalism to poetry and story writing. Hikes, meditations, talks and readings supplement the writing workshops. The workshop offers 4 days of activities. The Earth Writers Intensive is a 1-day event during the workshop, for those who can come for only a day.

The location draws writers, artists, seekers and naturalists year-round. Amongst spiritually oriented individuals, Ojai has a reputation similar to Sedona, Arizona, as a geographic spot known for certain mystical qualities. The Center's 276 acres include meadows, streams and canyons, as well as an Australian and a South African botanical garden.

Foothill College Writers' Conference

For fiction and nonfiction writers, poets In the hills between Palo Alto and San Jose — 12345 El Monte Rd., Los Altos Hills, CA 94022 **Voice:** 415-949-7316 **Founded:** 1976 **Open:** Late June **Admission:** Registration form only **Cost:** $75 **Size-Attendees:** 200

A N INEXPENSIVE 6-day conference featuring numerous accomplished writers on panels and reading from their works. Programs are distributed on the first day of the conference. Special topics to be explored may include: "nature and art, the dark side, the writing process, the state of the book, creative autobiography, moving between genres, the persona poem, men's poetry, women's issues, multicultural literature, and rural poetry."

Request the list of writers currently participating as guest faculty to whet your appetite. In 1996 Alan Cheuse and James D. Houston were among the authors offering readings. Each day there are 2 seminars, a choice of manuscript workshops, and one-on-one sessions for poets. Academic credit is available.

Glenessence

For all writers In the desert NE of LA — 1447 W. Ward Ave., Ridgecrest, CA 93555 **Voice:** 619-446-5894 **Fax:** 619-446-6782 **Contact:** Allison Swift **Open:** Mar.–May, Sept.–Nov. **Admission:** Reservation **Deadlines:** First come, first served **Cost:** $565 per month **Financial Aid:** Loans; Fellowship **Size-Attendees:** 5

G LENESSENCE, A HYBRID retreat and B & B, is a private home that's made available for writers. There are 5 bedrooms, each with a separate bath. You cook and clean for yourself here. There is also a laundry room, exercise equipment, library, dining and living room on the property, as well as a swimming pool. Some rooms have their own phones and cable TV.

The high desert provides a unique environment, appearing stark and even severe to newcomers from greener environs. The owner of Glenessence is the dean of the local college and volunteers that she can arrange access to its computer lab, library and bookstore. Death Valley National Monument is only a 2-hour drive away and intrigues most visitors.

Gordon Burgett—Communication Unlimited

For nonfiction writers primarily
Various colleges — P.O. Box 6405, Santa
Maria, CA 93456 **Voice:** 805-937-8711
Fax: 805-937-3035 **Contact:** Gordon
Burgett, Pres. **Admission:** Registration form
only **Cost:** $50 per session

BURGETT OFFERS seminars through the extended-education programs at colleges in California at various times during the year. Topics include "How to Sell 75% of Your Freelance Writing," "Writing Travel Articles That Sell" and "How to Publish Your Niche Marketed Book and Earn $50,000 Plus." He also sells tapes and books on the same subjects. In 1996 workshops took place in Aptos, Los Altos Hills, San Francisco, Santa Rosa, Sacramento, Chico, San Mateo, Redwood City, Rocklin, San Diego and Long Beach.

Headlands Center for the Arts

For fiction and nonfiction writers,
playwrights, poets Northern edge of SF Bay
— 944 Fort Barry, Sausalito, CA 94965
Voice: 415-331-2787 **Fax:** 415-331-3857
Founded: 1987 **Open:** Feb.–Dec. **Admission:** Application, writing sample, personal
statement **Deadlines:** Early June **Size-Attendees:** Varies

FOR MANY YEARS the northern edge of San Francisco Bay was off-limits, U.S. Army property. When the army left, the Golden Gate National Recreation Area was formed to protect the windswept rolling hills, beaches, cliffs and coves of the Marin Headlands. In 1982 Headlands Center for the Arts was founded to "investigate the relationship between human and natural systems through the arts." Money was raised, and 2 of the forts were transformed into a center for the arts.

Headlands provides a variety of programs, including residencies, for artists. Call to learn who may apply this year. In the past, the residencies have at times been open only to Bay Area residents, or only to residents of a particular state that has funded the year's program. Artists can also rent studio space here and attend readings and performances.

International Black Writers & Artists Los Angeles Conference

For fiction and nonfiction writers, poets, screenwriters, journalists Central
LA — P.O. Box 43576, Los Angeles, CA 90043
Voice: 213-964-3721 **Founded:** 1974 **Open:**
2 days in July **Admission:** Registration form
($25) **Cost:** $75–$150 (lunch incl.)

THE ANNUAL International Black Writers & Artists Los Angeles Conference focuses on a significant theme of concern to the LA arts community, for example "Diversity—Valuing Differences, Creating Visions." The conference always attracts a wide range of featured speakers and participants, including poets, journalists, television producers, professors, grant writers, playwrights, actors and visual artists.

Saturday workshops take place at a high school, where the facilitators include educators as well as writers and artists. To broaden the impact of the conference beyond established writers and artists, there is a special arrangement for teachers: Each can sponsor 1 student at a special rate of only $25 to encourage attendance by those who can't afford the conference but could greatly benefit from the inspiration and training provided.

When artists, educators and writers meet in Los Angeles, the focus naturally includes the worlds of television and film. There is an explicit emphasis here on creating artistic visions, as well as improving one's craft. On Sunday afternoon in 1996, there was a Play and Talent Expo at the William Grant Still Art Center, a co-sponsor of the conference.

Jack London Writers' Conference

For fiction and nonfiction writers, poets *Holiday Inn, San Francisco Airport — 512 Alameda de las Pulgas, Belmont, CA 94002* **Voice:** Conference: 415-342-9123; Registration: 415-593-2054; Membership: 415-572-2348 **Contact:** Howard Kraus, Registration Chair **Founded:** 1988 **Open:** 1 day in Mar. **Admission:** Registration form only **Deadlines:** Early Mar. **Cost:** $80 (lunch incl.); manuscript critique $10

W HO WAS Jack London? A popular writer, an adventurer and a socialist, London also joined with fellow writers to found the California Writers' Club, whose Peninsula Branch sponsors this conference. The CWC describes him as a skilled sailor who "transcended his life of poverty to become one of America's most beloved writers." Want to know more? Attend the conference and you will probably get to hear the popular presentation by Greg Hayes, a ranger at the Jack London State Historic Park in Glen Ellen, who describes how London became famous for his stories, such as *The Call of the Wild* and *The Sea Wolf,* inspired by his fantastic adventures.

In 1996 writers Isabel Allende and Elizabeth Tallent, director of the Stanford University Creative Writing Program, were among the keynote speakers. Morning and afternoon workshops

featured writers, editors and agents, and focused on writing poetry, romance/ fantasy, travel, children's literature and suspense fiction.

"Ask-A-Pro Consultations" (15-minute sessions) with professional editors on a first-come, first-served basis—are available all day.

Mendocino Coast Writers Conference

For fiction and nonfiction writers, poets *Mendocino coast — 1211 Del Mar Dr., Fort Bragg, CA 95437* **Voice:** 707-961-1001 **E-mail:** marlis@vm1.ucc.okstate.edu **Web Site:** http://www.okstate.edu/artsci/mcwc **Contact:** Marlis Manley Broadhead, Dir. **Founded:** 1990 **Open:** 2 days in June **Admission:** Registration form only **Cost:** $130–$150 **Size-Attendees:** 105–130

G OURMET FOOD draws folks to this writers' conference, which appears to be almost as much about the Mendocino area as it is about writing. The building that houses the College of the Redwoods, home to the conference, sits a block or so from the spectacular coast.

The annual 2-day conference features a combination of workshops facilitated by local writers, an editor and an agent. The fee includes a Friday night gourmet dinner, lunch on Saturday, and a "beachfire reading" Saturday night (participants are encouraged to bring poems to read at this event).

The college is just south of downtown Fort Bragg, a small fishing and logging town as nondescript as Mendocino, just 7 miles farther south, is gentrified and charming. The rocky coast and striking redwoods have attracted visitors to this area for decades. In the 1960s many artists, writers and other assorted urban refugees started settling in the area and created an arty culture. Tourism remains an important source of income for the area; consequently there are expensive restaurants, art galleries and shops for browsing.

Mount Herman Christian Writers Conference

For fiction and nonfiction writers In the redwoods near Santa Cruz — P.O. Box 413, Mount Herman, CA 95041 **Voice:** 408-335-4466 **Fax:** 408-335-9218 **Contact:** David Talbott **Founded:** 1970 **Open:** Fri.–Tues. over Palm Sunday weekend **Admission:** Registration form only **Deadlines:** Early Mar. **Cost:** $435 (meals incl.); $30–$215 housing **Financial Aid:** Loans; Scholarship

FOR THE CHRISTIAN writer, this is a conference not to miss. Set in the redwoods near the beaches of Santa Cruz, the Mount Herman conference draws representatives from major Christian publishers and publications to provide beginning and advanced writers with 5 days of stimulating sessions. There are worship services, communal meals and writing workshops.

With over 30 faculty teaching, the conference offers workshops on a wide variety of subjects, including fiction, nonfiction, poetry, children's books, interviewing, the advantages and perils of self-publishing, as well as specialized workshops in devotional writing and Christian curriculum writing.

If you are a professional Christian writer, consider applying for the advanced track, an exclusive series of workshops for those who meet the criteria.

Sensitive? Beware of Workshop Feedback

You've sweated it out for months, and finally you have a manuscript that makes you proud. You think, and your best friend agrees, that what you have written is good. Maybe not best-seller material, but worthy of publication. Certainly as good as, if not better than, most everything else out there in print.

You spend hard-earned money to get to a conference, where you share your manuscript with a writer or editor you respect. As you wait for a response, you're scared. You're excited. This may be the Big Break. And what happens? The much-admired expert does not share your judgment. In fact, the expert writer not only thinks it "needs work" but implies that maybe even work cannot save it.

At moments like this it would be better if you weren't so sensitive. But then if you weren't so sensitive you wouldn't have become a writer. You wouldn't have known what to write about. You wouldn't have noticed all sorts of oddities about human beings and places and your life would be much duller.

Okay, you're sensitive, but does that mean you have to cry at a conference? Can you control those tears, you wonder? Please, not now, you counsel yourself, as you fight the flood. You try valiantly to think about something else—anything except what you just heard.

Beware. The feedback from experts may be valuable even when it hurts. Can you write it down? How does one receive withering criticism and learn from it?

Timing is critical. Do not go to a workshop or conference before you are ready to be brutally criticized. Do not imagine that "feedback" means a positive response, or even constructive criticism. If you are lucky, it might mean that. Writers and editors are born critical—it's in their genes—and then they receive training to sharpen their skills.

Many (many, many) tears have been shed by writers at workshops. Too often people confuse the value of a manuscript with their value as a person. Yes, you wrote it; and yes, it may even be based on your very own life experiences. But whatever it is that you wrote, it is not you. You—the person—are more (for better and worse) than your writing.

Napa Valley Writers' Conference

🖋️ 💬 **For fiction writers, poets** *Wine country — Napa Valley College, 1088 College Ave., St. Helena, CA 94574* **Voice:** 707-967-2900 **Fax:** 707-967-2909 **Contact:** Anne Matlack Evans **Founded:** 1981 **Open:** 1 week in late July **Admission:** Registration ($10), writing sample, personal statement **Deadlines:** June 1 **Cost:** $450 **Financial Aid:** Loans; Scholarship **Size-Attendees:** 80

HERE IN THE HEART of California wine country—rolling hills, live-oak trees and vineyards—intoxication can come from concentrating on fine writing under the tutelage of a faculty of well-known poets and fiction writers. The small size of the conference and the high quality of the faculty—as teachers as well as writers—has made admission to this conference competitive, so apply early and submit your best work.

In the New Poetry Workshop you work exclusively with 1 faculty member for the week. The emphasis is on writing new poems. In the Craft of Fiction Workshop you work with each of the faculty writers, selecting 1 to review your manuscript. There are also panels featuring visiting editors and agents.

What distinguishes this gathering is its focus on developing literature, art and craft, as opposed to promoting commercialism. The background of the faculty demonstrates this artistic orientation. Program director John Leggett was director of the Writers' Workshop at the University of Iowa. This is not the conference for panel discussions on how to market yourself and your manuscript.

It is recommended that participants have a car to drive to the various vineyards hosting the special events. Transportation also makes San Francisco, the East Bay, Muir Woods and the Point Reyes National Seashore accessible.

Palm Springs Writers Conference

🖋️ 💬 **For fiction and nonfiction writers, poets, screenwriters** *A Palm Springs resort — 646 Morongo Rd., Palm Springs, CA 92264* **Voice:** 619-864-9760 **Fax:** 619-322-1833 **Open:** 3 days in May **Admission:** Registration form only **Cost:** $350 (some meals incl.); manuscript evaluations extra

NATURALLY MONEY is of concern at a conference held at a "world famous" resort in Palm Springs, best known for its celebrities and golf courses. These workshops and panels emphasize the marketplace: "How to Write Magazine Articles That Sell," "Selling That Mystery," "What's Hot and What's Not in Fiction and Nonfiction" and "The Finances of Publishing: Expectations vs. Reality in the Marketplace" were among the 1996 offerings.

Agents, editors and publishers, fiction and nonfiction writers, TV writers and screenwriters gather for workshops and panels led by best-selling authors, novelist-screenwriters, screenwriter-producers, and assorted hyphenates who make a living, or try to make a living, in Hollywood. A conference this close to Los Angeles necessarily reflects the dominance of television and movies in the marketplace.

Manuscript evaluations and agent and/or editor consultations can be scheduled in advance.

The resort offers a special rate for conference participants. As a guest you can take advantage of the spas, tennis courts, gym facilities and golf course. There is also a tram from Palm Springs into the San Jacinto mountains, where you can go hiking. In May, wild winds frequently stir up the arid landscape, blowing enormous tumbleweeds across the highways, and some of the flowers may still be in bloom on the ocotillos and cholla.

San Diego State University Writers' Conference

For fiction and nonfiction writers, screenwriters College of Extended Studies, SDSU, 5250 Campanile Dr., San Diego, CA 92182 **Voice:** 619-594-2514 **Fax:** 619-594-8566 **E-mail:** ealcaraz@mail.sdsu.edu **Contact:** Erin Gray Alcaraz **Founded:** 1984 **Open:** 3rd weekend in Jan. **Admission:** Registration form only **Cost:** $200 **Size-Attendees:** 390 **Handicapped Access**

A FULL 2 DAYS of activities for writers, sponsored by San Diego State University's College of Extended Studies. Dozens of speakers share their experiences of writing and publishing fiction, nonfiction, mysteries, children's books, screenplays, suspense and thrillers, westerns, women's fiction, historical fiction, fantasy and science fiction. There are plenty of opportunities to meet literary agents as well as senior editors from publishers such as Simon & Schuster, Harlequin, Berkley, Ace, Doubleday, Bantam, HarperCollins, Dutton Children's Books and Penguin.

A special feature is the Research Emporium, where experts from a variety of fields, from costume history to forensic anthropology, help nonfiction and fiction writers to do the research their projects require. "Digging Up The Bones—Forensics, How It Works and What It Can Tell Us," "Weaponry/Martial Arts" and "Beyond DNA and Bloody Gloves: Police Investigation" were among the 1996 presentations.

Participants may submit the first 7 pages of a manuscript for a critique. Remember that there are beaches galore in this area, as well as the popular San Diego Zoo and Sea World.

San Jose Center for Poetry and Literature

For poets The Monterey Peninsula — P.O. Box 221847, Carmel, CA 93922 **Voice:** 408-292-3254 **Contact:** Lequita Vance-Watkins, Exec. Dir. **Open:** 2½ days in Jan. **Admission:** Registration form only **Deadlines:** First come, first served **Cost:** $350 (room and board incl.) **Size-Attendees:** 46 **Handicapped Access**

D OES YOUR private fantasy go something like this: If only I could get away for a couple of days, escape to the Monterey Peninsula, stare at the sun as it sets, walk among the cypress trees, write, read and listen to poetry? It is possible to make it happen by attending the annual Asilomar Retreat in Pacific Grove, sponsored by the San Jose Center for Poetry and Literature. Poet, raconteur and men's movement guru Robert Bly is frequently the featured writer at this very popular event, so if you're interested, sign up early. He draws a big crowd.

The Center, which was founded in 1975, also sponsors 1- and 2-day workshops for poets throughout the year, as well as poetry readings; all take place in the San Jose area. Write for a schedule.

Santa Barbara Writers' Conference

For fiction and nonfiction writers, poets, playwrights, screenwriters Montecito (S of Santa Barbara) — Box 304, Carpinteria, CA 93014 **Voice:** 805-684-2250 **Contact:** Mary Conrad **Founded:** 1973 **Open:** 1 week in late June **Admission:** Registration form only **Cost:** $350 **Size-Attendees:** 350 **Handicapped Access**

T HE WEEKLONG Santa Barbara Writers' Conference has sparked raves from successful and well-known authors: "A most stimulating time — a glorious week!" says Eudora Welty. "A lovely time," comments Gore Vidal. "Very valuable!" raves Sidney Sheldon. "The best in the nation," claims James Michener. What does it do to earn this praise?

Ray Bradbury is the keynote speaker, and has been every year since the conference began in the early 1970s.

Workshops meet every morning and afternoon for 2 hours: fiction, nonfiction, biography, science fiction, mystery, screenwriting, dramatic writing, poetry, juveniles, romance, humor, marketing and the right-brain experience. Famous writers, screenwriters and teachers speak every afternoon and evening—in 1996, T. Coraghessan Boyle, Anne Lamont, Elmore Leonard and cartoonist Charles Schulz.

The setting, Hotel Miramar on the beach in Montecito, provides quiet comfort. In your free moments you can walk, explore Santa Barbara, bicycle, sample the many restaurants in the area, check out the local bookstores, go to a movie, visit the Mission or drive into the hills.

Society of Children's Book Writers and Illustrators National Conference

For fiction and nonfiction writers 22736 Vanowen St., Suite 106, West Hills, CA 91307 **Voice:** 818-888-8760 **Web Site:** http://www.scbwi.org **Founded:** 1968 **Open:** 3 days in Aug. **Admission:** Registration form only **Deadlines:** Varies **Cost:** $300 **Size-Attendees:** 500 **Handicapped Access**

THIS CONFERENCE attracts over 500 writers, illustrators, editors, educators, agents and librarians to the Los Angeles area for lectures and panel discussions. While there are some breakout sessions, for the most part everyone gathers in 1 room to listen to the various speakers discuss issues related to the craft and the business of children's literature. Luminaries in the field lecture and may offer individual manuscript consultations.

The faculty includes fiction and nonfiction authors and editors from publishers such as G. P. Putnam and Morrow Junior Books. The lectures address such issues as on listening to children, writing the novel, research, working with agents and creating the picture book. Groups affiliated with SCBWI sponsor local events, including regional conferences, around the country year-round (see *Associations and Organizations*).

Squaw Valley Community of Writers

For fiction and nonfiction writers, poets, screenwriters Close to N shore of Lake Tahoe — Summer: P.O. Box 2352, Olympic Valley, CA 96146; Winter: 10626 Banner Lava Cap, Nevada City, CA 95959 **Voice:** 916-583-5200; 916-274-8551 **Contact:** Brett Hall Jones, Exec. Dir. **Founded:** 1970 **Open:** July, Aug., Oct. **Admission:** Manuscript ($15 reading fee) **Deadlines:** Early May; early July for Travel Writing **Cost:** $555 (evening meals incl.); Travel Writing $385 (evening meals incl.) **Financial Aid:** Loans; Scholarship **Size-Attendees:** 15–120

AT SQUAW VALLEY, natural beauty and literary excellence combine to make these workshops an attractive option for serious writers. Participants live at Olympic House—site of the 1960 Winter Olympics—near Lake Tahoe. Mountains tower over the meadows and streams. This is a landscape to captivate, inspire and delight. Perhaps there is also an extra charge of some sort in the air, a special residue from the accumulated successes of the past participants in these workshops.

There are 4 distinct workshops, and each is selective (admission is based on manuscript submissions): The Fiction Workshops are taught by well-known writers, such as novelists Richard Ford and Amy Tan. "The task of the Fiction Program is to assist participants in the arduous passage from writer to author." The core activity—the workshops—is supplemented by panels on editing, publishing and the craft of writing. Non-fiction writers are now included in the fiction program, with a special workshop to meet their needs.

The Poetry Workshop, designed by Galway Kinnell, requires each participant to write a fresh poem every day— a poem that aims at "something new and daring." Emphasis is on creating a community of poets to encourage risk taking, freedom of expression, truth telling and depth.

The Travel Writing Workshop for Poets and Writers meets in the fall, at the

Learning On-Line

Everyone agrees that learning on-line is quite different from sitting face-to-face with one's peers and an instructor in a classroom. But many argue that for writers, the anonymity and the absence of a set class time actually facilitate the learning process.

The UCLA Extension On-Line Writing Program currently serves primarily Southern Californians, but no matter where you live, if you have access to the Internet, you can enroll in a course. The 1996 courses included the basics: "Fiction Fundamentals," "Writing the First Novel," "Writing the Novel the Professional Way," "Journal Writing" and "Screenwriting."

What makes these classes unique is the method of instruction. Students receive assignments, do homework, perform exercises, and get instructors' and classmates' feedback, all through e-mail. You do the work on your own time schedule, within the parameters of the course. Established in 1995, the program differentiates itself from conventional correspondence courses by offering dialogue throughout the week. Teachers pro-vide a "lecture" and an assignment on-line. Students e-mail their assignments to the teacher, which begins the conversation. Other students have an opportunity to engage or not. Faculty comment not just once on a finished assignment, but regularly throughout the writing process. Students can alter what they have written, which may evoke more comments, revisions, and conversation.

One pleased student commented: "The instructor's feedback was always timely, supportive, and pragmatic. I felt he took my writing and my questions seriously. He kept to the role of coach, offering suggestions to help me solve dilemmas, but ultimately encouraging me to work out my own solutions."

On-line classes may not replace the traditional classroom, but already the convenience of these courses attracts students and teachers from places far away from the host institution. And the locals appreciate them, too. As one student comments: "Now I don't have to worry about a babysitter, or parking, or driving. I just do the lesson when I have a free moment."

River Ranch in Alpine Meadows, a few miles from Squaw Valley, providing informal interactions with the faculty of travel writers, as well as workshops on the art, craft and marketing of literary travel writing. A Screenwriting Workshop is also available.

See also The Art of the Wild, offered in collaboration with UCDavis.

UC Berkeley Extension

For fiction and nonfiction writers, poets, screenwriters *Various Bay Area locations — UCB Extension, 1995 University Ave, #7002, Berkeley, CA 94720* **Voice:** 510-642-4111 **Fax:** 510-642-0374 **Web Site:** http://www-cmil.unex.berkeley.edu/ **Open:** Year-round **Admission:** Registration form only **Cost:** $180–$300 **Size-Attendees:** Varies

WHETHER YOUR interest is in writing news, poetry, mysteries, travel reportage, magazine articles, short stories, screenplays or novels, there is probably a course for you at UCB's extension program. While extension courses cannot offer a retreat from daily life, they do provide an opportunity to work on your writing, especially if faraway conferences in exotic locales do not fit into your budget or schedule.

The San Francisco Bay Area offers intellectual stimulation, wonderful bookstores, readings, cultural events, libraries galore, and nearby natural wonders from Point Reyes to the Monterey Peninsula. With these sorts of resources, who needs to travel elsewhere to concentrate on writing? Enroll in a course at the hometown university; there are courses in various locations throughout the Bay Area. Some courses have limited enrollments, so do sign up early.

In 1996 UCB joined with America Online to provide courses on-line; in addition, they offer courses by mail and fax. Call the Center for Media and Independent Learning to receive a catalog (510-642-4124), or visit the Web site.

If you can carve out a week of time, there is an intensive fiction workshop retreat during the summer for $1,000, which includes room and board and an opportunity to work with a published author on your manuscript.

UCLA Extension Writers' Program

For fiction and nonfiction writers, poets, screenwriters, journalists, playwrights *West L.A., Burbank, Santa Monica — 10995 Le Conte Ave., Los Angeles, CA 90024* **Voice:** 310-825-9415 **Fax:** 310-206-7382 **E-mail:** CTEW@UNEX.UCLA.EDU **Contact:** Chad Tew **Open:** Year-round **Admission:** Registration form, writing sample and/or prerequisites for some classes **Cost:** $175–$400 **Financial Aid:** Loans; Scholarship **Size-Class:** 15–25 **Degree or Certification:** Certificate in Creative Writing, Certificate in Screenwriting

UCLA EXTENSION offers the largest, most comprehensive and most diverse continuing-education writing program in the country. Be prepared to be overwhelmed. Over 400 courses are offered per year, several designed for the absolute beginner, many for experienced writers. Every genre is represented. Reading the catalogue can be an education in itself.

In LA the emphasis tends to be on writing for the film and television industries, and writing for whatever is "new," which today means the interactive media. Following your muse may be less important than following what is hot in the marketplace. Most of these classes meet weekly, but some are half-day workshops and some are intensive weekend courses, including in 1996 "Making Your Good Novel Great," "Creating Compelling Comic Characters" and "Stomping the Blues."

Making connections is often as important as the content of a course. Some classes are taught by representatives of television or movie production companies, publishing houses or literary agencies, and many others are led by published authors.

University of California, Santa Cruz Extension

For fiction and nonfiction writers, poets UCSC campus and Santa Clara — 740 Front St., Suite 155, Santa Cruz, CA 95060 **Voice:** 408-427-6600 **Fax:** 408-427-6690 **Web Site:** http://www.ucsc.edu/unex **Admission:** Registration form only **Cost:** $100–$150

UCSC EXTENSION offers a variety of workshops year-round, from "Story Crafting for Traditional and New Media" to "Taming the Inner Critic." Several blend writing, personal and psychological explorations: "Release the Writer Within You," "Writing Your Life History," "Self-Actualization and Creativity." Others focus on poetry. Some meet for a weekend; others meet weekly for a quarter.

Villa Montalvo Artist Residency Program

For all writers 1 hr S of San Francisco — P.O. Box 158, 15400 Montalvo Rd., Saratoga, CA 95071 **Voice:** 408-741-3421 **Fax:** 408-741-5592 **Founded:** 1942 **Open:** Year-round **Admission:** Application ($20), writing sample **Deadlines:** Mar. 1 (for Oct.–Mar.); Sept. 1 (for Apr.–Sept.) **Cost:** $100 security deposit **Financial Aid:** Loans; Fellowship **Size-Attendees:** 5

INSPIRED BY Italian academies, U.S. Senator James D. Phelan built Villa Montalvo in the style of a Mediterranean villa in the 1930s to promote art, music and literature. He invited prominent artists to his home, creating an informal artists' retreat, which became a formal program open to applicants in 1942. Today the retreat provides 1- to 3-month-long residencies in private apartments (with kitchens) for a fortunate 16 to 18 artists a year.

There are 2 seasons at Villa Montalvo: Active (spring/summer) and Quiet (fall/winter). Choose your season wisely. If you need solitude, apply for a winter residency. If you thrive on literary readings and workshops, exhibition openings and concerts, come during the Performing Arts Season, in spring/summer, when Montalvo hosts over 40 events at its 2 theaters. Residents receive complimentary tickets to all events.

At Montalvo, residents live and work independently, coming together only once a week for an informal dinner. Artists shop and cook for themselves. It is not for those seeking a communal experience.

Set in the foothills of the Santa Cruz Mountains, surrounded by redwood groves, creeks and nature trails, Villa Montalvo is open to the public year-round as an arboretum and Audubon Society bird sanctuary. During the active season, weekends are particularly lively.

Villa Montalvo

Writers Connection Seminars and Conferences

For fiction and nonfiction writers, screenwriters *Santa Clara* — *P.O. Box 24770, San Jose, CA 95154* **Voice:** 408-445-3600 **Fax:** 408-445-3609 **E-mail:** writer-scxn@aol.com **Contact:** Steve Lester, Pres. **Founded:** 1983 **Open:** Year-round **Admission:** Registration form only **Cost:** $115–$125 for seminars, $45 annual membership

THESE MARKETING-ORIENTED seminars are sponsored by an organization that aims to serve writers through a monthly newsletter and a grammar hot line. The 1-day conferences are held throughout the year in a hotel in Santa Clara. In 1996 the topics included "Book Publishing," "The Basics of Mystery Writing," "Making a Good Script Great," "Young Adult Novels" and 2 days on "Writing for Interactive Multimedia." A conference on "Selling to Hollywood" takes place in the LA area.

Writing Workshop with Poet Galway Kinnell

For poets *Tor House Foundation, Box 2713, Carmel, CA 93921* **Voice:** 408-624-1813 **Fax:** 408-624-3696 **E-mail:** hawk-tower@aol.com **Founded:** 1991 **Open:** 1 weekend in May **Admission:** Registration form only **Deadlines:** First come, first served **Cost:** $150 (meal incl.) **Size-Attendees:** 22 **Handicapped Access**

THIS WORKSHOP is an annual 2-day event featuring Pulitzer Prize-winning poet Galway Kinnell, who teaches poetry at New York University and has pioneered the poetry workshop at a number of conferences. Participants write, listen to, and read poems, as well as engaging in discussions on writing poetry. The sponsor—The Tor House Foundation—was created to preserve poet Robinson Jeffers's unusual stone home with its 40-foot-high stone-studded Hawk Tower, which he built as a retreat for his wife.

Yosemite Field Seminars

For fiction and nonfiction writers, poets *Yosemite National Park* — *Yosemite Association, P.O. Box 230, El Portal, CA 95318* **Voice:** 209-379-2321 **Fax:** 209-379-2486 **E-mail:** YOSE_Yosemite_Association@nps.gov **Founded:** 1973 **Open:** Feb.–Nov. **Admission:** Registration form only **Cost:** $145–$175 per seminar **Size-Attendees:** 10–15

THE YOSEMITE Association sponsors a variety of field seminars, some exclusively for writers, and dozens for bird watchers, photographers, naturalists, artists and backpackers.

Imagine walking through the meadows of the Sierras in Yosemite National Park—wildflowers, waterfalls, birds, towering trees, rocky moutainsides—and then sitting down with a group of writers to focus on developing your craft. In 1996 Robin Drury, coordinator of the Central California Writing Project at UC Santa Cruz, led a workshop designed for teachers that included hikes, writing exercises, response partnerships and lots of time for writing. Poet-naturalist Kristina Rylands has led a poetry workshop that mixed hikes, readings, free-writing exercises and solitude. The workshops change from year to year; contact the Association to discover what is available.

ZYZZYVA Master Classes

🖊 *For fiction and nonfiction writers, poets* Various hotels in San Francisco — 41 Sutter St., Suite 1400, San Francisco, CA 94104 U.S. **Voice:** 415-752-4393 **Fax:** 415-752-4391 **E-mail:** zyzzyvainc@aol.com **Contact:** Howard Junker, Ed. **Open:** Various fall weekends **Admission:** Registration form only **Cost:** $250 per weekend

ZYZZYVA IS A quarterly journal that has begun to sponsor weekend master classes. Each weekend session can stand alone, or you can enroll in the series. The focus is on issues, not on manuscripts. A faculty of fiction and nonfiction writers and poets lead discussions on how to create and maintain a career as a writer, what to read, how to select subjects and how to sustain a community. In 1996 Adam Hochschild and David Rains Wallace were among the teachers. Call for information on the current subject, location and dates.

🏠 California Academic Programs

California State University:
CSU Chico, Dept. of English, Chico, CA 95929; 916-898-6824; MA English (creative writing minor)
CSU Fresno, English Dept., Fresno, CA 93740; 209-278-3919; MA English, MFA Creative Writing (pending)
Cal State Hayward, English Dept., Hayward, CA 94542; 510-885-3153; MA English (with creative thesis)
Humboldt State University, English Dept., Arcata, CA 95521; 707-826-5939; MA Literature, MA Teaching Writing
CSU Long Beach, English Dept., 1250 Bellflower Blvd., Long Beach, CA 90840; 310-985-4223; MFA Creative Writing, MA English
Cal State Northridge, English Dept., Northridge, CA 91330; 818-885-3433; MA English (creative thesis)

CSU Sacramento, English Dept., Sacramento, CA 95819; 916-278-6586; MA English (creative writing concentration and creative thesis)
San Diego State University, English and Comparative Literature Dept., San Diego, CA 92182; 619-594-5443; MFA Creative Writing, MA English
San Francisco State University, Creative Writing Dept., 1600 Holloway Ave., San Francisco, CA 94132; 415-338-1891; MFA Creative Writing, MA English (concentration in creative writing)
San Jose State University, English Dept., San Jose, CA 95192; 408-924-4425; MA English (concentration in writing)
Sonoma State University, English Dept., Rohnert Park, CA 94928; 707-664-2140; MA English
Cal State Web site: http://www.cal state.edu
University of California, Davis, English Dept., Davis, CA 95616; 916-752-1658; MA Creative Writing, PhD English
University of California, Irvine, English Dept., Irvine, CA 92717; 714-824-6718; MFA English
Chapman University, English Dept., Orange, CA 92666; 714-997-7-6750; MFA Creative Writing
Mills College, English Dept., 5000 MacArthur Blvd., Oakland, CA 94613; 510-430-2217; MFA Creative Writing
New College of California, Poetics Program, 766 Valencia St., San Francisco, CA 94110; 415-626-0884; MFA Poetics & Writing
Saint Mary's College of California, Creative Writing Program, Moraga, CA 94575; 510-631-4088; MFA Creative Writing
Stanford University, Creative Writing Program, Stanford, CA 94305; 415-725-1208; no degree
University of San Francisco, Lone Mountain 212, 2130 Fulton St., San Francisco, CA 94117; 415-666-6208; MA in Writing
University of Southern California, Professional Writing Program, WPH 404, Los Angeles, CA 90089; 213-740-3252; Master of Professional Writing (MPW)

Colorado

Aspen Writers' Conference

For fiction and nonfiction writers, poets Aspen Institute — Drawer 7726, Aspen, CO 81612 **Voice:** 970-925-3122; 800-925-2526 **Fax:** 970-920-5700 **Contact:** Jeanne McGovern, Dir. **Founded:** 1976 **Open:** 2 weeks in June **Admission:** Application, manuscript **Deadlines:** Apr. 15 **Cost:** $495; housing $300–$450 **Financial Aid:** Loans; Scholarship **Size-Attendees:** 12

FOR OVER 20 YEARS, this conference has attracted 60 or so writers to the dazzling environment of Aspen— snow-capped mountain peaks, lush meadows, valleys overgrown with wild-flowers, and workshops led by well-known writers. In 1996 David Guterson, author of the award-winning novel *Snow Falling on Cedars,* gave the keynote speech at the conference.

Each morning there are workshops in poetry, fiction and nonfiction, led by an impressive faculty of prize-winning writers. Applicants select the writer they would like as their teacher, so apply early; enrollment is limited, and placement in the workshops is based on the space available as well as manuscript submissions. During the afternoons there are lectures by writers, editors and agents, and in the evenings there are readings.

Workshop days are full, but there is time for hiking, and if you're energetic and determined, horseback riding, river rafting, swimming, tennis, golf, fishing. Plus there are movies, restaurants and shops. Hard to believe that not that long ago Aspen was an unpretentious mining town.

Colorado Gold Conference

For fiction writers Rocky Mountain Fiction Writers, P.O. Box 260244, Denver, CO 80226 **Voice:** 303-252-7520 **Open:** 3 days in Sept. **Admission:** Registration form only **Deadlines:** First come, first served **Cost:** $145–$180 (2 dinners incl.) **Size-Attendees:** 300

ROCKY MOUNTAIN Fiction Writers, a nonprofit organization, sponsors the annual Colorado Gold Conference to advance its members' commercial writing careers. Literary agents attend, as do editors representing publishing companies, including Bantam, Kensington, Zebra, Pinnacle, St. Martin's, Dutton/Signet, Fawcett and Harlequin. The participating writers here are going for the gold (dollars).

Days are packed with concurrent workshops on the craft of writing, as well as on practical issues such as queries, proposals, and marketing on the Internet. Best-selling authors, RMFW members, and various experts— doctors, criminal investigators, historians—lead workshops. Award-winning mystery writer Nancy Pickard spoke on "Techniques of Handling Romance in the Mystery Genre" in 1996.

Manuscript workshops with editors are available to RMFW members (for an additional fee). Appointments with editors and agents are possible on a first-come, first-served basis. RMFW members are published and unpublished writers of commercial fiction—romance, suspense, historical fiction, science fiction/fantasy and westerns.

Inkwell Intensives

For fiction writers Resort in Aspen — P.O. Box 271798, Fort Collins, CO 880527 **Voice:** 800-613-1465 **Fax:** 970-225-3735 **Open:** 1 weekend in Sept. **Admission:** Personal statement **Deadlines:** First come, first served **Cost:** $695 **Size-Attendees:** 30

D O YOU YEARN for an intense weekend somewhere glorious—such as Aspen—to concentrate on your writing? *"Writing Fiction: How to begin, How to keep going, How to finish"* was offered here in 1996. Rebecca Hill and Judith Guest provided 20 hours of instruction, which aimed at helping participants "clarify ideas you don't quite have yet, identify what's working in your writing, refine your grasp of the elements of fiction. ..."

Beginners are welcome—this workshop is open to anyone. That is, anyone with $700 plus the money for room and board in Aspen, which can be expensive. With blocks of time during the weekend set aside for writing, this workshop also offers attention to the process of writing. Workshop goals include learning how to "Stop intending to write and get started" and "Keep going when you think you can't finish despite obstacles and perils."

Naropa Institute Summer Writing Program

For fiction and nonfiction writers, poets 2130 Arapahoe Ave., Boulder, CO 80302 **Voice:** 303-546-5296 **Contact:** Max Regan, Dir. **Founded:** 1974 **Open:** June–July **Admission:** Registration form ($10) **Deadlines:** First come, first served **Cost:** $315 per week non-credit; $500–$700 per week for credit **Handicapped Access**

F OUNDED BY Allen Ginsberg and Anne Waldman, "The Jack Kerouac School of Disembodied Poetics" offers a series of weeklong summer workshops. Participants work with "some of the most accomplished and notoriously

provocative writers of our times— scribes and performers currently charting the directions American writing is taking. The tradition emphasized is of the 'outrider' or left-hand lineage, which operates outside the cultural mainstream."

Naropa is the first American college to be founded on Buddhist principles. It offers BA, MA and MFA degrees in the arts, social sciences and humanities. During the summer, each week of workshops has a theme, such as "Eco/ Darma-Poetics," "Performance & Publication" or "Experimental / Wild Form." Participants select 1 workshop—these have equally colorful titles—per week. In 1996 there were workshops in "Feminafesto: Writing the Body" and "Lists, Dialogue, Fragments: Story Writing and Revising," among others. Sign up early as the workshops fill up quickly.

Dedicated to "contemplative education," NI aims to stimulate, inspire and provoke beginning as well as experienced writers. The summer workshop can be taken for credit and is attended by Naropa MFA students as part of their third year of studies.

In its literature, the Jack Kerouac School of Disembodied Poetics describes itself as "less a college department than an itinerant community of writers and scholars. It reinstates the old Greek akademi, 'a walking grove of trees,' in which elder and younger writers collect to exchange ideas and share concerns of craft. Or it conjures classical India

The Naropa MFA

While this is an unusual MFA program indeed—founded on Buddhist principles, aligned with the rebels and outriders—it is NCA accredited. The Allen Ginsberg Library houses an archive of 20 years of video and audio recordings. Think about what that means. You could listen to the original daring poets read, hear the lively sounds of culture in the making. There is also a letterpress print shop, a student literary magazine, a meditation hall and a Japanese teahouse among the facilities.

where poets, philosophers, yogins and poets sat alongside one another to practice and debate their various arts."

The school offers a full range of courses in Arts & Creativity; Environment, Wisdom & Culture; and Health, Healing & Psychology. Plus there are special musical and literary events as part of a performing arts series during the summer, and this includes readings by many of the poets on the faculty.

National Writers Association Summer Conference

For fiction and nonfiction writers *Varies — 1450 S. Havana, Suite 424, Aurora, CO 80012* **Voice:** 303-751-7844 **Fax:** 303-751-8593 **Founded:** Revived 1993 **Open:** 2nd weekend in June **Admission:** Application **Cost:** $350 nonmembers, $325 members (lodging, meals incl.); $195–$225 without meals **Size-Attendees:** 300–400

ACH YEAR THIS conference has a different theme and location. In 1996 "NWA Reveals the Mystery of Success" brought hundreds of writers to Denver. The fund-raising event and many of the workshops had a "mystery" flavor in their titles and a "success" theme—meaning how to derive monetary rewards from your writing. In 1995 writers attended workshops on the craft and business aspects of writing while on a cruise through the inland passage, the waterway between Vancouver Island and British Columbia.

Rocky Mountain National Park Artist-in-Residence Program

For fiction and nonfiction writers, poets *Cabin overlooking Moraine Park — Rocky Mountain National Park, Estes Park, CO 80517* **Voice:** 970-586-1225 **Fax:** 970-586-1256 **Contact:** Dianna Wiggam, Coord. **Open:** Mid-May through Sept. **Admission:** Application, work sample, personal statement **Deadlines:** Early Feb. **Cost:** Transportation, food **Size-Attendees:** 1 at a time

ROCKY MOUNTAIN National Park's Artist-in-Residence Program reminds participants that artists can play an active role in promoting the creation and use of our national parks. Their paintings, photographs and words inspire the public to discover and explore, as well as to protect and prize our parks as national treasures. This program aims to deepen the relationship between artists and parks. The park offers 2-week stays for artists and requests that in exchange, the artists make a contribution to the park.

Artists are asked to donate a piece of their work that reflects their time at the park, and to give an hour or two to the public while in residence. Artists have given talks, led hikes and given performances.

Residents live and work in a rustic cabin that once belonged to William Allen White, a Pulitzer Prize-winning journalist. The cabin includes a living/dining area with a large fireplace, a small kitchen, a bedroom and bath, but no central heat. The Rocky Mountains of Colorado will surround you, captivate you, may even take your breath away. Stare at them, stroll, hike, become entranced.

Rocky Mountain Women's Institute

For all writers Park Hill Campus, University of Denver — 7150 Montview Blvd., Denver, CO 80220 **Voice:** 303-871-6923 **Founded:** 1976 **Open:** Sept. 1–Aug. 31 **Admission:** Application, project description, writing sample, personal statement **Deadlines:** Apply Jan. 1–Mar. 15 **Cost:** Housing, meals, materials **Financial Aid:** Loans; Stipend **Size-Attendees:** 7

THE RMWI provides that essential "room of one's own" for a full year to the fortunate few who are selected to participate in the Associates Program. While you must house, transport and feed yourself, you receive a $1,000 stipend and support services in addition to the work space, in which you can concentrate on completing a creative project within a community of artists, scholars and writers.

This is not for the loner, or for that time in your life when you want to be left alone. The RMWI was established to create a community of artists, writers and scholars. Associates participate in biweekly meetings and attend special events sponsored by the RMWI. There's even an Open Studio Tour when the public is invited to come watch the Associates—which would be you—at work.

The RMWI hosts readings, discussions, seminars and showcases. Associates include visual artists as well as writers. You might want to attend one of their events to determine if this is the community for you.

Colorado Academic Programs

Colorado State University, English Dept., Fort Collins, CO 80523; 970-491-6428; MFA Creative Writing
University of Colorado at Boulder, English Dept., Campus Box 226, Boulder, CO 80309; 303-492-7922; MA Creative Writing
University of Denver, English Dept., Denver, CO 80208; 303-871-4387; MA and PhD English/Creative Writing
Naropa Institute, 2130 Arapahoe Ave., Boulder, CO 80302; 303-546-3572; MFA Writing & Poetics

Connecticut

Eugene O'Neill Theater Center National Playwrights Conference

For playwrights and screenwriters Waterford — 305 Great Neck Rd., Waterford, CT 06385; 234 W. 44th St., Suite 901, New York, NY 10036 **Voice:** 212-382-2790 **Fax:** 212-921-5538 **Contact:** Mary McCabe, Admin. **Founded:** 1965 **Open:** July **Admission:** Application ($10), script (send for guidelines) **Deadlines:** Dec. 1 **Financial Aid:** Stipend **Size-Attendees:** 10–15

THE NATIONAL PLAYWRIGHTS Conference offers emerging and experienced playwrights an opportunity to develop a play in a noncompetitive atmosphere. Invited playwrights receive a stipend, room, board and transportation to the conference. Prior to the conference, each playwright is assisted by an assigned dramaturge or story editor to develop his or her work, which is later read aloud before the conference during a pre-conference session. A discussion of the play and what will be presented at the conference follows the reading.

At the conference, there is a short rehearsal period during which plays are given 2 staged readings in front of an audience of conference participants. Professional actors participate, but performances have limited production values—minimal lights, no costumes.

This is a competitive residency administered from the Theater Center's

New York City office. The administration requests that applicants send for the guidelines, because they may change, and encourages early application. Screenwriters may also apply.

Stead Museum, a co-sponsor of the conference, works by Monet, Manet, Degas, Whistler and Cassatt are on display. In nearby Hartford one can visit the Mark Twain and Harriet Beecher Stowe houses.

Sunken Garden Poetry Conference

For poets *Miss Porter's School, near Hartford — 104 Trumbull Ave., Plainville, CT 06062; 21 Goodrich Rd., Simsbury, CT 06070* **Voice:** 860-793-9300 **Fax:** 860-793-0050 **E-mail:** RMcquil@aol.com **Contact:** Pit Pinegar, Dir. **Open:** 5 days in July **Admission:** Application ($15), poems **Deadlines:** May 29 **Cost:** $175–$200; room and board at Miss Porter's, $40 a day **Size-Attendees:** 35

AWARD-WINNING poet/teachers read, lecture and provide individual consultations at the Sunken Garden Poetry Conference. This is a small gathering, organized around a theme that changes annually. Lively exchanges take place in morning workshops, afternoon seminars and lectures, and late afternoon individual conferences. Each of the evenings spotlights one of the poet/teachers, reading poetry and answering questions.

"Poetry of the Political Imagination" was the theme of the 1996 conference. Conference organizers defined "political" in "the widest possible sense. Any poem in praise of the human spirit at odds with circumstance is, after all, a political poem." The instructors included poets Martin Espada, Marge Piercy and Kate Rushin, who directs the Center for African American Studies at Wesleyan.

The workshop coordinator, poet Pit Pinegar, also offers her own workshops—"Writing From the Inside Out" and "Writing to Heal"—throughout the year.

Rural Farmington offers hiking, swimming and canoeing. At the Hill-

Wesleyan Writers Conference

For fiction and nonfiction writers, poets, journalists *Wesleyan campus, 2 hr. from NYC and Boston — Wesleyan University, Middletown, CT 06459* **Voice:** 860-685-3604 **Fax:** 860-347-3996 **E-mail:** agreene@wesleyan.edu **Contact:** Anne Greene, Dir. **Founded:** 1956 **Open:** 5 days in June **Admission:** Registration form ($75) **Deadlines:** Apr. for financial aid **Cost:** $450; $740 with room and board **Financial Aid:** Scholarship; Fellowship **Size-Attendees:** 100 **Handicapped Access**

WHAT TURNS A GOOD learning experience into a phenomenal one? Is it the quality of the teachers, or is it the quality and motivation of the students? Some combination, no doubt, which is why the Wesleyan Writers Conference stands out. A remarkably distinguished faculty serve as instructors attracting talented serious

A manuscript review at Wesleyan Writers Conference.

beginning and experienced writers to its workshops. The passion for literature is omnipresent. Keynote speakers have included one of China's foremost woman writers, Zhang Jie, and award-winning novelist Robert Stone.

Participants are encouraged to concentrate on one of the seminars (each meets every day) and to visit several of the others (they are scheduled consecutively to facilitate this). Topics include "The Short Story," "Fiction Techniques," "Literary Journalism and Memoir," "Fiction and Film" and "The Novel." During the evenings there are guest speakers—publishers, agents, authors—and readings. Wesleyan draws on the New York and Boston literati to serve as guest readers and speakers.

Applicants may compete for one of many scholarships, which are awarded on the basis of "promise shown" in submitted manuscripts. For those interested, manuscript critiques are available.

Wesleyan University is a classic New England college, with picturesque rolling lawns, handsome mature trees, a mix of traditional and modern buildings, an impressive library, and an archetypal chapel. The nearby Atticus bookstore features books by the conference faculty and guests.

Wisdom House Writers & Artists Retreat

For fiction and nonfiction writers, and artists in selected other disciplines
40 mi. W of Hartford — 229 E. Litchfield Rd., Litchfield, CT 06759 **Voice:** 860-567-3163 **Fax:** 860-567-3166 **Founded:** 1985 **Open:** Year-round **Admission:** Letter, resume, project description **Cost:** $45 per day Mon.– Thurs.; $55 Fri.–Sun.; weekly and monthly rates available **Size-Attendees:** 115 maximum

Wisdom House provides rooms and meals for writers, visual artists and performing artists on a 54-acre property of meadows and woods. Residents live in either a 19th-century New England farmhouse or a large colonial-style brick building that can house 115 people in semi-private, private or dorm rooms. The rural setting encourages meditation and creative thinking.

The Daughters of Wisdom, a community of Catholic sisters who once used Wisdom House as a center for their own spiritual development, have transformed the place into an interfaith center for women and men. There are gardens residents can work in, and sunporches to relax on. An art gallery, swimming pool and a state forest are within walking distance of the center.

Connecticut Academic Programs

University of Connecticut, English Dept., Storrs, CT 06269; 840-486-2141; MA English

District of Columbia

Smithsonian Associates

For fiction and nonfiction writers In museums on the Mall — Mail: Smithsonian Institution, Dept. 0603, Washington, DC 20073; In person: 1100 Jefferson Dr., SW, Suite 3077, Washington, DC 20560 **Voice:** 202-357-3030 **Fax:** 202-786-2034 **Web Site:** http://www.si.edu/tsa **Contact:** Mara Mayor, Dir. **Founded:** 1846 **Open:** Year-round **Admission:** Application form only **Cost:** About $70 for members; about $95 more for non-members. **Handicapped Access**

AMIDST A whirlwind of other cultural activity at the sprawling Smithsonian Institution (more museums than you can visit in a week) are a few well-thought-out writing courses. Summer 1996 offered, for instance, "Writing (and Selling) Feature Articles," a 6-meeting workshop covering research, interviewing, organizing and selling the work. Instructor Alice Powers, with scads of freelance magazine, newspaper and book credits, is typical of the Smithsonian staff. The 1996 program also demystified the suspense novel with "How to Write a Mystery and Suspense Novel and Get It Published," another 6-session affair. Classes meet 1 night per week.

If you can stand the city's infamous heat and humidity, this program is a fine summer evening activity. Otherwise, inquire about fall–winter–spring course offerings. The Smithsonian catalogue is as rich as chocolate mousse, and the $45 annual membership offers a banquet of delights.

Updike on Discipline

Prolific fiction writer John Updike answered interviewer Charlie Rose's query about discipline:

"I work 6 days a week, 3 hours a day, and try to squeeze out 3 pages or a thousand words. If I don't, it is like bile backing up inside me."

Washington Independent Writers

For all writers 220 Woodward Bldg., 733 15th St. NW, Washington, DC 20005 **Voice:** 202-347-4973 **Fax:** 202-347-0298 **E-mail:** netwrite@cais.com **Contact:** Isolde Chapin, Dir. **Founded:** 1975 **Open:** Year-round **Admission:** Application form only

HIGH MARKS IN every respect for Washington Independent Writers. It's good to know that something is being well run in the nation's capital. Over 2,300 members strong, this service-oriented association sponsors workshops, lectures (formal and informal "Pubspeaks"), a spring writers' conference, a technology conference, professional development seminars, a course

SMITHSONIAN INSTITUTE

Smithsonian Institution Castle, Washington, DC

on freelance careers and a host of small groups (of members) who meet monthly to discuss their writing work and socialize.

Full membership is for those with publishing credits, in any genre. Anyone hoping to move into the writing world may become an associate member. University-level students are welcome, a nice touch, setting up some good mentoring opportunities no doubt.

The workshops tend to be business-oriented, covering selling your work, protecting intellectual property, and the care and feeding of agents. At the spring conference, seminar topics range widely across the literary and business of writing spectrum, drawing on Washington's (and New York's) plethora of publishing professionals for leaders. Many of Washington's writers are heavy-duty researchers for whom the new electronic tools (from Internet browsing to database management) are important. WIW's technology conference aims to keep the membership abreast of new developments. If you need help polishing a book proposal or want to fine-tune your negotiating skills (for contract time), look into WIW's annual freelance careers course. There's also an extensive job bank, accessible by telephone, and a small library of writer's reference tools at the WIW office. Icing on the cake includes availability of group health insurance and a legal services program.

All told, an extraordinary bargain and no hype. Every city should have such an organization for writers.

Atlantic Center for the Arts, New Smyrna Beach

Florida

Atlantic Center for the Arts

For poets, playwrights, fiction and nonfiction writers, and artists in selected other disciplines E coast, between Daytona Beach and Kennedy Space Center — 1414 Art Center Ave., New Smyrna Beach, FL 32168 **Voice:** 904-427-6975; 800-393-6975 **Fax:** 904-427-5669 **Contact:** Nick Conroy, Dir. **Founded:** 1977 **Open:** Year-round **Admission:** Each resident master artist defines criteria for his or her associates **Deadlines:** Revolving; usually 2 mo. before residency **Cost:** $100 per week; housing $500 for 3-week residency **Financial Aid:** Scholarship **Size-Attendees:** About 30 **Handicapped Access**

SURELY ONE OF THE most sophisticated artists' residency programs in the country, if not the world, ACA sponsors 4 to 6 residencies of 3 weeks each throughout the year. Each period brings 3 "Master Artists" from different disciplines together to work and teach. Each Master in turn selects up to 10 "Associates," who carry on their own work and enjoy the rigors of apprenticeship, splitting their time about 50–50.

Founder Doris Leeper, an artist and environmentalist, had a vision of interdisciplinary interaction among highly talented artists as a matrix for fresh work and productive social intercourse. The program is a huge success. The roster of Master Artists is a who's who of contemporary artistic leaders. In the writing field, playwright Edward Albee, critic/novelist Doris Grumbach and poet Ntozake Shange have served. Composers, choreographers, sculptors—you name it—also thrive at ACA.

The campus of typically "old Florida" buildings, with a few stunning contemporary structures too, is set on a 67-acre site by a tidal bay, something of an en-

vironmental education center in itself. An extensive program of readings, exhibitions and performances opens the center to the public. Thus ACA is a lively place—not a retreat for those seeking isolation.

Caribbean Writers Summer Institute

For fiction writers, poets, dramatists, translators and scholars who write in English Urban greater Miami — English Dept., University of Miami, Coral Gables, FL 33124 **Voice:** 305-284-2182 **Fax:** 305-284-5635 **Contact:** Sandra Pouchet Paquet, Dir. **Founded:** 1991 **Open:** 1 month, late June–late July **Admission:** Application form only **Deadlines:** Late Feb. **Cost:** Tuition $1,900; dormitory housing about $500 **Financial Aid:** Scholarship; Fellowship

I F THE LITERATURE of the Caribbean is your passion—as writer, scholar or translator—this is a solid program for you. The workshops, for writers working in English, cover fiction, poetry and drama, with classes meeting twice per week. Participants' new writing is reviewed in class. Faculty come from the islands (Trinidad, Jamaica, others) as well as the U.S. mainland. The atmosphere around the institute gets a de-

cided intellectual lift from the presence of scholars and translators in residence, some of whom give readings and lectures; these are open to workshop people and the public. And Miami is a Latin-Caribbean festival in itself.

FIU/Seaside Institute Writers Conference

For all writers Florida Panhandle — Creative Writing Program, Florida International University, North Miami Campus, North Miami, FL 33181 **Voice:** 305-919-5857 **Contact:** Les Standiford, Dir. **Founded:** 1986 **Open:** 4 days in mid-Oct. **Admission:** Registration form only **Cost:** $300 (late registration penalty); for manuscript consultation $25

P LAYING NONFICTION expert and batting first in the 1996 lineup at this fine conference was Dan Wakefield. Next was Pulitzer Prize–winning poet Maxine Kumin. Vying for third spot and cleanup were several other well-credentialed writing teachers and published writers, covering the fields from screenwriting to short story writing and beyond. With a 10-year record of success and imagination, this is one of the East Coast's better small conferences, worth the trip to an out-of-the-way locale in northern Florida.

Though you may not have much time for it during the conference itself (tightly scheduled with seminars, readings, manuscript reviews and a gala wrap-up affair on Saturday), there are miles of dunes and beaches near this neo-Victorian-style Gulf Coast town. The town of Seaside (closest airport, Panama City) has won architectural awards as a planned community.

Lodging ranges from rooms in private homes to motels and condos.

Florida Suncoast Writers' Conference

For fiction, science fiction, mystery and childrens' book writers West coast — Univ. of South Florida, St. Petersburg Campus, St. Petersburg, FL 33701; Univ. of South Florida, Div. of Lifelong Learning, 4204 E. Fowler Ave., MGZ 144, Tampa, FL 33620 **Voice:** 813-974-1711 **Contact:** Edgar Hirschberg, Steven Rubin, Co-Dirs. **Founded:** 1972 **Open:** 1 weekend in early Feb. **Admission:** Registration form only **Deadlines:** First day of conference **Cost:** $110 (teachers', students' discounts available); manuscript reading fee $35–$50; banquet $25

A VIRTUAL 3-RING circus of workshops—54 of them packed into 48 hours—makes this long-running hit a somewhat frenetic event. With an emphasis on fiction that sells in the popular market (adult and kids'), FSWC has a decidedly how-to flavor. Among the more interesting workshops may be those for absolute beginners, such as "Fear of Fiction: Taking the First Step."

Faculty in 1996 included poets Carolyn Forché and Marge Piercy, and a host of perhaps less well knowns with either academic credentials, publishing credits or both. Are you wrestling with nuts-and-bolts questions about your writing (structuring a plot, finding an agent, querying potential publishers)? Then this one's for you.

To recover from all the talk, enjoy the harbor in downtown St. Pete or head for the beaches on the Gulf of Mexico, minutes way. There is also the Florida Suncoast Writers' Weekend Workshop (same organization, in late April) for those who prefer discussion in a small-group setting.

Hemingway Days Festival

For fiction writers and poets S tip of state — P.O. Box 4045, Key West, FL 33041 **Voice:** 305-294-4440 **Contact:** James Plath, Dir. **Open:** 3 days in mid-July **Admission:** Registration form only **Deadlines:** June 15 **Cost:** $105 before 6/15; $120 guaranteed admission **Size-Attendees:** 60–100

WE SUSPECT even Papa Hemingway himself would have preferred this conference more if it were scheduled in midwinter, but what the hey, the program is rich and the setting (and, yes, the ambiance) is delightful, particularly for those who love the tropics and a cool drink at an outdoor bar. The overall event, which includes fishing and golf tournaments, plus a jazz festival, is touted by *Vacations* magazine as one of America's 10 best summer festivals. Looks like a sun-drenched party to us.

As for writing, discussions of fiction and poetry take place at various bars and grills, a refreshing variation from the standard college lecture hall. Several noteworthy authors have staffed the workshops, such as poet (and master teacher) Kenneth Koch and fiction writers Russell Banks and Peter Matthiessen. A short story competition (for writers who have not yet hit the big time) is a nice touch. This is not a Hemingway parody contest, and there is a real prize ($1,000) plus airfare. Inquire for submission details.

Hemingway lookalikes at the Hemingway Days Festival, Key West

Key West Literary Seminar and Writers' Workshops

For playwrights, poets, nonfiction and fiction writers S *tip of state —* 419 Petronia St., Key West, FL 33040 **Voice:** 305-293-9291 **Fax:** 305-293-0482 **E-mail:** keywestlit@earthlink.net **Contact:** Monica Haskell, Dir. **Founded:** 1983 **Open:** 1 week or weekend in early Jan. **Admission:** Registration form only **Deadlines:** None **Cost:** $275 before 9/30; $295 thereafter

T HEMES VARY FROM year to year, but if the 1997 program is any indication, this is an unusually fine opportunity to gather with serious professional writers to discuss matters of substance. The 1997 conference topic, "Literature in the Age of AIDS," attracted staff such as novelist Ann Beattie, psychohistorian Christine Downing, and playwright Tony Kushner. Registration tends to close early (in November), so call ahead. A separate 4-day writers' workshop precedes the seminar and involves some of the seminar's leading speakers. With a resort-marina as conference headquarters, no matter how serious the discussion, there's bound to be an element of lightness and play surrounding this attractive event. Inquire about discounted lodging.

Southwest Florida Writers' Conference

For all writers Southwestern coast — Edison Community College, Div. of Continuing Education, P.O. Box 60210, Fort Myers, FL 33906 **Voice:** 941-489-9226 **Fax:** 941-489-9051 **Contact:** Joanne Harkke, Dir. **Founded:** 1980 **Open:** 1 weekend in late Feb. **Admission:** Registration form only **Deadlines:** Mid-Feb. **Cost:** $80 for both days, all-inclusive (workshops, 2 meals, T-shirt!) **Financial Aid:** Scholarship **Degree or Certification:** Teachers' in-service credits

P OTPOURRI. Two days of talks and workshops ranging from the hard-nosed business approach to writing ("What to Expect from an Agent") to an inspirational speaker who may goose you into believing in your work. Plus a touch of class with visiting lecturers such as the urbane nonfiction writer and editor (Paris Review) George Plimpton. For Florida residents or those wishing a literary vacation weekend on the Suncoast, this conference is a good bet.

Indulge Yourself: You Deserve It

A far cry from the romantic image, the starving artist, scribbling in a garret, Levenger's catalogue, *Tools for Serious Readers*, is fun for any writer—though it teeters on the brink of being effete and hyper-bourgeois. The fountain pens are truly *objets d'art* as are the monogrammed hardwood boxes to store or display them. The lamps, chairs, writing desks, bookends, and everything else you can imagine for the reader-writer come in styles from Victorian to Danish modern. In an age given more to bytes and pixels than to words, it is refreshing to see someone pay attention to the tradition of writing with fine pens, in a rainbow of inks, on elegant note paper. Among our grandfathers were a carpenter and a mechanic who worked with their hands. They kept their drill bits and Allen wrenches in nifty hardwood boxes and well sewn leather pouches. Why shouldn't a writer stow his pens in a similarly precious, durable case? If, for you, the bookmark, pen, desk and reading lamp are sacred objects, then seek no further: Levenger is ready to sell you any number of personalized holy grails.

Visit Levenger on the Internet at http:\\www.levenger.com

Space Coast Writers Guild Conference & Workshop

*For fiction and nonfiction writ-
ers Central E coast — P.O. Box 804, Mel-
bourne, FL 32902* **Voice:** 407-727-0051
Contact: Edwin Kirschner, Dir. **Open:** 1
weekend in early Nov. **Admission:** Registration form only **Deadlines:** None **Cost:**
About $75 for nonmembers

WITH AN EMPHASIS on the practical side of writing (how to get
published, how to run your local writers' workshop, how to work with
an agent), this affair serves those who
want to see their work in print. There
are some sessions on the mechanics of
writing fiction and children's stories. A
useful event, no doubt, but a bit formulaic (hotel, hors d'oeuvres, networking,
book fair). If you're living in the Mel-
bourne area, however, check it out. The
price is right.

Write for Success Workshop: Children's Books

*For children's book writers and illus-
trators Central W coast — 3748 Harbor
Heights Dr., Largo, FL 34644* **Voice:** 813-
581-2484 **Contact:** Theo Carroll, Dir. **Open:**
1 day in mid-Mar. **Admission:** Registration
form only **Cost:** $85 (meals and materials
incl.) **Size-Attendees:** 90–100

LEADER THEO CARROLL has a world of
children's book experience behind
her—as author, editor, adapter (of
adult stories for children) and workshop
leader. This workshop should be valuable simply for the exposure to her voice
of authority. The 1-day session covers
the mechanics of story construction and
the business side of marketing your material. In the past, a guest speaker from
the current editorial ranks has provided
the benefit of describing what publishers may be looking for currently in the
children's department.

Florida Academic Programs

Florida International University,
English Dept., North Miami
Campus, 3000 NE 145th St., North
Miami, FL 33181; 305-919-5857; MFA
Creative Writing
University of Florida, English Dept.,
4008 Turlington Hall, P.O. Box
117310, Gainesville, FL 32611; 353-
392-0777; MFA Creative Writing
University of Miami, English Dept.,
P.O. Box 284145, Coral Gables, FL
33124; MFA Fiction and Poetry

Georgia

Curry Hill Writer's Retreat

*For fiction and nonfiction writers,
journalists 6 mi. E of Bainbridge — P.O. Box
514, Bainbridge, GA 31717; 404 Crestmont
Ave., Hattiesburg, MS 39401* **Voice:** 601-
264-7034; at Curry Hill 912-246-3369 **E-
mail:** jminn@whale.st.usm.edu **Contact:**
Mrs. Elizabeth Bowne, Dir. **Founded:** 1977
Open: 2 weeks in the spring **Admission:**
Application, personal statement **Deadlines:**
Call in early Oct. to learn dates **Cost:** $500
(room and board incl.) **Size-Attendees:** 8

WRITER AND TEACHER Elizabeth
Bowne opens her ancestral
home for a 2-week writers' retreat each spring. Eight participants live
and work in the large plantation house,
gathering for meals and evening conversation. The emphasis in the evening
discussions is on what participants are
writing and their work plans.

Bowne is available for individual
consultations with each resident. She
has published books for adults and children, many articles and short stories,
and currently teaches creative writing
at the University of Southern Mississippi. Curry Hill, listed on the National
Registry of Historical Sites, was built before the Civil War by Bowne's great-

grandfather. Residents may roam the 400 acres and find a shady place to work under the pine trees.

Hambidge Center

For all writers, and artists in selected other disciplines Blue Ridge Mountains — P.O. Box 339, Rabun Gap, GA 30568 **Voice:** 706-746-5718 **Fax:** 706-746-9933 **E-mail:** jbarber@purple.tmn.com **Contact:** Judith Barber, Dir. **Founded:** 1988 **Open:** Year-round **Admission:** Application ($20), manuscript or published work, resume, personal statement **Deadlines:** Jan. 31 for May–Oct.; Aug. 31 for Nov.–Apr. **Cost:** $125 per week **Financial Aid:** Fellowship **Size-Attendees:** 7 at a time

ARTISTS COME from around the world to live and work at the Hambidge Center in Nantahala National Forest, located in the Blue Ridge of northeastern Georgia. Residents live in private cottages, eat communally at dinner 5 days a week, and when not working are free to roam the 600 acres of these beautifully wooded Appalachian mountains. Most residents stay for 4 weeks.

Established as a studio and cottage weaving industry in 1934 by Mary Hambidge, whose handwoven fabrics won medals in the 1930s, Hambidge Art Center has been transformed since her death in 1973 into an artists' residency program and an art gallery featuring the work of folk artists and craftspeople. The Center's property and its 13 buildings are listed on the National Register of Historic Places.

The Rock House at Hambidge Center, Rabun Gap

The Hambidge Center Nature Trail offers hiking through a variety of ecosystems, with streams, springs and waterfalls galore.

(Note: The Center is closed from November through April, but the residency program continues to operate. This means residents during those months must prepare all their own meals.)

Jane Todd Cooper, a past resident, summarized her Hambidge experience: "Every day I went forth like one who paints from life and wrote what I saw. Regardless of how I felt, emotionally or physically, I rode a current of joy here, a joy that was not 'my own' but a result of participation with Nature in this place."

Moonlight & Magnolias: Georgia Romance Writers' Conference

For romance writers Hotel in Atlanta — Georgia Romance Writers, P.O. Box 941187, Atlanta, GA 31141 **Voice:** 770-945-2184 **Fax:** 770-977-2707 **Contact:** Lillian Richey **Founded:** 1982 **Open:** 1 weekend in Sept. **Admission:** Registration form only **Cost:** $105; banquet $35; discount for GRW members, early registrants **Size-Attendees:** 300

MOONLIGHT & Magnolias, one of the largest regional conferences for romance writers, has the sweetest, dreamiest title of any in this book. Three tracks have been established to serve the different needs of beginning to published romance writers: Basics, General Interest and Published Author Forums. Editors from romance publishers such as Bantam, Berkley, Dell, Harlequin, Kensington, Pocket Books, Silhouette and St. Martin's generally attend. Agents and local and national romance authors share their insights in workshops.

Appointments with agents and editors may be made in advance by mail on a first-received basis. A Saturday afternoon Romance Bookfair features book signings. Conference organizers make a special effort to introduce participants to the numerous local published romance authors.

Sandhills Writers' Conference

For fiction and nonfiction writers, poets, playwrights Augusta College campus — Division of Continuing Education, Augusta College, 2500 Walton Way, Augusta, GA 30904 **Voice:** 706-737-1636 **Contact:** Maxine Allen **Open:** 3 days in May **Admission:** Registration form only **Cost:** $105–$176 (reduced rates for conference only, without manuscript critique, and for early registration) **Financial Aid:** Scholarship **Size-Attendees:** 100–150

SPONSORED BY Augusta College's Division of Continuing Education, the Sandhills Writers' Conference brings at least 1 nationally prominent author, such as poet and National Public Radio commentator Andrei Codrescu, to the campus to read their work and participate with a staff of regionally rooted writers. Beginning and experienced writers may submit a manuscript for evaluation prior to the conference.

At the conference the emphasis is divided between individual consultations with the staff of professional writers and teachers and workshops in fiction, poetry, nonfiction and children's literature. Evenings feature public readings by members of the faculty.

Southeastern Writers Workshop

For fiction and nonfiction writers, poets St. Simons Island, 60 mi. S of Savannah — 4021 Gladesworth La., Decatur, GA 30035 **Voice:** 404-288-2064, after 6 p.m. **Contact:** Nancy Knight, Dir. **Founded:** 1976 **Open:** 6 days in June **Admission:** Registration form only **Cost:** $50–$60 a day, $195–$235 for the week (discount for SWA members); housing and meals for 6 days $242–$482 **Size-Attendees:** 60–80 **Handicapped Access**

THE SOUTHEASTERN Writers Association sponsors this annual event on St. Simons Island at an antebellum plantation turned hotel called Epworth-by-the-Sea. Writers are encouraged to submit unpublished manuscripts prior to the conference for an evaluation by the staff. The instructors, who include published authors and teachers based in Georgia, lead workshops in nonfiction, popular fiction, poetry, short story, inspirational writing, novels and playwriting.

"Writing for the Regional Market" was the theme at a special 3-day workshop-within-the-workshop in 1996. The topic for these special workshops changes annually. An Advanced Fiction Workshop is offered to a limited number of participants for an additional fee.

Spanish moss and oak trees cover St. Simons Island, just off the coast of southern Georgia, which has long been shared by the extremely wealthy who vacation there and a year-round black community. Epworth-by-the-Sea, the conference site, offers a pool and playground and easy access to golf and fishing. St. Simons Island has numerous historic and tourist sites.

Walker Woods

🏠 *For fiction and nonfiction writers, poets, international writers translating a work into English* 1397 La Vista Rd. NE, Atlanta, GA 30324 **Voice:** 404-634-3309 **Fax:** 404-634-3309 **E-mail:** writers@mind-spring.com **Contact:** Dalian Moore **Founded:** 1993 **Open:** Year-round **Admission:** Application ($20), manuscript, personal statement, references **Deadlines:** Jan. 15 for Jan.–Apr., Mar. 17 for May–Sept., June 1 for Sept.–Dec. **Cost:** $150–$600 per month **Financial Aid:** Scholarship; Work/Study **Size-Attendees:** 8 at a time

A COMMUNAL SPIRIT mixed with southern hospitality infuses Walker Woods. Once a private home on 1½ acres in North Atlanta, the house has been transformed into an international residence for writers. Participants are unpublished writers, who submit a sample of their current project. Two-week to 8-month residencies are available.

Founded by poet Dalian Moore and named for her late husband Richard Leigh Walker, a Reuters foreign correspondent, Walker Woods provides rooms equipped with computers and printers. Residents "live as a family," eat communally, may share a room and are expected to participate in the upkeep, cooking, and gardening. The grounds include a rose garden, hot tub, waterfall, pond and stream.

Monthly special events (open to the public) are held at Walker Woods, particularly around the holidays. Community arts leaders, writers and journalists often visit to share in dinners and readings.

🏠 Georgia Academic Programs

Georgia State University, English Dept., University Plaza, Atlanta, GA 30303; 404-651-2900; MFA Creative Writing

University of Georgia, English Dept., Athens, GA 30602; 706-542-2659; MA and PhD English (creative writing emphasis)

Hawaii

Kalani Honua Eco-Resort

🏠 *For fiction and nonfiction writers, poets, playwrights* SE coast of the Big Island — RR 2, Box 4500, Kehena Beach, HI 96778 **Voice:** 808-965-7828; 800-800-6886 **E-mail:** kh@ILHawaii.net **Web Site:** http://www.maui.net/~randm.kh.html **Open:** Year-round **Admission:** Application form, resume **Cost:** $30–$48 per night

N OT EXACTLY A residency program, this is a resort that offers much of what one seeks in a residency—a getaway in beautiful natural surroundings. It earns a mention in this book because there is a 50 percent reduction on lodging for "Artists-in-Residence." To qualify for this reduction, send a stamped, self-addressed envelope for an application form, which asks for a resume and basic information. The best time to apply is June through December, when rooms are more likely to be available.

Kalani Honua means "heaven on earth." On the sunny southeastern coast of the island of Hawaii, within a large conservation area, the resort includes private cottages, cedar lodges, dorms and a campsite. Food, including meals for vegetarians, is available. There are a pool and spa on the premises; beaches, warm springs and Volcanoes National Park are nearby.

Occasionally there are classes on writing, but mostly the resort is the site for yoga retreats, dance and musical events, and workshops with an emphasis on the "heart," including "Heart-Power Healing," "Shared Heart Retreat" and "Heart Awakening."

Volcano Art Center's Writers' Conference

For fiction and nonfiction writers, poets *Within Hawaii Volcanoes National Park* — *P.O. Box 104, Hawaii National Park, HI 96718* **Voice:** 808-967-8222 **Fax:** 808-967-8512 **Open:** 1 weekend in June **Admission:** Application ($25), writing sample **Deadlines:** Apr. 15 **Cost:** $225 **Financial Aid:** Loans; Scholarship **Size-Class:** 10

DISTINGUISHED award-winning writers teach at the Volcano Art Center's Writers' Conference. "The Fire Within: Writing at the Volcano" covers nonfiction, fiction and poetry. Workshops, the core activity of the weekend, meet for a total of 10 hours, providing time for a critique of each participant's manuscript.

The workshop leaders have credentials as teachers and writers. In 1996 a Hawaiian author, Darrell Lum, "noted for stories and plays which speak to issues of family and culture, and are rooted in the vernacular language of the islands and a strong sense of place," led the fiction workshop.

There is time for informal socializing at lunch and dinner, and evening readings by the faculty round out the weekend.

If you have been searching for a way to justify a trip to Hawaii, this may be it. The Volcano Art Center is actually within Volcanoes National Park on the Big Island, and quite near the top of the 4,000-foot-high Kilauea volcano, the world's most active volcano. Nearby there are a variety of climatic zones to explore, including a native rain forest, an alpine forest, a lava desert and a gorgeous coastline. Think snorkeling, swimming, bicycling, hiking, sunsets, dramatic vistas and, yes, a writing workshop.

Hawaii Academic Programs

University of Hawaii at Manoa, English Dept., 1733 Donaghho Rd., Honolulu, HI 96822; 808-956-8956;

MA English (creative writing thesis), PhD (creative writing specialization)

Idaho

Sun Valley Writers' Conference

For fiction and nonfiction writers, poets, journalists *Conference: lodge in Sun Valley; Workshop: ranch N of Sun Valley* — *P.O. Box 957, Ketchum, ID 83340* **Voice:** 208-726-6670 **Fax:** 208-788-0106 **Founded:** 1995 **Open:** Conference: 4 days in Aug.; workshop: 3 days in early Sept. **Admission:** Conference: registration form; Workshop: registration form, manuscripts **Deadlines:** Workshop: May 15 **Cost:** Conference pass: $185; Workshop: $400 (meals, lodging incl.); discount for both **Size-Attendees:** 125 per conference; 8–10 per workshop

AFTER ATTENDING the first Sun Valley Writers' Conference for Readers and Writers, a program launched in 1995, novelist Ethan Canin reported: "A splendid week, as satisfying as they come." Wide-ranging discussions with Canin, W. P. Kinsella, Anne Lamott and other invited writers were the heart of the workshops and panel discussions. Plus there were picnics overlooking a river, hikes in the glorious surrounding countryside, and evening speakers on a terrace during the sunset.

The morning gatherings are designed to be "hands-on sessions," more craft oriented, but they also may include discussions about social issues in film. Afternoon sessions include panel discussions, lectures and readings.

In 1996 the Sun Valley Writers' Conference initiated its second program, a fiction writing workshop led by Canin and Lamott. The setting, a guest ranch located an hour north of Sun Valley in the Sawtooth Wilderness, provides hundreds of miles of trails, pine-covered mountains, meadows with a profusion of wildflowers, and trout-filled lakes. While the workshops are demanding, there is also time for swimming, canoeing and sitting around the hot springs.

Each participant works with one of the writer/teachers and can audit the other's workshop because they meet at different times. Each participant may contribute one manuscript to the workshop for critiquing and must present critiques of other participant's stories. Evenings include readings, social events and live music.

Writers & Readers Rendezvous

For fiction and nonfiction writers, poets Lakeside lodge in McCall, 100 mi. N of Boise — Boise State University Division of Continuing Education, 1910 University Dr., Boise, ID 83725 **Voice:** 208-385-4092 **Fax:** 208-385-3467 **Contact:** Rick Ardinger **Founded:** 1992 **Open:** 3 days in Oct. **Admission:** Registration form **Deadlines:** Mid-Sept. **Cost:** $110 **Financial Aid:** Loans; Scholarship **Size-Attendees:** 150 **Handicapped Access**

MANY OF IDAHO's finest writers converge on Shore Lodge on Payette Lake to participate in the annual Rendezvous. Nationally celebrated writers give readings, sit on panels and participate in discussions of the business and craft of writing. Marilynne Robinson, who wrote the award-winning novel *Housekeeping,* about a family living in Idaho, was featured in 1996. Publishers and editors join with numerous authors and poets to share their experiences.

If you need to write, if you love to read, or if you want to lead a more literary life, this is your chance to follow your bliss," states the invitation to the 1995 Rendezvous.

A beautiful setting for mixing it up with very literary folk. Often there are films in the evenings that link with the theme, say a film based on a visiting writer's novel, and book signings and readings throughout the day.

Idaho Academic Programs

University of Idaho, English Dept., Moscow, ID 83844; 208-885-6873; MFA Creative Writing

Illinois

Blooming Grove Writers' Conference

For fiction and nonfiction writers, poets Illinois Wesleyan University campus — P.O. Box 515, Bloomington, IL 61702 **Voice:** 309-828-5092 **Fax:** 309-829-8369 **E-mail:** bettstory@aol.com **Contact:** Bettie Story **Founded:** 1977 **Open:** 5 days in July or Aug. **Admission:** Registration form ($25), $25 for each manuscript submitted **Deadlines:** First come, first served **Cost:** $225–$240; housing $165–$180 **Financial Aid:** Loans; Scholarship

FOUNDED AND INITIALLY sponsored by Illinois Wesleyan University, this 5-day conference became an independent entity in 1994, but it still takes place on the IWU campus. Supported by the Bloomington public library, McLean County Arts Center and friends, the conference organizers encourage participants to mail manuscripts in ahead of time if they are interested in receiving a careful reading by an instructor. Afternoon workshops are designed to focus on these early submissions.

The daily schedule includes classes in nonfiction, poetry, fiction and children's fiction that everyone can attend in the mornings, and then the more selective workshops in each genre in the early afternoon. Late-afternoon seminars focus on special subjects, such as electronic publishing, and talks given by agents and editors. Evenings feature readings by writer/instructors.

Mississippi Valley Writers Conference

For fiction and nonfiction writers, poets On the Mississippi River — College Center, Augustana College, Rock Island, IL 61201 **Voice:** 309-764-5540 **Contact:** Bess Pierce **Founded:** 1974 **Open:** First week in June **Admission:** Registration ($25), manuscript **Cost:** $90 for 2 workshops; $40 each additional workshop; $25 audit only

WRITERS MAY SIGN up for 1 or more of the 9 hour-long daily workshops in poetry, nonfiction, short story or novel writing at Augustana College, the sponsor of this conference for over 20 years. Participants may bring a manuscript for the faculty of professional writers to critique during the week. Special evening events, book signings and an awards banquet are part of the week's schedule.

Of Dark and Stormy Nights

For mystery and true crime writers Rolling Meadows, a Chicago suburb — Mystery Writers of America, Midwest Chapter, P.O. Box 1944, Muncie, IN 47308, IL **Voice:** 317-288-7402 **Contact:** Bill Spurgeon, Dir. **Founded:** 1982 **Open:** 1 day in June **Admission:** Registration form only **Cost:** $120 ($95 for MWA members; meals incl.); manuscript critique $30 **Size-Attendees:** 150–200

THE ANNUAL Mystery Writers of America (MWA) national conference attracts mystery lovers, both members and nonmembers. "What Coroners Do," "In the Minds of Killers," "Fire Investigations and Arson," "Medical Situations," "True Crime," "Frank and Ernest Discussion of Poisons," and "Interactive Mysteries: A Stopover and a Destination" are some of the workshops that have been offered at past conferences.

MWA, based in New York with chapters across the country, promotes mystery writers and writing, awards "Edgars" (named for Edgar Allan Poe) for the best mysteries of the year, and publishes a monthly newsletter. The several thousand members of MWA include published mystery and true crime writers, while the associate members may be in related fields and include academics, publishers, editors and writers from other genres (see *Associations and Organizations*). The Illinois conference packs its workshops and panels into 1 intensive day in a hotel near Chicago. Small-group sessions alternate with panel discussions.

Ragdale Foundation Residency

For all writers, and artists in selected other disciplines Near Lake Michigan — 1260 N. Green Bay Rd., Lake Forest, IL 60045 **Voice:** 847-234-1063 **Fax:** 847-234-1075 **Contact:** Michael Wilkerson, Dir. **Founded:** 1976 **Open:** Jan. 2–Apr. 30, June 1–Dec. 15 **Admission:** Application ($20), project description, work sample, references **Deadlines:** June 1 for Jan.–Apr., Jan. 15 for June–Dec. **Cost:** $15 a day **Financial Aid:** Loans; Fellowship **Size-Attendees:** 13

RAGDALE IS THE fourth largest haven for artists in the country. Residents include writers, composers, visual artists, filmmakers, dancers. Writers live in the Arts and Crafts–style Ragdale House, built in 1897 by Chicago architect Howard Van Doren Shaw for his family, and in the Barnhouse; both are on the National Register of Historic

Ragdale Foundation, Lake Forest

Places. Dinners are the only scheduled event. During their 2- to 8-week stay, residents (usually 8 writers and 5 artists) create their own schedule, cook breakfast and lunch from the well-stocked kitchens and share their work only by choice. Upscale Lake Forest's stores and library are a mile away. There is an hourly train to Chicago's museums, galleries and theaters.

Ragdale borders a nature preserve that includes a large stand of virgin prairie. The estate's original landscaping remains mostly unchanged. A garden, a wide lawn, and trails through meadow and prairie enhance the residents' stay. The Ragdale Foundation actively promotes the arts, sponsoring programs on its grounds and recruiting support from Chicago-area residents. Writing workshops take place throughout the year, taught by local writers. And "Second Sundays at Ragdale" is a monthly event that features works-in-progress by artists, composers and writers. Additional special events attract the public, promoting the new artistic endeavors that Ragdale encourages.

Illinois Academic Programs

Columbia College Chicago, 600 S. Michigan Ave., Chicago, IL 60605; 312-663-1600; MFA Creative Writing

Illinois State University, English Dept., Campus Box 4240, Normal, IL 61790; 309-438-3667; MA English (creative writing specialization), MA Writing

University of Illinois at Chicago, English Dept., 601 S. Morgan St., Chicago, IL 60607; 312-413-2240; MA and PhD Creative Writing

Indiana

Indiana University Writers' Conference

For fiction writers, poets
Ballantine Hall 464, Bloomington, IN 47405
Voice: 812-855-1877 **Contact:** Maura Stanton, Dir. **Founded:** 1940 **Open:** 5 days in June **Admission:** Application ($25), manuscript for workshop conferees **Deadlines:** Mid-May for workshop conferees **Cost:** $180, plus $100 per workshop **Financial Aid:** Scholarship **Size-Attendees:** 110–120

NATIONALLY PROMINENT writers have come to teach workshops at the Indiana University Writers' Conference for over 50 years. There are 2 tracks for participants: If you want to work on a manuscript in a workshop, submit the manuscript by the deadline and state your instructor preference. This option is selective, based on the quality of your submission. Otherwise opt for the other track, which enables you to attend all of the classes, readings and panel discussions, but does not require attendance in a workshop.

Past faculty have included novelists Andre Dubus and Charles Johnson, distinguished instructors and writers from Indiana's college campuses, and editors of *Crazyhorse*, *The Illinois Review*, *Indiana Review*, and *TriQuarterly*. The fiction and poetry workshops meet daily (some are concurrent), as does the combined poetry and fiction workshop.

Mary Anderson Center for the Arts

For all writers, and artists and scholars in selected other disciplines Monastery 15 min. from downtown Louisville, KY — 101 St. Francis Dr., Mount Saint Francis, IN 47146 **Voice:** 812-923-8602 **Contact:** Sarah Yates, Exec. Dir. **Founded:** 1989 **Open:** Year-round **Admission:** Application ($15), writing sample, personal statement **Cost:** $350 per week (some discounts available, based on need) **Financial Aid:** Fellowship **Size-Attendees:** 6 at a time **Handicapped Access**

THANKS TO THE Franciscans of Mount St. Francis Friary, there is an artists' retreat on 400 wooded acres just 15 minutes outside Louisville, Kentucky. Residents are selected for 2-week to 2-month residencies based on the description of their project, their artistic vision, and the promise of their work. This residency mixes quiet time, when residents retreat to their individual rooms within Loftus House, with communal meals across the street at the Mount St. Francis Retreat Center. Because the residents at the friary and the retreat center are there for contemplation, the atmosphere could not be more serene. There is no radio, television, or daily newspaper. And there is only 1 telephone.

The center sponsors special events—everything from potlucks on Monday nights with Center board members to symposiums. (In 1995 "Working Without a Net: Risk-Taking, Failure, and Creativity" featured 4 prominent artists including, novelist Kurt Vonnegut.)

Bluebirds, hawks, pileated woodpeckers, skunks and foxes share the woods that once belonged to 19th-century Louisville actress Mary Anderson. She gave the land to the friars to preserve its natural environment, and in 1989 the friars helped found the Mary Anderson Center and the artists' residency as a secular program. Since then the friars and the visiting artists have coexisted, sharing a vision of promoting cultural development while protecting the environment.

Midwest Writers Workshop

For fiction and nonfiction writers, poets Dept. of Journalism, Ball State University, Muncie, IN 47306 **Voice:** 317-285-8200 **Fax:** 317-285-7997 **Contact:** Dr. Earl Conn, Dir. **Founded:** 1972 **Open:** 4 days in late July, early Aug. **Admission:** Registration form ($50), writing sample **Deadlines:** Mid-July (mid-June for scholarships) **Cost:** $185; manuscript critique $20 **Financial Aid:** Scholarship **Size-Attendees:** 130

THIS MIDWEST Writers Workshop takes place in Muncie, Indiana, and is sponsored by a nonprofit committee of writers from east central Indiana and Ball State University. (There's another program with the same name in Canton, Ohio.) There are daily workshops in fiction, nonfiction and poetry, plus 2 concurrent afternoon sessions that focus on marketing your writing. Each year there is a special theme, such as "Getting Fit for Writing" or "Getting on the Write Road." The instructors include an editor, a literary agent and several authors, all with a well-developed commercial orientation. Evening programs have featured panel discussions or a special appearance by a guest writer, such as George Plimpton, editor of the *Paris Review*, in 1995.

Twenty-minute consultations with the agent-in-residence may be scheduled, and manuscript critiques are available (for a fee). Note: This workshop uses the required writing sample to help its teachers structure their workshop rather than to screen out applicants.

Midwest Writers publishes a bimonthly newsletter and sponsors additional writing programs throughout the year.

RopeWalk Writers Retreat

For fiction writers, poets Historic New Harmony, 40 min. NW of Evansville — Continuing Education, University of Southern Indiana, 8600 University Blvd., Evansville, IN 47712 **Voice:** 812-464-1989; 800-467-8600 **Founded:** 1989 **Open:** 6 days in June **Admission:** Registration form only **Cost:** $395 (2 meals per day incl.); $200 for 2nd workshop **Financial Aid:** Scholarship **Size-Attendees:** 60 per retreat

HISTORIC New Harmony, the site of two 19th-century utopian experiments, is also home to the Rope-Walk Writers Retreat, a program of the University of Southern Indiana. Conference organizers chose New Harmony for its "history of creative and intellectual achievement," to encourage writers to develop their own creativity. The faculty of published writers, most of whom also teach at universities throughout the country, lead the daily writing workshops, provide individual consultations, and give readings from their work in the evenings. Workshops are limited to 12, so if this is your program of choice, send in your instructor preference as early as possible. One daily lecture on the craft of writing is open to everyone.

In New Harmony, restored buildings from the Harmonist and Owenite utopian communities stand near the modern award-winning Athenaeum, designed by Richard Meier. Workshops and readings take place in various historic and contemporary buildings.

Indiana Academic Programs

Indiana University, English Dept., 442 Ballantine Hall, Bloomington, IN 47405; 812-855-1543; MFA Creative Writing

Iowa

Iowa Summer Writing Festival

For fiction and nonfiction writers, poets, journalists, screenwriters, playwrights Downtown — Division of Continuing Education, 116 International Center, Univ. of Iowa, Iowa City, IA 52242 **Voice:** 319-335-2534 **Fax:** 319-335-2740 **Contact:** Peggy Houston **Founded:** 1987 **Open:** May–July **Admission:** Registration form **Cost:** $350–$375 per week, $150 per weekend **Size-Attendees:** 1,000 per conference, 12 per workshop

IOWA IS extraordinary. Not only is there the famous and highly competitive Iowa Writers Workshop, but also since 1987 there has been a summer program open on a first-come, first-served basis for beginning as well as advanced writers. Exceptional writers, many graduates of the Workshop, teach and study here, creating a stimulating, lively community. Come for a week or a weekend: workshops are offered from May through July.

Send for the descriptive catalogue as soon as possible, for there are over 100

Novelist/screenwriter Wayne Johnson reads at Iowa Summer Writing Festival

workshops to consider. The 1996 catalog included photographs of the teachers along with short bios that offered the individual's writing and teaching credits as well as occasional personal tidbits. You will probably get a better sense of the personality of the faculty from these descriptions than in the standard university catalogue. A wide range of genres is offered, including short fiction, novels, plays, humor, poetry, memoirs, mystery and romance. The workshop instruction style means the emphasis will be on writing, rather than on lectures or readings.

In addition to the workshops, there are readings by famous writers, theater events and concerts throughout the summer, as well as special workshops called "The Elevenses." The Elevenses get their name from when they meet—11 a.m. daily. All workshop participants can attend them. Discussions in past sessions included a variety of subjects, from "Overcoming Writer's Block" to "Becoming a Book Reviewer."

🏠 Iowa
Academic Programs

Iowa State University, English Dept., Ames, IA 50011; 515-294-2477; MA English (creative writing specialization)

University of Iowa, Writers' Workshop, English Dept., 436 English Philosophy Bldg., Iowa City, IA 52242; 319-335-0416; MFA Creative Writing

Iowa Writers' Workshop

For years, the Iowa Writers' Workshop was considered the number one academic program for creative writers in the country. It is, after all, the birthplace of the MFA in Creative Writing. What makes this program extraordinary? Certainly the teachers are a key ingredient, but also it must be their philosophy. The debate over whether or not writing can be taught began before the Workshop was created—and continues.

Here's how the Iowa Workshop describes its approach: "Though we agree in part with the popular insistence that writing cannot be taught, we exist and proceed on the assumption that talent can be developed, and we see our possibilities and limitations as a school in that light. If one can 'learn' to play the violin or to paint, one can 'learn' to write, though no processes of externally induced training can ensure that one will do it well. Accordingly the fact that the Workshop can claim as alumni nationally and internationally prominent poets, novelists, and short story writers is, we believe, more the result of what they brought here than of what they gained from us. We continue to look for the most promising talent in the country, in our conviction that writing cannot be taught but that writers can be encouraged."

Yes, Iowa is where magic happens—in a mid-size midwestern town in a state known for its cornfields. This is where Robert Penn Warren, Kurt Vonnegut, Wallace Stegner, Mary Lee Settle, Philip Roth, Flannery O'Connor, John Irving, Robert Lowell, John Cheever and Nelson Algren studied and/or taught writing. When considering where you would like to study, remember that the Workshop is large, exceedingly competitive, and in Iowa. Some thrive in this environment; others wilt.

Kansas

Center for the Study of Science Fiction Writers Workshop

 For science fiction writers 40 mi. from Kansas City — Dept. of English, University of Kansas, Lawrence, KS 66045 **Voice:** 913-864-3380 **E-mail:** jgunn@falcon.cc.ukans.edu **Contact:** James Gunn, Dir. **Founded:** 1984 **Open:** 2 weeks in July **Admission:** Application, manuscript **Deadlines:** June 1 **Cost:** $400 **Size-Class:** 15

I F SCI-FI IS YOUR GENRE, this workshop may be the perfect introduction to the resources at the University of Kansas's Center for the Study of Science Fiction. Led by sci-fi author and scholar James Gunn, the Center's director, the workshop is designed for writers who are just beginning to sell their work. The daily morning critique session lasts 3 hours. Each participant brings a manuscript to the workshop, and it is this work that is the center of attention. These conference organizers are serious about their commitment to seeing participants' work published. The afternoons and evenings are unscheduled so that participants can write, study, consult and relax.

Established in 1982 to promote science fiction, the Center itself houses special collections and sponsors 2 additional events that you might want to attend: The Campbell Conference, which immediately follows the Workshop, awards prizes for the best science fiction novel and short story of the year. The Intensive English Institute on the Teaching of Science Fiction follows the conference.

Science fiction has had a mixed reputation within academic and literary circles. The Center aims to help define the genre while it promotes it: "Science fiction ... attempts to domesticate the unknown and to estrange the commonplace. The pulp tradition, during which science fiction explored its territory and perfected its methods, gave it a raffish reputation that had to be overlooked or overcome before it could be accepted into the academy. But its readability, the provocativeness of its ideas, and its ability to comment on contemporary and future social problems made it useful to a variety of disciplines."

Heart of America Writers' Conference

 For fiction and nonfiction writers, poets Suburb of Kansas City — Johnson County Community College, 12345 College Blvd., Overland Park, KS 66210 **Voice:** 913-469-3837 **Contact:** Judith Choice, Dir. **Founded:** 1985 **Open:** 2 days in Apr. **Admission:** Registration form only **Cost:** $95 (lunch incl.) **Size-Attendees:** 140

J OHNSON Community College puts on an annual writers' conference and also provides workshops for credit in a variety of genres from "The Journal: The Discovery of Your Lifetime" to "There's an Angel in Your Inkwell: Writing the Inspirational Article." A useful series of courses offered in 1996 was titled "Fiction Fixers—Four Techniques to Conquer Common Problems," including a session each on "Show Don't Tell," "Details, Details, Details," "Who Tells Your Story" and "Spherical Characters."

The conference features at least 1 well-known author among many writers, editors and bookstore owners. Panels and workshops run one right after another for 2 days and have a practical edge. From "Ha Ha Fiction," on writing with humor to capture attention, to "What Does *Redbook* Really Want?" this conference aims to help beginning and more polished writers develop their craft and their careers.

Novelists, Inc., National Conference

For popular-fiction writers
Various cities around U.S. — *P.O. Box 1166, Mission, KS 66222* **Voice:** 816-561-4524 **E-mail:** muttering@juno.com **Contact:** Randy Russell **Founded:** 1989 **Open:** 4 days in Oct. **Admission:** Registration form; open to members only **Cost:** $175

FOR WRITERS OF popular fiction—romance, science fiction, fantasy, horror, mystery, suspense, young adult and westerns—this is an exciting and useful conference. To attend you must be a member of Novelists, Inc., which means you must have published (by "bonafide publishers") at least 2 novels.

The location for the national conference changes every year. Workshops feature writers, agents and editors who specialize in popular fiction. There are oodles of chances to network, formal and informal. Everyone at this conference has published, so the emphasis is not on how to get published but how to advance your career. There are discussions on contracts, clauses and rights, "Friends in High Places," self-promotion, book signings and tours, "The Perils in Publishing," changes in bookselling and movie sales. There are also opportunities for appointments with agents.

Members of Novelists, Inc., receive a monthly newsletter, which publishes such articles as "Auditing Your Publisher," "Professional Jealousy," "Guerrilla Marketing," "On-line" and "Incorporation for Writers." NI does not publish "how-to" articles; this group assumes its members already know how to write. (See *Associations and Organizations*).

Kansas Academic Programs

University of Kansas, English Dept., Lawrence, KS 66045; 913-864-4520; MA English (creative writing option)

Wichita State University, English Dept., Box 14, Wichita, KS 67260; 316-978-3130; MFA Creative Writing

Kentucky

Appalachian Writers Workshop

For fiction and nonfiction writers, poets Rural community SE of Lexington — Hindman Settlement School, Forks of Troublesome Creek, Hindman, KY 41822 **Voice:** 606-785-5475 **Contact:** Mike Mullins, Exec. Dir. **Founded:** 1978 **Open:** 5 days in late July, early Aug. **Admission:** Application ($50), manuscript **Deadlines:** First come, first served **Cost:** $350 (room and board incl.) **Size-Attendees:** 60–65 **Handicapped Access**

DO REGIONAL cultural differences persist in the United States? If so, is this desirable? The Appalachian Writers Workshop serves as an example of how one nurtures and promotes the development of a regional culture, demonstrating the value of such efforts. The workshop focuses on writing by and about the Appalachian region. The staff consists of writers who are either "from, have roots in or have writings that deal with this region." Daily workshops are organized by genres: short story and nonfiction writing, novels and poetry, children's writing and Appalachian literature.

Hindman Settlement School, a private nonprofit education and community service center, is located in a hilly rural community southeast of Lexington. Poets and novelists from the region continue to deepen their relationship to Hindman and the workshop over the years, returning to teach, read from their works and promote the development of Appalachian literature. Poet and novelist James Still (*River of Earth*) has been connected to Hindman for more than 60 years.

Eastern Kentucky University Creative Writing Conference

For fiction writers, poets 350-acre campus S of Lexington — English Dept., Eastern Kentucky University, Richmond, KY 40475 **Voice:** 606-622-5861 **Contact:** Dorothy Sutton, Dir. **Founded:** 1963 **Open:** 5 days in June **Admission:** Application, manuscript **Cost:** $80 (credit extra) **Size-Attendees:** 15–20

D ISTINGUISHED WRITERS staff this small 5-day conference at Eastern Kentucky University in the Bluegrass Region of the state. With only 15 to 20 participants, admission is selective, based on the quality of the submitted manuscript. The schedule includes daily manuscript workshops with the staff, who have included the editor of *TriQuarterly* and teachers from Kentucky's colleges. Each of the visiting writers gives a public reading during the week.

While the heart of this event is the daily manuscript workshop, the surrounding countryside is an additional attraction. This is thoroughbred horse country. Nearby is Berea, the arts and crafts center of Kentucky, and not far off are the scenic mountain ranges of the Cumberland Plateau.

Green River Writers' Workshops

For fiction and nonfiction writers, poets University of Louisville Shelby campus — 11906 Locust Rd., Middletown, KY 40243 **Voice:** 502-245-4902 **Contact:** Mary O'Dell, Pres. **Founded:** 1984 **Open:** Workshop and retreat: 3rd week in July; Novels-in-Progress: 1 week in winter **Admission:** Registration form, manuscript; For Novels-in-Progress: application ($25), manuscript, synopsis **Deadlines:** Early July **Cost:** $65–$75 weekend and retreat; $40 weekend or retreat only; $300 for Novels-in-Progress **Size-Attendees:** Workshop and retreat: 50–60

G REEN RIVER WRITERS' motto, "Writers Helping Writers," captures the spirit behind its events. A nonprofit grassroots organization, GRW sponsors an annual summer weekend of workshops, followed by an unstructured weeklong retreat. At the weekend workshop, published authors lead editing sessions for participants who have submitted fiction, poetry or essays ahead of time. During the retreat, by contrast, there are no scheduled events. Instead, everything is left up to the participants, who may initiate impromptu workshops and critique sessions, lead discussions or give readings. Participants may choose to attend both the workshop and the retreat or just a single event.

GRW's "Novels-In-Progress-Workshop" usually takes place in March. This workshop is for writers who are in the midst of a novel and need encouragement to complete the work. The faculty of authors includes those who have published novels, children's literature, romances, mysteries and short stories. Agents and editors from Atlanta and New York attend. There are panels and discussions, and individual consultations are available.

Writers for Racing Workshops

For fiction and nonfiction writers, poets Churchill Downs, KY, and elsewhere — P.O. Box 3098, Princeton, NJ 08543 **Voice:** 609-275-2947 **Fax:** 609-275-1243 **E-mail:** MBCD26B@prodigy.com **Contact:** Karl Garson, Dir. **Founded:** 1992 **Open:** Varies **Admission:** Application ($25), writing sample **Deadlines:** Varies **Cost:** $850 (lunches at the track incl.) **Size-Attendees:** 12 per workshop

LOVE HORSES? The Kentucky Derby? Racetracks in general? Here is an unusual opportunity for horse aficionado writers to spend 2 weeks exploring horse racing—the breeding farms, horse auctions, museums, training centers and racetracks. Not only do you soak up the atmosphere and interview horse trainers, owners, breeders and jockeys, but you spend your mornings in writing seminars with award-winning authors who share your passion for horses. Past teachers have included Jim Bolus, official historian of the Kentucky Derby, and Jana Harris, a 2-time Pulitzer Prize nominee for poetry, who raises horses on her farm and teaches creative writing at the University of Washington.

There are 2 workshops each year, one at Churchill Downs, home of the Kentucky Derby, the other out west. In 1996 Ruidoso Downs Racetrack in New Mexico was the second workshop site.

Workshop founder and director Karl Garson wrote for *The Daily Racing Form* and taught creative writing at 3 universities before he established the Writers for Racing Project. Garson believes horse racing deserves better coverage, and that means improving the skills of those who write about it. Participants can receive academic credit for these workshops. Participants book their own lodging at a hotel designated by the director; rates typically run $40 per night.

Bringing serious writing workshops in fiction, nonfiction and poetry to such an unconventional site is popular: admissions are selective, so apply early.

Louisiana

Deep South Writers Conference

For fiction writers, poets Mainly on the USL campus — English Dept., Box 44691, University of Southwestern Louisiana, Lafayette, LA 70504 **Voice:** 318-482-5478 **Contact:** Jerry McGuire, Dir. **Founded:** 1961 **Open:** Last weekend in Sept. **Admission:** Registration form only; manuscript for intensive workshop **Cost:** $40–$50; $40 per intensive workshop **Size-Class:** 8–10

AT THE DEEP SOUTH Writers Conference, well-known regional writers mingle with guest authors, editors, agents, publishers and USL students and teachers. Animated talk surely must flow at a conference that highlights the literature and culture of the Deep South. There are plenty of scheduled readings, panel discussions and workshops, as well as unstructured time for informal networking.

Panel discussions generally focus on the craft of creative writing but sometimes include special topics, such as "Poetry: Electronic Collaborative Writing: Strategies, Resources and Aims" and "Folklore: Oral Traditions and Their Effects on Creative Writing."

Optional Intensive Writing Workshops offer participants a chance to work on a manuscript with peers and with an instructor who is an experienced writer. Both local and visiting writers have led intensive workshops in poetry and short fiction, meeting for 2 hours on Friday and Saturday.

Entertainment may include readings by Louisiana-based poets and collaborations between musicians and writers, as well as guest authors reading from newly published works.

Since 1995, USL has also sponsored a Deep South Spring Literary Festival, which features visiting writers, readings and workshops.

🏠 Louisiana
Academic Programs

Louisiana State University, English Dept., Baton Rouge, LA 70803; 504-388-2236; MFA Creative Writing
McNeese State University, English Dept., Lake Charles, LA 70609; 318-475-5326; MFA Creative Writing
University of New Orleans, Creative Writing Workshop, New Orleans, LA 70148; 504-286-7454; MFA Creative Writing
University of Southwestern Louisiana, English Dept., P.O. Box 44691, Lafayette, LA 70504; 318-231-6908; MA and PhD English (creative writing)

Maine

Acadia National Park Artist-in-Residence Program

🏠 *For all writers, and artists in selected other disciplines* An island off the central coast — P.O. Box 177, Bar Harbor, ME 04609 **Voice:** 207-288-5459 **Contact:** Coordinator **Open:** Spring and fall **Admission:** Resume, brief manuscript, project description, references **Deadlines:** Early Jan. **Cost:** Transportation, meals **Size-Attendees:** 6–8

IDYLLIC, PLAIN AND simple. As a setting for artistic work, Acadia National Park is about as inspiring as it gets. The sea crashes against Maine's rocky coast; Cadillac Mt. rises up into the sunshine (or fog), providing spectacular vistas for those who make the modest climb; miles of woodland trails invite the pensive walker; and nearby villages overflow with charm. If you can resist all this and still get some writing done, then by all means apply.

You'll be among a select few, however, with only a half dozen or so artists (writers usually among them) in residence in each of the 2 seasons. Housing is in simple (shared) cottages. Blessedly, you'll also miss the hordes of summer tourists. Resident artists are asked to make a public presentation and to give at least 1 work of art to the park's collection. Otherwise the artist's time is unstructured and all his or her own. For an intense 2-week stint of hard work on a developing manuscript, this program offers a rare opportunity because of its location, although financially it is not as rich as several of the private residential programs for which stipends and travel money are available.

The application process (and review by a professional jury) is serious. Beginning writers must earn their first credits elsewhere before having a shot at this fine target.

DownEast Maine Writer's Workshop

✒️ *For fiction and nonfiction writers, and children's writers* Near Belfast, on mid-coast — P.O. Box 446, Stockton Springs, ME 04981 **Voice:** 207-567-4317 **Fax:** 207-567-3023 **E-mail:** 6249304@mcimail.com **Contact:** Janet Barron, Dir. **Open:** Memorial Day weekend, July 4th week, Columbus Day weekend **Admission:** Registration form only **Cost:** From $115 for 1 day to $675 for a week; some discounts available **Handicapped Access**

BREATHLESS PROSE ON the flyer ("wonderful," "sensational") promises insider info available "nowhere else" about writing and getting published. A little hype, perhaps? Emphasizing children's story writing and adult fiction, this how-to set of workshops on 3 major holidays is open to novices and others. Director Janet Barron ("author, editor, publisher, agent") leads most of the sessions. New twist: you can take 1 day or more to suit your specific needs. Accommodations off-site (inquire early).

Molasses Pond Retreat/Workshop

For fiction and nonfiction writers *NE of Ellsworth, not far from coast* — *RR 1, Box 85C, Millbridge, ME 04658; Oct. 1–May 1: 36 Manning St., Portsmouth, NH 03801* **Voice:** 207-546-2506; off-season 603-431-6306 **Contact:** Martha Barrett, Dir. **Founded:** 1987 **Open:** 1 week in mid-June **Admission:** Manuscript, personal statement **Deadlines:** Mar. 1–15 only **Cost:** $350 (housing, workshop, evening meals incl.) **Size-Attendees:** 10

ESCHEWING THE celebrity-driven style of the tonier workshops, Molasses Pond opts for self-directed learning (with help from two University of New Hampshire creative writing teachers— Martha Barron Barret, a novelist and columnist, and Sue Wheeler, a short story writer. Both women have strong credits with serious publishers. This is a quiet weeklong retreat for serious writers at a site hidden in the woods. The glorious Maine coast is only minutes away.

Participants share 5 lakeside cottages, where mornings are spent at writing. Afternoon technique classes are followed by manuscript critiques. A social hour and community dinner usher in the evening. Few distractions mean that writing at night is also possible.

No poetry or children's stories are accepted for review at Molasses; adult fiction and nonfiction are the menu. Most participants come from northern New England.

State of Maine Writers' Conference

For all writers *Coastal village, 15 mi. S of Portland* — *P.O. Box 7146, Ocean Park, ME 04063* **Voice:** 207-934-9806 **Contact:** Richard Burns, Chairman **Founded:** 1941 **Open:** 3 days in late Aug. **Admission:** Registration form only **Deadlines:** None **Cost:** $75 in advance, $85 at the door; students 22 and under, $40

VENERABLE YET MODEST, the State of Maine Writers' Conference is perhaps the oldest of its kind in the country. Associated in the early days with the Chatauqua movement (it still has a partial inclination toward the spiritual), the conference has humble yet admirable intentions in trying to bring together diverse writers for a few days of intense discussion and mutual support. An emphasis on camaraderie is important here. It's not a place where national stars and their devotees strut their stuff or fawn, respectively.

Sessions vary from year to year and cut across the genres. There is much discussion of participants' material, and a long list of writing contests fills out the bill. Apply early for contest rules. Certain thematic interests predominate, such as nature and the environment. Contest deadlines and submission rules vary (confusingly). Call ahead.

Housing and most meals during the conference are catch as catch can. Remember that August is high season on the Maine coast. Reserve your accommodations well in advance.

Nearby Portland ranks as one of the East Coast's most attractive arts-friendly communities.

Stonecoast Writers' Conference

For fiction and nonfiction writers, and poets On Casco Bay — University of Southern Maine, 96 Falmouth St., P.O. Box 9300, Portland, ME 04104 **Voice:** 207-780-4076 **Contact:** Barbara Hope, Dir. **Founded:** 1979 **Open:** 10 days in late July **Admission:** Manuscript **Deadlines:** Late June **Cost:** $435 **Financial Aid:** Scholarship **Size-Class:** 15

BOTH STAFF AND setting make this conference a good bet. More than 2 dozen widely published writers and experienced editors, plus the occasional literary publisher such as David Godine, provide a wealth of useful advice for writers in several genres. Teachers here have won the Delmore Schwartz poetry award, the Iowa Short Fiction award and many others. Yet the conference is not elitist; anyone—novice to advanced—with a serious manuscript may apply.

Located at an estate on the Maine coast, Stonecoast's water views and heather gardens may distract you from your pages, but the university-based program will bring you back to serious work. "Courses" are rated intermediate and advanced; placement follows acceptance to the conference. (In-state undergraduate credit is available.) Consider carefully the manuscript submitted as application—it will be reprinted for use in workshop discussions.

Housing and meals are extra—not on the estate; dormitory accommodations are available at the university. For writer-insomniacs, a special opportunity: all-night shopping at Freeport's famous outdoor retailer, L. L. Bean.

Maine Academic Programs

University of Maine, English Dept., 5782 Winslow Hall, Orono, ME 04469; 207-581-3218; MA in English (concentration in creative writing)

Maryland

Mid-Atlantic Creative Nonfiction Summer Writers' Conference

For nonfiction writers Goucher College campus, 8 mi. N of downtown Baltimore — Center for Graduate and Continuing Studies, Goucher College, 1021 Dulaney Valley Rd., Baltimore, MD 21204 **Voice:** 410-337-6200; 800-697-4646 **Fax:** 410-337-6085 **E-mail:** nmack@goucher.edu **Contact:** Noreen Mack **Founded:** 1996 **Open:** 6 days in early Aug. **Admission:** Registration form only **Cost:** $495 (lunches and dinners incl.); $200 extra for room and breakfast; Sat. only, $150 **Size-Attendees:** 90–100 per conference **Size-Class:** 15 **Handicapped Access**

EXCELLENT NEWS. Finally, the burgeoning genre of "creative nonfiction" gets a conference of its own, thanks to the efforts of Goucher College's Center for Graduate and Continuing Studies. Initiated in 1996, this conference brings a distinguished faculty of writers and editors together for workshops and panels focused exclusively on creative nonfiction. Featured guest writers in its debut session included 2 indisputable champions in this genre: John McPhee, staff writer for *The New Yorker,* and Diane Ackerman, author of *A Natural History of the Senses.*

Daily workshops—"Literary Journalism," "The Memoir," "The Personal Essay," "Writing for Major Magazines"—meet concurrently in the mornings. "A Guide to Literary Publishing on the Internet," "Understanding Copyright," "Profiling Famous People" and special sessions with the guest writers fill out the afternoon meetings. Evening readings by the faculty and guests are a highlight of the event.

Writers unable to come during the week may attend the Saturday session, which is designed to stand on its own. Editors from book publishers (Viking

Penguin, Putnam) and from major magazines (*The New York Times Magazine, Harper's, National Geographic, The Smithsonian, Vogue*) participate in panel discussions. Individual manuscript consultations are available for an extra fee.

The Center for Graduate and Continuing Education at Goucher College plans to offer an MFA in Creative Nonfiction beginning in September 1997. A low-residency program, it will require only 2 weeks a year on campus.

CNF: Does Anyone Know What This Is?

There's a new kid in town named "creative nonfiction," and he's feisty. In recent years some of the best books seen on the American market have come from this colorful, rambunctious category.

John McPhee may be its unanointed leader, but if so he shares the throne with Annie Dillard, Diane Ackerman, Gary Wills, George Plimpton, Norman Mailer, Joan Didion and other writers who may or may not have made names for themselves in more traditional genres.

What are the creative nonfiction writers up to? For subjects they will choose anything. McPhee roams from geology to basketball. Dillard and Ackerman see magic in the natural world. Wills brought literary analysis and historiography together in *Lincoln at Gettysburg*. Plimpton gracefully merges memoir and sports writing with cultural comment. Mailer's nonfiction is a hearty brew of politics, psycho-history and, well, Mailer. Didion chronicles the underbelly of the culture with the literary finesse of Flaubert. One could go on: Sven Birkerts' *The Guttenberg Elegies,* a meditation on "the fate of reading in an electronic age" or Ian Frazier's *Family*, a zany marriage of autobiography and sociology, are two other notable examples.

Our current favorite, *An Adirondack Passage: The Cruise of the Canoe "Sairy Gamp,"* by Christine Jerome, can serve to define the creative nonfiction enterprise. Jerome seized upon the story of a real man, George Washington Sears, a Gilded Age sports writer who had paddled the "Sairy Gamp," a 10½ pound canoe, through the Adirondack wilderness, on an epic 180-mile voyage. Jerome decided to reenact the voyage and to see the Adirondack world of today through her subject's highly perceptive eyes and through her own. The result, a double-perspective narrative, rich as chocolate mousse, blending biography, history, sociology, literary criticism, and the author's personal memoir. Like *cinema verité*, creative nonfiction plunges us into the scene, eschewing authorial distance, and then, like traditional documentary film, backs off to a carefully researched, thoughtful analysis. No tool or technique of the fiction writer, dramatist, screen writer or poet is off limits to the writer of creative nonfiction. Vividness, a sense of immersion in a flood of detail and a sense of real time inform the narrative (for Jerome and Sears some days, and on some pages, this meant paddling upwind in a cold rain). The reader shares the chill. Like an unforgettable character one meets in real life, those we encounter in creative nonfiction are quirky and impassioned, and are often driven by forces larger than themselves. Creative nonfiction writers insinuate themselves as intimate fellow travelers with their subject, and the reader plunges subjectively into the tale or the analysis as well, for better or for worse.

St. Mary's Writing Workshops and Retreat

For fiction writers, poets St. Mary's College campus, 70 mi. SE of Washington, DC — Literary Festival, St. Mary's College of Maryland, St. Mary's City, MD 20686 **Voice:** 301-862-0239 **Contact:** Dr. Michael Glaser, Dir. **Founded:** 1979 **Open:** Workshops 2 weeks, retreat 10 days, end of May **Admission:** Weekend events: registration form only; Retreat and workshops: application, writing sample **Deadlines:** First come, first served **Cost:** $500–$600 for workshops; $425 for retreat (dorm room incl.) **Size-Attendees:** 16 per workshop **Handicapped Access**

L ITERATURE TAKES center stage at St. Mary's College of Maryland in May, when the annual Literary Festival brings inspiring poets and writers to the campus for 2 weekends of readings, workshops, seminars and discussions. Each festival is organized around a theme, such as "The Stories We Tell: The Myth into the World" (1996), which brought Vietnamese and American writers to campus for readings and discussions on Vietnam.

Each weekend of the festival (which is free and open to the public) includes at least 1 workshop for writers, led by a guest author. Past topics have included: "History, Family, and the Imagination" and "Writing Through the Senses."

The festival now also includes 2-week workshops in poetry and fiction, which meet simultaneously. Enrollment in these workshops is limited. Most of those enrolled are students at St. Mary's.

To top it all off, a retreat for writers has been established in conjunction with the festival. Writers may opt for a 10-day stay in a single dorm room during the festival. Weekdays are unscheduled, though the retreat coordinator will set up workshops for those who would like them.

Maryland Academic Programs

John Hopkins University, Writing Seminars Dept., Baltimore, MD 21218; 410-516-7562; MA Creative Writing

University of Maryland, English Dept., College Park, MD 20742; 301-405-3820; MFA Creative Writing

Massachusetts

Amherst Writers & Artists

For all writers "Five-College" area, central MA — P.O. Box 1076, Amherst, MA 01004 **Voice:** 413-253-7764 **Fax:** 413-253-7764 **Contact:** Pat Schneider, Dir. **Founded:** 1980 **Open:** Year-round **Admission:** Application **Financial Aid: Size-Class:** Varies **Degree or Certification:** Workshop Leadership Certificate

M ORE LIKE A collective (remember the '60s?) than a school, AWA leans left, and with a heart. Its workshops in creative writing, offered in the university town of Amherst (central Massachusetts) and in Ireland, emphasize writing "rooted in the language of home." Open to all but especially inviting to women, AWA sponsors a Leadership Certificate Program for those who want to lead writing workshops elsewhere. A concern for women and children in low-income families is a theme here. AWA also runs AWA Press and *Peregrine,* a literary journal. The AWA workshop method is explained in *The Writer as Artist,* by Pat Schneider.

Cambridge Center for Adult Education

For all writers *Brattle St., just off Harvard Square* — *P.O. Box 9113, Cambridge, MA 02238* **Voice:** 617-547-6789 **Fax:** 617-497-7532 **Web Site:** http://www.ccae.org /CCAE **Contact:** James Smith, Exec. Dir. **Founded:** 1938 **Open:** Year-round **Admission:** By permission of instructor **Cost:** Varies with length of workshop ($35–$150) **Financial Aid:** Scholarship **Size-Class:** About 15 **Handicapped Access**

D ID YOU FORGET to attend Harvard, or did your rich uncle cancel that trust fund at the last second? No matter, there's a place in Cambridge, just off famed Harvard Square, waiting for you to come by and write your heart out. One of the most colorful, extensive and best-run adult education programs in the country, CCAE offers a cornucopia of writing courses and workshops. Indeed, a cornucopia of learning opportunities, period: arts, humanities, crafts, domestic skills, computers, business, finance, personal growth, movement and leisure.

With that backdrop, and the Boston-Cambridge community to draw on for teachers, it's no surprise that the writing workshops here run the gamut from the nuts-and-bolts "Intro to Proofreading" to the esoteric "Transparent Minds: Presenting Consciousness of Fictional Characters." Are you into Zen? Are you gay, lesbian or bi-? At CCAE there's a writing workshop tailored for you. A recent catalogue listed no fewer than 41 courses, clearly something for every level of adult scribbler.

Instructors are published writers, professional editors and academics or those on the fringe of the university, though you'll find few big names on the list. Costs are reasonable; the setting, a few steps from Harvard Yard, is lively to say the least. The clientele are generally sharp and motivated. After class, cruise the cafes and bookshops around the square (more books per capita here than anywhere in North America). One drawback: parking is impossible, or at least pricey (take the subway).

Camel River Writing Workshops

For all writers, including children *The Berkshires, western MA* — *22 School St., Lenox, MA 01240* **Voice:** 413-637-0505 **Contact:** Karen Chase **Founded:** 1995 **Open:** Year-round **Admission:** By permission of the instructor **Cost:** $200 **Size-Class:** Small groups

H OW COULD A writing workshop be anything but good with a brochure displaying these two quotes: *"Stare, pry, listen, eavesdrop. Die knowing something."* (Walker Evans); and *"Forget grammar and think about potatoes."* (Gertrude Stein). A 1-woman enterprise, run by poet and story writer Karen Chase, Camel River workshops serve beginners, advanced and blocked writers. Chase's rich background includes 15 years as writer-in-residence at New York Hospital–Cornell Medical Center. A story of hers made the top 100 list in *Best American Short Stories*, 1993. Workshops meet once a week for 10 weeks and thus serve primarily a regional audience. Children's workshops come around twice yearly.

Cape Cod Writers' Center

For fiction and nonfiction writers, poets, screenwriters *Lower Cape Cod* — *P.O. Box 186, Barnstable, MA 02630* **Voice:** 508-375-0516 **Contact:** Joseph Ryan, Dir. **Founded:** 1963 **Open:** 1 week each, in August **Admission:** Application **Cost:** Workshop, $325 per class; Conference, $85 per class; plus $70 registration fee **Size-Class:** 12 maximum

I F YOU CAN BEAR to stay off the beach, a writing workshop on the Cape is a fine way to use some holiday time. Typically CCWC offers 2 programs per summer, somewhat confusingly labeled "Workshop" and "Conference." In each case it's small classes with hands-on work led by respectable instructors. The nonfiction class, for instance, is directed by Robert Finch, whose natural history essays about Cape Cod are a must. Classes in biography, mystery, even "cyberspace" (not that we know it, as yet, as a genre), fill out the bill.

Apply early and ask for help in finding housing. While you wait for summer, read Henry Beston's *The Outermost House,* the ultimate Cape Cod writing story.

Chilmark Writing Workshop

For all writers *Martha's Vineyard Island, off Cape Cod — Chilmark, MA 02535* **Voice:** 508-645-9085; 800-368-2292 **Contact:** Nancy Aronie, Dir. **Open:** Spring through fall **Admission:** Apply by letter **Cost:** 1-week session, $250 **Financial Aid:** Scholarship

YOU MAY HAVE heard Nancy Slonim Aronie's commentaries on National Public Radio. If you were intrigued, if you are a writer, and if you can swing some time on the (expensive) island of Martha's Vineyard, Aronie's writing workshop may be worth some research on your part. Certainly the setting could not be better, the Vineyard being one of the most beautiful and intensely popular offshore spots in the country. But consider the style of the workshop first.

If brochure copy can be trusted, the emphasis here would seem to be much more on nurturing and building self-esteem than on the skills and techniques of writing. For those who find their writing suffering because something inside them says "Stop"—a little demon chirping "You can't do this, put that pen down now!"—Aronie's therapeutic approach may appeal. To those who find the idea of sharing their inner angst in a group setting just shy of nauseating, this is not the right place to bring your manuscript.

That much said, one writer whose songs we have admired (Carly Simon, a fellow Vineyarder) took Aronie's workshop and gave it high praise: "She is clear and powerful and very real. ... She

reminds us that we are all in the same boat rather than isolated ships passing in the night."

Cummington Community of the Arts

For writers and other artists *Western Massachusetts — Mail is not being accepted, Cummington, MA 01026* **Founded:** 1923 **Open:** Closed until further notice

OBITUARY: AFTER YEARS as a well-respected arts colony, Cummington closed its doors in 1995 due to financial troubles. We hope that it will soon announce, as did Samuel Clemens, that the rumors of its death have been greatly exaggerated.

Eastern Writers' Conference

For beginning- to intermediate-level writers *Salem State College, 45 min. N of Boston — Div. of Graduate & Continuing Education, Rm. 102, Sullivan Bldg., Salem State College, 352 Lafayette St., Salem, MA 01970* **Voice:** 508-741-6330 **Contact:** Prof. Rod Kessler, English Dept. **Founded:** 1976 **Open:** Mid-June **Admission:** Open **Deadlines:** 1 week prior **Cost:** $55 (readings, seminars, meals); manuscript conference $40/hr.

PROXIMITY TO BOSTON and a charming town, dripping with seaside history, make this annual mid-June 1evening/1-day writing workshop a good bet. The focus is on the beginning- to intermediate-level writer. Manuscript conferences can be arranged if you apply by late May. The conference is primarily a set of readings and talks by well-seasoned writers and editors. Recently C. Michael Curtis, a senior editor at the *Atlantic Monthly,* joined Katha Pollitt (National Book Critics Circle Award winner) on the conference faculty. The price is certainly right, and evaluations bear out that attendees come away satisfied: "My first writers' conference—it was excellent! Superbly organized, friendly, relaxed. Most helpful: concrete marketing tips." Brush up your Hawthorne before arriving; then squeeze in a visit to the real house of the seven gables in downtown Salem.

Fine Arts Work Center in Provincetown

For fiction writers, poets
Outermost Cape Cod — 24 Pearl St., Provincetown, MA 02657 **Voice:** 508-487-9960 **Fax:** 508-487-8873 **Contact:** Michael Wilkerson, Exec. Dir. **Founded:** 1968 **Open:** Year-round **Admission:** Written application ($35), portfolio **Deadlines:** Feb. 1 **Cost:** No fees for Oct.–May resident artists; Summer program $800/wk. residency, $400 tuition only **Financial Aid:** Fellowship; Stipend **Size-Attendees:** 20 seven-month residencies; other programs vary

I F YOU COME HERE in the summer, expect to be intoxicated by delicious sunshine and tempted to walk miles on the rolling dunes and endless beaches of outermost Cape Cod. If you hunker down here in winter to complete your novel, bring a hot-water bottle and your sou'wester; it can be grim. Fear not, though, for FAWC's program is so well honed after 25-plus years that if you're among the lucky few to win a place here, you will be (a) well looked after and (b) left alone to do your thing.

The October–May session is restricted to writers (fiction or poetry only) and visual artists in the early stages of their careers (20 recipients win 7-month fellowships each year, about 10 of these for writers—obviously very competitive). In 1995 FAWC initiated summer workshops and residencies on an open-enrollment basis (200 participated in the trial year). New also in '95

was a program for accomplished artists and writers aged 50 and above.

Facilities are top-notch. Writers live and work in 2- or 3-room apartments, in a contemporary building cloaked in appropriately weathered shingles, grayed by the persistently salty seaside air. A common room suitable for public readings and a gallery provide on-site outlets for resident and visiting artists' work. Among the latter (it's a long list by now) are John Ashbery, Amiri Baraka, Margaret Atwood, Robert Creeley, Annie Dillard, Galway Kinnell and Norman Mailer, just for starters. In such a rarefied atmosphere, admission is, as you might expect, by juried panel. Best news of all: In addition to fellowships covering room and board, winter-term resident artists receive a modest stipend—though off-season in Provincetown there's little to spend it on besides clam chowder and beer.

PAT DE GROOT

Writing Fellow Jacqueline Woodson at Fine Arts Work Center, Provincetown.

Harvard University, Extension School & Summer School

📝🏠 *For expository, technical and professional writers* Harvard campus — Writing Program, 51 Brattle St., Cambridge, MA 02138 **Voice:** 617-495-4024 **Fax:** 617-495-2921 **Web Site:** http://dcewww.harvard. edu/ext/ or http://dcewww.harvard.edu/summer/ **Contact:** David Gewanter, Dir. **Open:** Extension: fall and spring terms; Summer School, mid-June to mid-Aug. **Admission:** Open enrollment; contact director for information **Deadlines:** Extension: Fall, Aug. 14–Sept. 18; Spring, Dec. 11–Feb. 2. Summer School: early June **Cost:** $25 registration fee per term; $975 per graduate class **Financial Aid:** Loans; Scholarship; Work/Study **Size-Class:** Varies considerably **Degree or Certification:** Certificate in Publishing & Communications; Master of Liberal Arts in Literature & Creative Writing **Job Placement:** Yes **Handicapped Access**

A S YOU WOULD expect, even the Extension School at Harvard is top-rank. Offering undergraduate and graduate credit, the HUES writing program can be enjoyed for a random course or an official academic degree. The Certificate in Publishing & Communications (new in '95–'96) prepares students for careers in the book or magazine world, or in media production. The MLA in Creative Writing (new in '95) requires not only course work but also a full-length thesis with a critical introduction: not an easy ride. All creative writing courses here include critical writing, and the emphasis appears to be on fiction writing. Most HUES students are working adults, living locally.

Summer School is perhaps more serious, for those pursuing degrees or other professional advancement. Few classes are graduate students only; most mix undergrads as well. Dormitory housing available during summer, a boon in pricey Cambridge.

Into the hallowed halls of Widener Library, Harvard University, Cambridge.

Medicine Wheel Artists' Retreat

🏠 *For all writers, and artists in other disciplines* N central Massachusetts, 1 hr. NE of Boston — P.O. Box 1088, Groton, MA 01450 **Voice:** 508-448-3717 **Fax:** 508-448-3717 **E-mail:** medwheel@tiac.net **Founded:** 1989 **Open:** Late Aug.–mid-Sept. **Admission:** Resume, project description, writing samples **Deadlines:** None **Cost:** $175 per week ($125 double room; meals incl.) **Financial Aid:** Scholarship **Size-Attendees:** 20 per week

A WELL-KEPT SECRET, Medicine Wheel Artists' Retreat is a low-pressure program for artists of many stripes, writers included. Retreat sites vary. Sometimes it's rustic (a boys' summer camp). At others it's more comfortable (a prep school), or even beautifully inspiring (an abbey in Still River, MA, with a long view from the hilltop). This is not the fast track to publication but rather just what the name "retreat" implies: an escape for serious artists (who may not yet be self-supporting from their art) to a quiet place where work can be done in an unstructured environment. Collegiality here is key.

With private rooms and all meals provided, a lot of work can get done during a Medicine Wheel residency. Volunteer efforts by all the artists help to run this refreshingly low-keyed, inexpensive show (there is very limited financial aid). Writers working solo here are likely to be in the company of a dance or theater troupe that is creating new performance works. A film animation festival was in the works as of fall 1996. Cross-fertilization is nearly inevitable.

MIT Summer Professional Programs

For technical and multimedia writers MIT campus — *Office of Summer Session, MIT, Cambridge, MA 02139* **Voice:** 617-253-2101 **Fax:** 617-253-8042 **E-mail:** summer-professional-programs@mit.edu **Web Site:** http://web.mit.edu.org/s/summer programs/ **Contact:** Frederick McGarry, Dir. **Open:** June **Admission:** Application form **Deadlines:** 2 weeks prior to workshop **Cost:** $1,500 for 2 workshops; lodging at nearby hotels or MIT dormitory (single $50/night) **Degree or Certification:** 5.0 CEUs

SURPRISE: MIT is not just for computer geeks who speak only ASCII or dBase. Both the undergraduate and graduate programs offer many solid humanities courses, and the Summer Professional Programs for writers are top-notch. They are aimed primarily at technical writers and editors, scientists and engineers who want to strengthen their skills and corporate-communications trainers seeking to beef up their skills. In 1995 two seminars were offered, each a 2- to 3-day affair: one on Communicating Technical Information (grammar, style, documentation); the other on Multimedia Project Development (computer geeks, and others, welcome here).

MIT is smack between Harvard and downtown Boston, on the subway line (leave your car at home), with convenient, though Spartan, dormitory accommodations (or hotel arrangements, if the boss is paying).

Nantucket Island School of Design & the Arts

For all writers, and artists in selected other disciplines 30 mi. off the coast of Cape Cod — *P.O. Box 1848, Nantucket, MA 02554* **Voice:** 508-228-9428 **Fax:** 508-228-2451 **Contact:** Kathy Kelm, Dir. **Founded:** Early 1970s **Open:** Year-round, principally summer **Admission:** Application form ($20), writing samples **Deadlines:** Apply in spring for fall–winter residencies **Cost:** Varies by season, length of stay and accommodations, from $140 to $300 per week; July–Aug–Sept. substantially higher **Financial Aid:** Scholarship; Work/Study **Size-Attendees:** 15 resident artists **Degree or Certification:** Workshops can earn graduate credit via Massachusetts College of Art

FROM TINY ACORNS do great oaks grow. In the early 1970s two pioneering arts educators on Nantucket developed an interdisciplinary arts program for teachers, linking the arts and the environment, science and culture. A quarter century later, the program has expanded to include everything from a residential arts colony in the off-season to a bustling arts-o-rama school and cultural entertainment center in the summer. A veritable supermarket of arts practice and learning opportunities, NISDA has something for almost everyone, from kids to professionals.

Writers are most likely to want the isolation and quiet of the 2-, 4-, 6-, and 8-month residencies during the fall-to-spring period, when the swarms of tourists are gone. One-month residencies are infrequently available, too. Time is unstructured but residents may join in the weekly lecture and film series and potluck gatherings; informal sessions to read and share work spin off from these events. Each resident is provided with a private housekeeping cottage (from 1 room to 2-bedroom affairs) in Nantucket town. You're on your own for daily meals.

Nantucket off-season can be hauntingly beautiful, with wild, windy beaches and rain-swept cobblestone streets ... or a lonely, chilly ordeal. If you'd rather be in Greenwich Village, think twice. If you relish an island town with no multiplex cinema, you can't do better than Nantucket, redolent with history and architectural charm.

New England Writers' Workshop

For novelists and short story writers *Simmons College, central Boston — Simmons College, 300 The Fenway, Boston, MA 02115* **Voice:** 617-521-2090 **Contact:** C. Michael Curtis, Dir. **Founded:** 1977 **Open:** 5 days in early June **Admission:** Manuscript (if review at workshop is desired) **Deadlines:** Mid–May **Cost:** Workshop about $525; housing in dorm $150 single, $105 double **Size-Class:** Small groups

FOCUS AND INTENSITY, that's the name of the game in this 5-day fiction workshop at Boston's Simmons College. Drawing heavily on Boston and New York literati (editors, agents, published writers), the staff and guest lecturers are top-rank. Nonfiction and fiction writers as diverse as William F. Buckley and Betty Friedan, Jayne Ann Phillips and John Updike, have spoken here. Participants say they appreciated the opportunity to read to an audience, and the record of those who've gone on

to publish with big-league houses is impressive. A good place for manuscript evaluation and networking, starting with the conference director, who is a senior editor at the *Atlantic Monthly*.

Bonuses: Simmons is on the green, meandering Fenway in downtown Boston, with the Museum of Fine Arts nearby and the Red Sox a pop fly away; the college offers cheap dormitory housing, and a week's parking for $10!

Novel Enterprises

For fiction writers *Suburban Boston — P.O. Box 563, Pepperell, MA 01463* **Voice:** 508-433-2092 **Fax:** 508-433-9297 **E-mail:** NOVELENT@AOL.COM **Contact:** Floyd Kemske, Dir. **Open:** 1-day events in spring and fall **Admission:** Registration form only **Cost:** $125

HERE'S THE FICTION writer's answer to Jiffy Lube: a 1-day workshop, repeated twice in the spring and fall, built around 7 steps toward creating a better novel. If a systematic approach to plot building, character development and finding the right voice appeal to you, this workshop may be a good fit. Some writers who believe the essence of fiction writing cannot be taught, or at least cannot be broken down into discrete parts, would find this approach unpalatable. But it's all a matter of taste.

Workshop leader Floyd Kemske, himself a novelist, writes in a genre he claims to have invented: "the corporate nightmare," where "sympathetic characters cope with the demands of a surreal workplace." Lots of readers could identify with that! Kemske's work has drawn the attention of reviewers from coast to coast. His assistant workshop leader is sociologist Barbara Shapiro, also a novelist (in the mystery vein), who teaches at the Cambridge Center for Adult Education (see its listing as well).

Open Road Writing Workshops

For fiction and nonfiction writers, poets *Varying sites in U.S. and abroad* — *P.O. Box 386, Amherst, MA 01004* **Voice:** 413-259-1602 **Fax:** 413-259-1602 **Contact:** Michael Pettit, Dir. **Founded:** mid-1990s **Open:** Varies; June in 1997 **Admission:** Manuscript and statement of goals **Cost:** About $400 per week **Size-Class:** Small groups

WALT WHITMAN—he of "Song of the Open Road"—would have loved this one. The Amherst, Massachusetts, base is only a jumping-off point for 2-week workshops and conferences elsewhere, "in a stimulating atmosphere." Would Provence in June suit you? The June 1997 conference is scheduled there. Readings, lectures and private manuscript conferences flesh out the program, fueled in the past by internationally recognized faculty such as Margaret Atwood, Joseph Brodsky, Tracy Kidder, Galway Kinnell and Peter Matthiessen. The list suggests a wide scope of genres, from poetry to fiction and nonfiction.

Perspectives in Children's Literature

For children's book writers and illustrators *Central MA* — *Children's Literature Conference, School of Education, 226 Furcolo Hall, Univ. of Massachusetts, Amherst, MA 01003* **Contact:** Marsha Rudman, Dir. **Founded:** 1970 **Open:** 1 day in mid-May **Admission:** Registration form only **Deadlines:** Mid-Apr. **Cost:** $50 **Size-Attendees:** 500 maximum **Degree or Certification:** Graduate credit or Prof. Dev. Pts. **Handicapped Access**

UMASS ISN'T FAMOUS just for its basketball team. Situated at the heart of the "five-college area" (Amherst, Mt. Holyoke, Smith, Hampshire, and the university), there are several good programs here for writers. This 1-day annual conference on children's

books attracts writers, illustrators, educators and librarians. Workshops (some on multiculturalism) focus on how-to skills in writing and getting published.

Ploughshares International Fiction Writing Seminar

For fiction writers *In the Limburg region of Holland, 20 mi. N of Venlo* — *European Programs, Emerson College, 100 Beacon St., Boston, MA 02116* **Voice:** 617-824-8495 **Fax:** 617-824-8618 **E-mail:** dgriff @emerson.edu **Contact:** David Griffin, Coord. **Founded:** 1989 **Open:** 1 week in late Aug. **Admission:** Short fiction manuscript; $20 fee **Cost:** $2,200 (tuition, double rm., meals, excursions, 4 graduate credits incl.) **Financial Aid:** Fellowship **Size-Class:** 10 maximum

DO YOU FANCY communing by night with the resident ghost of a Dutch castle and by day with the likes of novelist John Updike in a fiction writing seminar? If you can afford the ticket, the Ploughshares seminar for fiction writers may well be the most exotic and high-powered writing workshop you can find.

Typically the day includes workshops or lectures, writing time and meetings with mentors, and evening readings or discussions led by distinguished faculty or visiting writers and editors. The atmosphere is intense, the standards the highest. Kasteel Well, the castle, provides inspiration if your own runs short: There's a ruined medieval Dragon Tower and a royal curse, plus the chilly echoes of the Prisoners' Tower from the Nazi Occupation.

Participants are Emerson College (a co-sponsor) MFA candidates and other writers, both American and European. By design the group includes people of diverse occupations and viewpoints. Also co-sponsored by the literary magazine *Ploughshares*, the program attracts faculty with wide writing and teaching credits, as well as distinguished visitors like the prolific novelist Updike.

Rowe Camp & Conference Center

For writers especially interested in self-development NW MA, near Charlemont, about 18 mi. from North Adams — Kings Highway Rd., Rowe, MA 01367 **Voice:** 413-339-4216 **Fax:** 413-339-5728 **Founded:** 1924 **Open:** Year-round **Admission:** Registration form only **Deadlines:** Generally 2–4 weeks in advance **Cost:** Depends on income; $125–$185 for weekend workshops; meals and 2 nights lodging varies from camping ($80) to private room ($165) **Financial Aid:** Work/Study **Size-Attendees:** 25–50

SINCE THE 1920s Rowe Camp has attracted a clientele who see themselves as "out in front of the larger society no matter where the society happened to be." In today's terms that means lots of workshops for the New Age crowd on healing and self-improvement. Commingled with these are a few, often provocative, writing workshops, or programs tangent to writing anyway. Poet and cultural critic Robert Bly ran a men's workshop here in 1995. The 1996 offerings included workshops on "writing and the many selves within us" and "the meaning of life at mid-life," both with a heavy emphasis on exploratory psychology. Rowe is not so much for the professional writer as for the therapist (in each of us) who would use writing as a tool in healing. Be aware: a very rustic, deep backwoods setting in mountainous northwestern Massachusetts.

Truro Center for the Arts

For fiction and nonfiction writers, poets, playwrights Upper Cape Cod, near Provincetown — P.O. Box 756, Truro, MA 02666 **Voice:** 508-349-7511 **Fax:** 508-349-7513 **Contact:** Mary Stackhouse, Dir. **Founded:** 1971 **Open:** Year-round, primarily summer **Admission:** Application form only **Deadlines:** Apply early for summer workshops **Cost:** 4 sessions $110, 18 sessions $390; discounts to members of Castle Hill (parent organization) **Size-Class:** 25 maximum

THE LURE OF Cape Cod in the summer: sea breezes and sunsets. Here's an arts center, in a town known for its love of the arts, where serious work happens in an oceanside community where a lazy stroll on the beach is as important as morning coffee. TCA operates year-round, but its July-August workshops are the real draw for a wide range of artists, writers among them. In 1996 classes (usually meeting twice weekly for 6 weeks) were offered in poetry (by Alan Dugan and Marge Piercy), memoir, fiction and playwriting. TCA is for writers who do not seek the isolation of an artists' colony and who savor the charged atmosphere of a multi-disciplinary arts community. Caveat: no accommodations on site; plan far ahead if you hope to rent a cottage on Cape Cod (TCA provides advice).

Write It/Sell It Seminars & Workshops

For fiction writers *Varies; across the U.S. — P.O. Box 139, S. Lancaster, MA 01561* **Voice:** 508-368-0287 **Contact:** Gail Provost, Dir. **Founded:** 1987 **Open:** 10 days in late May **Admission:** Simple "Order Form" plus 1-paragraph project description **Deadlines:** None **Cost:** $1,595 first-timers (housing, meals incl.)

APPROACHING ITS 10th anniversary, this commercially oriented program for popular-fiction writers serves those who like highly structured how-to guidance. Practice and critiques of student work, in such "units" as "Hooks," "Subplotting" and "Pace," fill the days and evenings of a busy 10-day workshop. Featured teacher in 1996 was Alice Orr, author of romantic suspense novels published by Harlequin. Workshop locations vary; it was Marydale Retreat Center, Erlanger, KY, in 1996. Caveats: heavy deposit (only partially refundable) up front. The newsletter and brochure emphasize the participants' personalities more than their work. Special feature: workshops on video and audio writing and production (for an extra fee).

Massachusetts Academic Programs

Emerson College, Graduate Writing Program, 100 Beacon St., Boston, MA 02116; 617-824-8610; MFA Creative Writing, MA Writing and Publishing

University of Massachusetts, English Dept., Bartlett Hall, Box 30515, Amherst, MA 01003; 413-545-0643; MFA English

Michigan

Alden B. Dow Creativity Center Residency Program

For all writers, and artists in selected other disciplines *Northwood University campus — 3225 Cook Rd., Midland, MI 48640* **Voice:** 517-837-4478 **Fax:** 517-837-4468 **Founded:** 1979 **Open:** 8 weeks in summer **Admission:** Application ($10), project description, writing sample, references **Deadlines:** Dec. 31 **Size-Attendees:** 4 per summer

INDIVIDUALS IN ALL fields and disciplines who "have an innovative idea they wish to pursue" are welcome at the Alden B. Dow Creativity Center's summer residency program. Dow, the son of the inventor and entrepreneur who founded the Dow Chemical Company, "defined creativity as the way individuals express their uniqueness." Those fortunately chosen for one of the 8-week residencies live on the campus of Northwood University in a large apartment in a wooded environment. Weekday lunches are provided at the Center. There is a per diem allowance to cover additional meals, as well as a $750 stipend.

Residents are judged on the quality and uniqueness of the project idea submitted. Former residents have included a writer who worked on a creative writing program for prisoners and one who wrote poetry about scientific concepts.

The fellowship gives residents unscheduled time to pursue a specific project. At the end of their stay, residents give oral presentations to an audience of Creativity Center board members, evaluators, Northwood University staff and guests.

Isle Royale National Park Artist-in-Residence Program

For fiction and nonfiction writers, journalists, and artists in selected other disciplines Island in Lake Superior, 15 mi from Grand Portage — 800 East Lakeshore Dr., Houghton, MI 49931 **Voice:** 906-482-0984 **Open:** Mid-June to mid-Sept. **Admission:** Application, manuscript, resume, personal statement **Deadlines:** Feb. 15 **Cost:** Transportation, meals **Size-Attendees:** 4–5 per season

IF REMOTE WILDERNESS is what you crave, consider this residency: rustic living on an island wilderness in Lake Superior, miles away from civilization. The closest humans and power generators are 2 miles away by boat or foot in Rock Harbor, Isle Royale National Park's main development. Isle Royale measures 45 miles long, 8½ miles wide, and is situated near the Canada-Michigan-Minnesota border.

This is a 2- to 3-week residency for the robust and self-sufficient. There is no electricity or running water. Residents must bring food for their entire stay, any gear they might need, and clothes for cool temperatures. The park provides a canoe for transportation, a rustic cabin, basic cooking equipment, bedding, fuel, a pit toilet, a pump that draws water out of the lake and a guest house that can serve as a workroom.

Live amidst boreal forests of spruce and fir; watch for wolves, moose and colorful birds. Henry David Thoreau would have loved it. This is the perfect place for our favorite piece of office equipment, the woodstove-powered word processor, featured some years ago in a spoof of the L. L. Bean catalog.

Midland Writers' Conference

For fiction and nonfiction writers, poets 1710 W. St. Andrews, Midland, MI 48640 **Voice:** 517-835-7151 **Fax:** 517-835-9791 **E-mail:** Kred@vlc.lib.mi.us **Contact:** Katherine Redwine **Founded:** 1980 **Open:** 2nd Sat. in June **Admission:** Registration form only **Deadlines:** First come, first served **Cost:** $35–$75 **Size-Attendees:** 100 **Handicapped Access**

THE MIDLAND WRITERS' Conference is a rather plain name for a conference that takes place during (and is co-sponsored by) the annual Matrix: Midland Festival, a major celebration of the arts, sciences and humanities. Prominent writers and artists attend the festival and workshops. A well-known author gives the keynote address; Pat Conroy (*Prince of Tides*) and popular writers P.J. O'Rourke and Andrew Greeley have appeared to speak at both the conference and the festival.

Beginning and established writers gather to exchange ideas and discuss problems with professional authors in the concurrent workshop sessions. Novelist Nicholas Delbanco, who directs the MFA Writing Program at the University of Michigan, spoke and led a workshop in 1996: "Judgment: Fact and Fiction in the Writers' Trade." Other workshops may focus on children's literature, poetry, news reporting and "The Care and Feeding of a Literary Agent." The Matrix: Midland Festival offers a full weekend of theater, dance, jazz, popular and classical music, celebrated lecturers, art exhibits and family entertainment.

Oakland University and Detroit Women Writers Annual Writers' Conference

For fiction and nonfiction writers, poets Oakland University campus, Rochester — Division of Continuing Education, Oakland University, Rochester, MI 48309 **Voice:** 810-370-3120 **Fax:** 810-370-3137 **Contact:** Nadine Jakobowski, Dir. **Founded:** 1961 **Open:** 1½ days in October **Admission:** Registration form only **Deadlines:** Early Oct. **Cost:** $60 for conference; $35 for workshop; $45 for manuscript critique **Financial Aid:** Scholarship **Size-Attendees:** 400–450 per conference **Size-Class:** 10 **Handicapped Access**

HUNDREDS OF EAGER writers take advantage of the practical workshops offered at this annual weekend conference. On Friday there are "Hands-On Writing Workshops" organized by genre with published authors, editors and agents. Each participant receives 20 minutes of attention in these 4-hour sessions, reads for 10 minutes, and then hears a critique.

On Saturday, a series of concurrent workshops takes place. "Clues to the Mystery," "Diaries, Memoirs, and Journals," "Jump-start Your Poems," "Finding a Publisher," "Writing the Personality Profile" and "Historical Romance" are among the topics covered. At the luncheon, a commercially successful, award-winning Michigan-based writer speaks. Credit is available through the co-sponsor, Oakland University.

Third Coast Writers' Conference

For fiction writers, poets Western Michigan University, near downtown Kalamazoo — Dept. of English, Western Michigan University, Kalamazoo, MI 49008 **Voice:** 616-387-2570 **Fax:** 616-387-3999 **E-mail:** mclaughlindo@wmich.edu **Contact:** Michele McLaughlin **Founded:** 1988 **Open:** 3 days in early May **Admission:** Application, manuscript **Deadlines:** Early Mar. **Cost:** $125 **Size-Attendees:** 75–90 **Size-Class:** 8–10

FORGET THOSE HORRID dismissals of the Midwest and its culture. Attend the Third Coast Writers' Conference; meet a dynamic faculty of award-winning poets, novelists and short story writers; and let them help you improve your work. Short story writer Amy Hempel and poet Gerald Stern have been among the faculty, reading their work and leading morning workshops. Afternoons are devoted to panel discussions, such as "Getting Published: An Editors' Panel," which in 1996 had representatives from the Michigan Quarterly Review, Third Coast and Another Chicago Magazine.

Admission is selective, based on manuscript submissions. Participants may read their work during the open readings at the Third Coast Cafe in the afternoons. All events take place on the WMU campus, and inexpensive dorm housing is available. Fine restaurants and shops are accessible in nearby downtown Kalamazoo. Wondering what is meant by "third coast?" Could it be that the Great Lakes create a coast and a culture to compete with the East and West coasts?

Michigan Academic Programs

University of Michigan, English Dept., 7617 Haven Hall, Ann Arbor, MI 48109; 313-936-2274; MFA Creative Writing

Western Michigan University, English Dept., Kalamazoo, MI, 49008; 616-387-2584; MFA Creative Writing

Minnesota

Minneapolis Writers' Workshop Conference

🖉 📖 *For fiction and nonfiction writers* Area hotel — P.O. Box 24356, Minneapolis, MN 55424 **Voice:** 612-938-7029 **Founded:** 1985 **Open:** 2 days in Aug. **Admission:** Registration form only **Cost:** $50–$100 **Size-Attendees:** 100–125

OUNDED IN 1937, the Minneapolis Writers' Workshop serves local writers with weekly evening meetings aimed at building morale, breaking the isolation of the writer's life and supporting participants' efforts to get published. The annual conference, for beginning and experienced writers, offers 2 days of consecutive workshops on such topics as "Writing Commercial Fiction," "Getting Your Manuscript to Market" and "Getting Paid for Your Writing." Instructors include writers, editors and publishers based in the Minneapolis–St. Paul area.

Mississippi River Creative Writing Workshop

🖉 *For fiction writers and poets* St. Cloud State University, 72 mi. NW of Minneapolis — Dept. of English, 106 Riverview, 720 Fourth Ave. S, St. Cloud, MN 56301 **Voice:** 320-255-4947 **Fax:** 320-654-5524 **Contact:** Bill Meissner, Instructor **Open:** 2 weeks in June **Admission:** Registration **Cost:** $270

HIS WORKSHOP IS actually a summer extension course offered by St. Cloud State University; it meets 4 afternoons for 2 weeks. During the first week the emphasis is on poetry and fiction writing techniques. During the second week, 5 published authors serve as guest teachers. Each visiting instructor focuses on a specific topic, such as "Your Notebook As Your Playground" or "Writing About What Matters, or Some Ways to Hit into the Wind."

New York Mills Arts Retreat

🏠 *For fiction and nonfiction writers, poets* 180 mi. NW of the Twin Cities — 24 N. Main Ave, New York Mills, MN 56567 **Voice:** 218-385-3339 **Fax:** 218-385-3366 **E-mail:** nymills@uslink.net **Open:** Year-round **Admission:** Application, writing samples, personal statement/project description **Deadlines:** Apr. 1 for July–Dec.; Oct. 1 for Jan.–June **Financial Aid:** Loans; Stipend **Size-Attendees:** 5–7 per year

T NEW YORK MILLS, residents will find time for work—2- to 4-week residencies—combined with a rare opportunity to contribute to the life of a rural farm community. Residents may choose to live with a local family or opt for a comfortable bed and breakfast. There's a stipend that can be used to pay for transportation, meals and materials. Studio spaces are available for residents 3 miles from town in the New York Mills Regional Cultural Center.

Community outreach projects, which are required of participants, make this an unusual residency experience. A program coordinator will help you invent and develop a project. Artists in the past have led creative writing workshops for local students and have taught a variety of art classes in the local schools and senior centers. One compiled an anthology of regional writers. Another worked with students to create a mural for the town center.

The New York Mills Regional Culture Center sponsors gallery exhibits, literary, film, musical and theater events.

Norcroft, a Writing Retreat for Women

For fiction and nonfiction writers, poets 90 mi. NE of Duluth — 32 E. 1st St., Duluth, MN 55802 **Voice:** 612-377-8431 **Founded:** 1993 **Open:** May–Oct. **Admission:** Application, writing sample, project description, essay **Deadlines:** Dec. 1 **Cost:** Transportation only **Size-Attendees:** 4 **Handicapped Access**

CREATED AND FUNDED by Joan Drury and the Harmony Women's Fund, the mission of Norcroft is to encourage women to write. If you are selected to be one of the 4 residents at this retreat, you will live in a lodge on the north shore of Lake Superior, on the edge of the Boundary Waters Canoe Area Wilderness. Each resident has her own writing shed, which comes with a desk and chair, dictionary, thesaurus and rocking chair. Residents bring their own computer, typewriter, paper, pens and pencils. Each resident has access to a stocked kitchen for meals and snacks.

Residents are selected based on the quality of their writing and the depth of their commitment to feminism. Members of Drury's family have spent summers in the area for 5 generations. Drury believes her months in these woods helped her to become a better writer and more "in touch with her inner self." Her dream—to share her experience with other women writers—inspired her to create Norcroft.

Norcroft has a strict rule: there is absolutely no talking between 9 a.m. and 4 p.m. Sunday through Friday. Silence is imposed for many reasons, primarily as an attempt to interrupt women's tendency to listen to and care for others, often at their own expense. At Norcroft one is expected to listen to one's own voice and to put writing first. The silence is meant to encourage each resident to hear herself think. Drury found the silence crucial, increasing her ability to focus on her work. With silence one may hear the wind in the trees, as well as one's thoughts.

Split Rock Arts Program

For fiction and nonfiction writers, poets, and artists in selected other disciplines Univ. of Minnesota, 306 Westbrook Hall, 77 Pleasant St. S.E., Minneapolis, MN 55455 **Voice:** 612-624-6800 **Fax:** 612-625-2568 **E-mail:** srap@mail.cee.umn.edu **Founded:** 1983 **Open:** July–Aug. **Admission:** Registration form ($25 fee) **Cost:** $385; $65 extra for credit; $246 for room and board at Cloquet Forestry Center **Financial Aid:** Loans; Scholarship **Size-Class:** 16 **Handicapped Access**

AT SPLIT ROCK YOU immerse yourself in your art—which could be writing, drawing, pottery, quilting, tapestry, improvisational beadwork—with people who share your interests. The 6-day residential summer workshops require about 60 hours of concentrated work from each participant. Most workshops take place on the University of Minnesota campus in Duluth, which the catalog describes as "comfortably warm and fresh, not hot and sticky." A few workshops—"Writing Fiction/Essays in the Forest," "Poetry and Belief"—are held at the Cloquet Forestry Center in the north woods, where participants sleep in cabins and explore the forest.

Workshops during 1996 included "Writing an Annotated Life," "Autobiography of the Soul" and "Writing About Family and Loved Ones." There were also courses in writing poetry, biography and creative nonfiction, as well as writing for young adults and travel writing.

"The best fiction is not merely a narrative of words and ideas, it is an experience so alive that readers forget they are reading. They join the life of the story and are moved and persuaded and changed as though it was their own life. How can I move readers, or develop a deep understanding, if I haven't lived into the story myself?" writes Mary LaChapelle, the "Elements of Fiction" workshop teacher for 1996.

Phillip Lopate, who teaches "Creative Nonfiction," writes: "How the world comes at another person, the irritations, jubilations, aches and pains, humorous flashes—these are the classic building materials of the personal essay. We learn the rhythm by which the essayist receives, digests, and spits out the world, and we learn the shape of his or her privacy."

The Loft: A Place for Writing & Literature

For fiction and nonfiction writers, poets, screenwriters Pratt Community Center, Minneapolis — 66 Malcolm Ave. SE, Minneapolis, MN 55414 **Voice:** 612-379-8999 **Founded:** 1989 **Open:** 1 week during the summer **Admission:** Registration form ($25) **Deadlines:** Varies **Cost:** $375–$400 **Financial Aid:** Loans; Stipend **Size-Class:** 16 **Handicapped Access**

E STABLISHED IN 1974 by a group of writers who wanted a community that would nurture their writing and artistic growth, The Loft offers a tantalizing array of workshops and classes, as broad as that offered by large university extension and continuing education programs. The Loft's resources and activities include a small-press library, readings, special events, a monthly magazine, prizes and grants. Supported by its members, The Loft encourages writers to become members, to volunteer and to contribute to the development of the artistic community in the Midwest.

For beginners there are introductory courses. For more experienced writers there are almost infinite possibilities: courses in writing poetry, short stories, historical fiction, mystery novels, fantasy and science fiction, ghost stories, children's literature, as well as screenwriting and storytelling, creative nonfiction, the persuasive essay, journals and memoirs.

Many meet weekly. Some meet for only 1 Saturday morning. The half-day workshops in 1996 schedule included "Wrestling With Your Angels: A Spiritual Journey to Great Writing," "Composing Stories in The African American Tradition" and "Performance for Writers."

The Loft also sponsors Inroads, a special 8-week mentoring program for emerging writers from specific racial or cultural groups. For example, gay, lesbian, bisexual, Hispanic, Latino and Chicano writers were chosen one year, and were teamed with local authors who share their racial or cultural identity. In other years African American, Asian Pacific and Native Americans participated. Inroads offers seminars, public readings given by the mentors and individual manuscript consultations. Participants receive a stipend to enable

Novelist Philip Roth at The Loft, Minneapolis.

them to attend. The program serves different groups on a rotating basis; call to find out who is invited to apply this year.

Mississippi

🏠 Minnesota Academic Programs

University of Minnesota, English Dept., Minneapolis, MN 55455; 612-625-6366; MFA Creative Writing

🏠 Mississippi Academic Programs

University of Southern Mississippi, English Dept., Box 5037 USM, Hattiesburg, MS 39406; 601-266-4321; MFA Creative Writing, PhD (creative writing emphasis)

Can Creative Writing Be Taught?

The writer's legitimacy in the academy is more firmly established than is generally acknowledged. In *The Triggering Town* Richard Hugo reminds us that creative writing isn't new:

"For around 400 years [writing] was a requirement of every student's education. In the English-speaking world, the curriculum for grammar and high school students included the writing of 'verses.' In the nineteenth century, when literary education weakened or was dropped from elementary and secondary education, colleges picked it up, all but the creative writing. Creative writing was missing for 100 years or so, but in the past 40 years it has returned."

Student writers in an English department find themselves in a position to read, to come to know the tradition that will sustain, if not someday contain, them. Richard Howard's analysis of this benefit is succinct: "Read or fail." In return, literature students are confronted with living, breathing practitioners—constant welcome or rude reminders of where art comes from in the first place.

To the question, can creative writing be taught?, it's reasonable to remember that few in the academic world are disturbed over the possibility that their students will not produce the breakthrough scholarship, so it's perhaps unfair to require creative writing students to be instantly transformed into eminent artists. They can be taught something—reading, writing, thinking—just as traditional students can. And if we get distressed over the nonproduction of Eliots, we need only recall that if an Eliot came through the classroom we could be sure that we did not produce him.

Finally: What goes on? What goes on is that every student writer in a writing program gets readers: a luxury of them. Cursory readers, careful readers, sleepy or dopey or disgusted readers, stubbornly literal readers, readers who resolve to beat the writer at his/her own game and sometimes do. Writing students have the scarifying experience of being read at close range. They are chefs forced to join the diner to watch with fear and hope the progress of the fork toward the eager or reluctant mouth. Many things happen. Allegiances form: trusted allies defect; enemies unexpectedly embrace the text. Suggestions are made: Some stick to the work and enhance it, others are like bowling balls trying to decorate a hat. The readers applaud because the work is like—or unlike—their own. All this is, we hope, fit preparation for a wider, if no less volatile, public.

—ANGELA BALL, UNIVERSITY OF SOUTHERN MISSISSIPPI

Missouri

Investigative Reporters and Editors' National Conference

For journalists, investigative reporters Varies — UMC School of Journalism, P.O. Box 838, Columbia, MO 65205 **Voice:** 573-882-2042 **Fax:** 573-882-5431 **E-mail:** jourire@muccmail.missouri. edu **Web Site:** http://www.projo.com/ire/ **Founded:** 1976 **Open:** 3 days in June **Admission:** Registration form only **Cost:** $180; members $125 **Financial Aid:** Loans; Scholarship

INVESTIGATIVE REPORTERS and Editors (IRE) is a national organization dedicated to "improving the quality of journalism through intensive training and cooperative exchange of professional advice." Its annual conference focuses on "ferreting out great stories and telling them well."

Whether you need to learn about "Going Undercover," "Muckraking the Law" or "Interviews that Work," if investigative reporting is your field, this is the conference. While many conferences offer to give participants a critique of their writing, few declare that their "emphasis is ... on the positive, with the priority on improving, rather than criticizing, one's writing."

To attend the conference you must join IRE, which links you to its 4,000 members. The organization publishes the *IRE Journal*, provides help for on-line journalists, offers select publications at a discount and houses a resource center. IRE has greatly expanded its on-line activities recently and can assist you with yours.

Mark Twain Writers Conference

For fiction and nonfiction writers Resort between the Mississippi and Illinois Rivers — 921 Center St., Hannibal, MO 63401 **Voice:** 573-221-2462; 800-747-0738 **Contact:** Cindy Allison **Founded:** 1985 **Open:** 5 days in June, Aug. and Sept. **Admission:** Registration form ($50) **Deadlines:** First come, first served **Cost:** $465 (meals and lodging incl.) **Size-Class:** 25

AS OF 1997, the annual Mark Twain Writers Conference "goes on vacation," meeting in a luxurious resort rather than on the Hannibal–La Grange College campus as it has done in the past. (You'll have to inquire to see whether this becomes a tradition or the conference returns to the campus in 1998.) Four 5-day-long workshops are planned, each open to only 25 participants and each with its own focus.

The workshop topics in 1997 include "Writing for Children & Storytelling," "Travel Writing," "Adventure Writing," "Writing Your Autobiography" and "Books & Humor." The conference schedule includes lectures on the craft of writing, one-on-one consultations with the instructors and writing workshops.

University of Missouri Kansas City Writers' Workshops

For fiction and nonfiction writers, poets, journalists, screenwriters UMKC campus — *5100 Rockhill Rd., Kansas City, MO 64110* **Voice:** 816-235-2736 **Fax:** 816-235-5279 **E-mail:** mckinlem@smtpgate.umkc.edu **Contact:** James McKinley, Dir. **Open:** June **Admission:** Registration form only **Cost:** $110 (more if for credit) **Financial Aid:** Loans; Scholarship

UMKC OFFERS 2 programs for writers, both in June. The Mark Twain Creative Writing Workshop, begun in 1979, sponsors 3 weeks of intensive study. Meet with the faculty every weekday morning for 3 hours to study in one of several genres—fiction, nonfiction, screenwriting or poetry. Dormitory housing available.

The New Letters Weekend Writers Conference, offered over the final weekend in June, features best-selling authors reading from their work. Workshops with professional writers focus on creating and selling your work. Editors, authors, poets and a screenwriter shared their experiences over the 2 days in 1996, when the theme was "Writing for Love, Money and Immortality" and James Ellroy was the featured writer.

The setting, Kansas City, is a hub of activity and culture for the Midwest—museums, theater, symphony, jazz and blues clubs, steakhouses and barbecue.

Missouri Academic Programs

University of Missouri, Columbia, English Dept., 107 Tate Hall, Columbia, MO 65211; 573-882-4676; MA and PhD English (creative writing emphasis)

Washington University, Writing Program, English Dept., Campus Box 1122, St. Louis, MO 63130; 314-935-5190; MFA Writing

Montana

Environmental Writing Institute

For journalists, nonfiction writers, environmental essayists Teller Wildlife Refuge, 45 mi. S of Missoula — *Environmental Studies Program, Rankin Hall, University of Montana, Missoula, MT 59812* **Voice:** 406-243-2904 **Fax:** 406-243-6090 **E-mail:** hrh@selway.umt.edu **Contact:** Hank Harrington **Founded:** 1990 **Open:** 1 week in May **Admission:** $10, nonfiction manuscript **Deadlines:** Mar. 31 **Cost:** $550 (room and board incl.) **Size-Class:** 14

THIS WORKSHOP offers participants an opportunity to share their work with a handful of peers and to ready a manuscript for publication. Barry Lopez, Peter Matthiessen, Wen-

CHRIS MILLER

Writers (and Director Richard Nelson, on knees) at the 1996 Environmental Writing Institute, Missoula

dell Berry, Gretel Erlich, Terry Tempest Williams and Richard Nelson number among the EWI workshop faculty. You cannot ask for more inspirational leadership in the field of environmental writing.

To become one of the lucky 14 participants (essayists, natural historians, scientists, outdoor writers and journalists), submit an essay that is "in the final stages of revision, but unpublished." The essays of those selected are then distributed to all participants before the workshop for reading and evaluation.

Rustic remodeled farm buildings house the participants "on the edge of 1300 acres of timbered river-bottom, croplands, and uplands." There are float trips on the Bitterroot River, hikes and guided bird-watching.

Teller Wildlife Refuge, a co-sponsor of the workshop, was established by conservationist Otto Teller, past president and founding member of Trout Unlimited, to promote conservation and the preservation of wild lands and wildlife habitat. Deer, moose, otters, beaver, pheasant and waterfowl inhabit the refuge.

Glacier Institute

For fiction and nonfiction writers, poets Glacier Park Field Camp or Big Creek Outdoor Education Center — 137 Main Street, P.O. Box 7457, Kalispell, MT 59904 **Voice:** 406-755-1211 **Founded:** 1983 **Open:** June–Aug. **Admission:** Registration form only **Cost:** $200 (lodging & meals incl.)

THE GLACIER INSTITUTE offers a wide variety of Field Seminars providing adults and children with an opportunity to learn about wolves, grizzly bears, wildflowers, birds and geology. "When Wild Things Happen to Ordinary People" was the 1996 Special Workshop designed specifically for writers, "to explore human relationships to the wild places that surround us." There were other workshops for painters, naturalists and photographers.

Taught by a local outdoorsman and writer, the writers' workshop took place over a weekend in August at Big Creek Outdoor Education Center, adjacent to Glacier National Park. Days were spent in and around the park, one of the most striking natural environments on the continent. Workshops vary from year to year, so call to learn what is currently available.

Montana Artists Refuge

For all writers, and artists in selected other disciplines Downtown Basin, between Butte and Helena — P.O. Box 8, Basin, MT 59631 **Voice:** 406-225-3525 **Open:** Year-round **Admission:** Resume, writing sample, personal statement/project description **Cost:** $200–$400 per month plus heat, electricity and food **Financial Aid:** Loans; Stipend

IF YOU HAVE BEEN longing to live in a small town somewhere out in those wide-open spaces that have made the West famous, consider applying for a residency here, where you will live and work in one of the facilities provided by a group of artists who joined together to create the Montana Artists Refuge. (Residencies can be 3 months to 1 year.)

The tiny (pop. 250) town includes a grocery, cafe, two bars and a one-room school. Nearby there is infinite space with old mountain roads and game trails leading into the Rocky Mountain front range. If you want solitude you can find it. If you desire interactions with other artists, that, too, is possible.

The Refuge offers spaces in the old Hewett State Bank building and in another downtown location next door to a dry-goods store. Additional living and studio spaces for artists will be added to the Refuge's facilities as the artists continue to negotiate with local community members. Costs vary depending on the space you desire and on the season. In addition to rent, heat can cost $150 a month in winter, electricity $100 a month. But for this kind of quiet, the price isn't bad.

Yellow Bay Writers Workshop

For fiction and nonfiction writers and poets 85 mi. N of Missoula — University of Montana, Center for Continuing Education, Missoula, MT 59812 **Voice:** 406-243-2094 **Fax:** 406-243-2047 **E-mail:** Hynson@selway.umt.edu **Founded:** 1988 **Open:** 1 week in Aug. **Admission:** Application, writing sample, 1-page bio **Deadlines:** July 1 (early June for scholarships) **Cost:** $735 with room and board; $435 commuter **Financial Aid:** Loans; Scholarship **Size-Class:** 16 **Handicapped Access**

IMAGINE SPENDING a week working on a manuscript in rural Montana under the tutelage of a skilled creative writer. Submit your application early if you want to be assigned the teacher of your choice. In 1996 Bill McKibben (*The End of Nature*), 2 fiction writers and poet Pattiann Rogers were in residence.

Lodgings are rustic cabins at Yellow Bay, a biological research station. Lavatory and shower are nearby, but there are no typewriters.

Days are for workshops, writing, attending panel discussions, lectures and readings by participants. Evenings are given to socializing, informal discussions and special readings by faculty and guests. Hellgate Writers, a local writers group that co-sponsors the workshop, has hosted a reception, barbecue and readings in the past.

The wide variety of recreational activities near Yellow Bay include swimming, fishing, canoeing and hiking. The incomparable Glacier National Park is a mere 55 miles away.

Montana Academic Programs

University of Montana, English Dept., Missoula, MT 59812; 406-243-5231; MFA Creative Writing

Nebraska

Nebraska Sandhills Humor Writing Conference

For humorists, comedy writers and performers Broken Bow, 4 hr. W of Lincoln — Country Chuckles, Rt. 1, Box 96A, Merna, NE 68856 **Voice:** 800-484-9722 code 3100; 800-347-5237 **Fax:** 308-643-2286 **E-mail:** strout@unlinfo.unl.edu **Contact:** Steve Sommer or Shirley Trout **Founded:** 1995 **Open:** 1 weekend in June **Admission:** Registration form only **Cost:** $215 full conference; $70 meal and entertainment package; $150 Sat. only

NO JOKE. THERE really is a Humor Writing Conference in the Sandhills of Nebraska, and yes, it takes place in a small town called Broken Bow, 5 hours west of Omaha, 6 hours east of Denver. Not to worry—there is a $40 round-trip shuttle available from the Omaha and Lincoln airports.

This is a serious weekend conference for those who aim to make a living out of being funny, silly and amusing, or who simply want to use humor in their work, whether that work is as a writer, advertiser or storyteller or in the personnel department of a corporation. The conference offers 2 tracks—one for writers, the other for performers. The bulk of Saturday is spent in small "Creation Labs," where participants meet with 1 of the 5 instructors to receive critiques on their writing, explore personal performance styles, write and then rewrite their material. Those in the performers' track present their work in a "Comedy Concert in the Park" on Sunday afternoon.

Gene Perret, who was a head writer for Bob Hope, spoke in 1996 on "Successful Teams: What writers need to know about working with performers and what performers need to know about working with writers."

On Monday there is an optional canoe trip down the Niobrara River through the rolling Nebraska Sandhills. The entertainment and meals package includes a Saturday night barbecue, a prime rib luncheon and a buffalo burger supper. Seriously.

🏠 Nebraska Academic Programs

University of Nebraska, English Dept., 202 Andrews Hall, Lincoln, NE 68588; 402-472-3191; MA and PhD English (concentration in creative writing)

Nevada

Reading and Writing the West

📝 🌀 *For fiction and nonfiction writers, poets* Dept. of English, University of Nevada, Reno, NV 89557 **Voice:** 702-784-6755 **Fax:** 702-784-6266 **E-mail:** <stuchu@powernet.net> **Contact:** Stephen Tchudi **Founded:** 1992 **Open:** 2 weeks in July **Admission:** Registration form only **Deadlines:** May 15 **Cost:** $325 **Size-Attendees:** 40

THE UNIVERSITY of Nevada at Reno sponsors an annual summer institute on western life, literature and culture. At the institute, which is also a class for undergraduate and graduate credit through UNR, the emphasis is on examining the history and culture of the American West, as much as it is on writing. There is usually a field trip to a ghost town, but it is the discussions of literature and culture with humanities scholars, geographers, elders and historians that take center stage.

While writing itself may not be central here, reading before the workshop and discussions of that reading are. Assignments are given ahead of time. Those taking the class for credit contribute an article to an anthology that the teacher publishes.

New Hampshire

Seacoast Writers Association Conference

🌀 *For all writers* SE (near seacoast) NH — White Pines College, 40 Chester St., Chester, NH 03036; SWA, 33 Royal Crest Dr., Apt. 9, Marlboro, MA 01752, **Voice:** no phone **Contact:** Michael DiBattista, Registrar **Open:** 1 day in late Oct. **Admission:** Registration form only **Cost:** $50 ($60 at door); discount for SWA members

WITH A MEMBERSHIP including writers from Maine, Massachusetts, and New Hampshire, the Seacoast Writers Association serves a diverse group of writers, both beginner and advanced. This 1-day fall conference offers a panel, seminars and workshops. Some of the leaders are less than widely known, but a few, such as (in 1996) former Morrow publisher and editor-in-chief James Landis, certainly know the business side of the publishing racket.

Workshops concern both writing in certain genres and the ever-present question on writers' minds: how can I sell my work? If you're in the Portsmouth, NH, or Portland, ME, area, check it out. The price is certainly right.

Down Boston way, there are bigger, more sophisticated programs.

The Frost Place Festival of Poetry

🔄 *For poets* White Mountains, NW New Hampshire — Ridge Rd., Franconia, NH 03580 **Voice:** 603-823-5510 **Contact:** David Keller, Dir. **Founded:** 1979 **Open:** 1 week in midsummer **Admission:** 3 pages of poems, $25 reading fee (applicable to tuition) **Deadlines:** Jan.–early July **Cost:** $380; $295 audit only **Size-Attendees:** About 45 **Handicapped Access**

B E A SWINGER of birches for a week in the inspiring White Mts. house where Robert Frost composed many of his best poems. Each of the 6 days of this "festival" (actually a workshop) is presided over by a poet with solid credentials—Grace Paley, Hayden Caruth and Brad Leithouser have taught here. Morning lectures are followed by afternoon critique sessions. Participants' new work gets close scrutiny in groups of 6 to 8 writers (plus auditors).

Evening readings by guest faculty are a highlight. Poet Donald Hall commented, "There is no other poetic in-stitution in the United States that feels more consecrated to the poem itself." Former participants give rave reviews. The apply/accept ratio is 3:1, so inquire early and beat the rush for affordable accommodations. At workshop's end, head for the woods or scale a mountain, scribbler's notebook in hand.

The MacDowell Colony

🏠 *For all writers, and artists in se-lected other disciplines* S central NH, mid-way between Manchester, NH, and Brattle-boro, VT — 100 High St., Peterborough, NH 03458; 163 E 81st St., New York, NY 10028, **Voice:** 603-924-3886 **Fax:** 603-924-9142 **Contact:** David Macy, Resident Mgr. **Foun-ded:** 1907 **Open:** Year-round **Admission:** Application form ($20), project description, work sample **Deadlines:** Jan. 15, Apr. 15, Sept. 15–4 to 7 months ahead **Cost:** Volun-tary. Limited travel funds available. **Finan-cial Aid: Size-Attendees:** 30 resident writ-ers and artists

P ROGENITOR OF American art colo-nies, prestigious MacDowell has been a national historic site since 1913 (yes, 1913), providing hosts of

Cabin or Castle in the Woods

Since 1966 MacDowell has been on the National Register of Historic Places. James Baldwin called this most prestigious of American arts colonies a "refuge," but others see it as a 40-building conglomeration of architectural showpieces representing a wide spectrum of design styles popular in America over the past 2 centuries. As a resident you may find yourself scribbling away in a Revolutionary War-era wood frame house or a stone and masonry 20th-century bungalow. Local materials were diversely used, and some of the "cottages" are hardly that: they reflect the donors' elevated tastes and pre-tensions. Thus the formality of the neo-Federalist period with its echoes of Greek and Roman temples stands within shouting distance of a shingle-style house or even a log cabin. Perhaps this zany eclecticism is apt. The range of literary, musical and graphic arts styles practiced by residents at MacDowell is as wide as the horizon from a New Hampshire hilltop.

artists, well known and just beginning to fly, with peace, quiet, camaraderie and inspiration. Typical residencies last 4 to 8 weeks.

The MacDowell property, all 400 acres, approaches paradise regained for its "colonists." There are 28 secluded artists' studios for warm-weather use, many of them distinctive architecturally, the products of noted design firms in New York and Boston. Converted farmhouses and outbuildings form a social-administrative center, year-round lodgings and dining hall.

Who's on the MacDowell roster? No surprise: invitees have already demonstrated a high level of accomplishment or promise. The waiting list is long.

If you are accepted, you will be, historically, in good company indeed. Marian MacDowell founded the colony in '07 to honor her ailing husband, Edwin, the prominent composer. Among the nearly 2,500 resident artists who have benefited from MacDowell since then are Thornton Wilder, James Baldwin, Milton Avery, Aaron Copland and Leonard Bernstein, to drop just a few household names. If these fail to light up your board, try Willa Cather, Edwin Arlington Robinson and Studs Terkel; and then there was … well, you get the point. The Pulitzer Prize list and the MacDowell alumni list are more or less consonant.

Time at MacDowell is unstructured until the evening meal, after which in-

Lunch arrives in a basket at Chapman Studio, MacDowell Colony, Peterborough

tense socializing and sharing of new work is the nightly agenda. Cutting your teeth at other writers' colonies may enhance your application, but nothing is more important than the quality of your work. Take a number, get in line and work hard while you wait.

New Hampshire Academic Programs

University of New Hampshire,
English Dept., Hamilton Smith Hall, Durham, NH 03824; 603-862-3963; MA Writing

New Jersey

Metropolitan Writers Conference

For fiction and nonfiction writers On Seton Hall University campus, 14 mi. from NYC — Continuing Education, Bayley Hall, Seton Hall University, South Orange, NJ 07079 **Voice:** 201-761-9783 **Contact:** Jane Degnan, Dir. **Founded:** 1991 **Open:** Varies **Admission:** Registration form only **Cost:** $60; plus $20 per manuscript submission **Size-Attendees:** 100 **Handicapped Access**

POPULAR AUTHORS—Belva Plain in 1995, Mary Higgins Clark in 1996—kick off this 1-day spring conference in South Orange, sponsored by Seton Hall University's Continuing Education Department. The practical workshops that fill the schedule are aimed at writers in the early stages of their careers. "Writing and Publishing the Personal Memoir," "Understanding Plot" and "Characterization" have been among the basic workshops in the craft of writing offered here.

Published authors with track records in fiction and nonfiction lead the workshops. Many genres are covered, from children's books to creative nonfiction. At least 1 workshop in some aspect of the business of writing features literary agents and supplements the sessions on craft. Manuscript evaluations are available, but the work must be sent in prior to the workshop.

New Jersey Romance Writers' Fall Conference

For romance writers Hotel — 21 Wildhedge Lane, Holmdel, NJ 07733 **Voice:** 609-985-7192 **Fax:** 609-985-8515 **Contact:** Rainy Kirkland, Dir. **Founded:** 1984 **Open:** 1½ days in early October **Admission:** Application **Deadlines:** Early Sept. **Cost:** $135 **Size-Attendees:** 250

WHETHER YOU simply seek a glimpse into the world of romance writing or want serious instruction in the craft as well as the business side of this commercial genre, the 1-day regional conference sponsored by New Jersey Romance Writers deserves attention. Editors from a variety of presses, including Kensington, Berkley, Ballantine/Fawcett, Avon, Harlequin, Bantam and Silhouette, attend. Literary agents participate, offering appointments on a first-come, first-served basis (register early).

The conference caters to both experienced and beginning writers, and not only to romance writers. Members of NJRW also write mysteries, historical novels, children's books and young adult fiction. Well-known romance authors are among the faculty. Sessions have focused on a variety of subjects, including "The Credible Cupid: How to Make Your Characters Fall in Love," "Finding the Conflict," "Sex vs. Sexual Tension" and "Keep the Pages Turning."

NJRW holds monthly meetings and sponsors other workshops throughout the year.

Trenton State College Writers' Conference

For fiction and nonfiction writers, poets, playwrights, screenwriters, journalists Trenton State College campus — Dept. of English, Trenton State College, Hillwood Lakes, CN 4700, Trenton, NJ 08650 **Voice:** 609-771-3254 **Contact:** Jean Hollander, Dir. **Founded:** 1982 **Open:** 1 day in Apr. **Admission:** Registration form only **Cost:** $40, plus $10 per workshop, $5–$8 for special presentations **Size-Attendees:** 800–1,000

PROMINENT AUTHORS—Alice Walker (1996), Kurt Vonnegut (1995), Norman Mailer (1991), Erica Jong (1992)—attract hundreds of writers to the evening event that caps this day of workshops. The emphasis is on fiction and poetry in the concurrent workshops, readings and panels, facilitated by editors, novelists, journalists and poets. Sessions include "Magazine and Newspaper Journalism," "Breaking Writer's Block" and "Literature for the Young."

Additional panels overlap the workshops and focus on publishing and on making a living as a writer. Participants may sign up for an open reading, which takes place before the evening's guest speaker. Representatives from such publishing houses as Crown and W. W. Norton; fiction editors from *The New Yorker,* the *Atlantic Monthly* and *Redbook;* and members of the National Writers' Union have addressed this conference, which benefits from its proximity to New York.

New Jersey Academic Programs

Rutgers University, Camden, English Dept., Camden, NJ 08102; 609-225-6121; MA English (concentration in writing)

William Paterson College, English Dept., Wayne, NJ 07470; 201-595-2254; MA English (concentration in writing)

New Mexico

Helene Wurlitzer Foundation of New Mexico

For all writers, and artists in selected other disciplines Taos —Box 545, Taos, NM 87571 **Voice:** 505-758-2413 **Contact:** Kenneth G. Peterson, Exec. Dir. **Founded:** 1954 **Open:** Apr.–Sept. **Admission:** Writing sample, project description **Deadlines:** Rolling **Cost:** Transportation, meals **Size-Attendees:** 12 **Handicapped Access**

THESE 12 SEPARATE furnished studio residences are booked years in advance by creative artists who normally stay about 3 months. You set your own schedule, and cook and clean for yourself. This is a retreat for the self-sufficient and independently motivated. No communal lunches, dinners or orientation sessions. It is possible that you may not even be introduced to the other residents unless you take the initiative. At Wurlitzer, residents enjoy the luxury of time and a place to write. Beautiful mountains, incredible skies. A landscape to explore, to observe and to inspire.

Santa Fe Writers' Conference

For fiction writers, poets, playwrights Walking distance from the historic Plaza — Recursos, 826 Camino de Monte Rey, Santa Fe, NM 87505 **Voice:** 505-982-9301 **Contact:** Peter Eichstaedt, Dir. **Founded:** 19 **Open:** 1 week in late July, early Aug. **Admission:** Application ($35), writing sample **Deadlines:** Mid-June **Cost:** $380 ($470 with lunches) **Size-Attendees:** 60 **Handicapped Access**

THE SANTA FE WRITERS' Conference is an annual event that brings poets and fiction writers together at the Plaza Resolana Conference and Study Center in downtown Santa Fe. A program of the Santa Fe Literary Center and a component of Recursos, a not-for-profit organization that sponsors seminars and conferences, this conference features award-winning writers for 5 days of workshops. Admission is selective, based on manuscript submissions.

The emphasis is on the small group workshop with writer/teachers, although there are also discussions about publishing with editors and agents. Readings at a nearby Native American ruin, panel discussions with guest authors and individual conferences supplement the workshops. During unstructured moments, you can explore the pueblos, enjoy Santa Fe cuisine, hike in pine forests, lie spread-eagle and watch the sky.

Santa Fe continues to attract artists and writers from around the world to its historic 17th-century plaza, museums and art galleries. Native American, Hispanic and Anglo cultures clash, combine, conflict and commingle in Santa Fe, making it a stimulating place to study writing in the late 20th century.

The Santa Fe Playwrights Workshop, jointly sponsored by the Santa Fe Stages and Recursos, accepted 12 students in each of its 2 classes in 1996. The 6-day workshop concentrated on the presentation of staged readings of participants' manuscripts by the Santa Fe Stages Company. (The workshop overlapped the poetry/fiction conference.)

Contact Recursos for information about "Writing Your Self," a nonfiction workshop on writing memoirs (held in late August).

Shapes of Poetry in the 21st Century

 For poets *College of Santa Fe — College of Santa Fe, Humanities Dept., 1600 St. Michaels Dr., Santa Fe, NM 87505* **Voice:** 505-982-3765 **Fax:** 505-982-3765 **Contact:** Dottie Indyke, Coord. **Open:** 3 days in Mar. **Admission:** Registration form only **Deadlines:** Feb. 4 for early registration **Cost:** $150 (early registration $120)

THE FAMOUS AND the unknown are attracted to this "brainstorming session on poetry for the new millennium." Poets, editors, educators, scholars, critics, artists and thinkers come to Santa Fe to participate in lively, passionate dialogues and discussions.

From the open invitation on the brochure: "Why You Should Come: Poetry is important to people: There are more practicing professional poets in the United States than have ever existed at any time in any culture. ... All of us, professional and amateurs alike, share a profound sense that poetry is vital not merely to art or education, but as a quest for meaning, as a way to live sanely and fully in a violent and disordered world. "Questions are plentiful, answers few: How should poetry deal with today's astonishing technologies? Can it deal with them? How can poetry tap into vision in a fresh way? Can it become the voice for a new age of realistic mystics and down-to-earth metaphysicians? Is poetry a part of the natural or-

der, or yet another example of humanity's disastrous divorce from nature?"

Whether or not you have written a line of poetry, the organizers of this event want you to participate. This is not one of those exclusive, send-in-your-manuscript-and-we'll-tell-you-if-you-can-come affairs; these poets want you to join them.

Southwest Writers Workshop Conference

For fiction and nonfiction writers *Hotel in Albuquerque — 1338 Wyoming Blvd. NE, Suite B, Albuquerque, NM 87112* **Voice:** 505-293-0303 **Fax:** 505-237-2665 **Founded:** 1982 **Open:** 3 days in Aug. **Admission:** Registration form only

STARTED BY A GROUP of romance writers who met in each other's homes to learn more about the craft, the Southwest Writers Workshop (SWW) has grown to over 1,000 members. Its annual conference provides workshops in almost every genre. Not only can you learn about writing mysteries, children's books, historical novels, humor books and New Age tracts, but there are dozens of how-to sessions on everything from query letters, to what to expect from your publisher, financial planning, and the advantages of self-publishing. One workshop offered to explain "Sex Across the Genres: How sex scenes differ among genres and how to write for your category."

Editors, authors and agents, mostly from the region, participate on panels and are also available for appointments. There are "Meet the Speakers" sessions and luncheons with speakers (Thomas Keneally in 1994, Deanne Stillman in 1995).

SWW invites writers to join its ranks, come to the twice-monthly meetings, sign up for health insurance, read the newsletter, volunteer.

Taos Institute of Arts

For fiction and nonfiction writers, poets, and artists in selected other disciplines 1½ hr. N of Santa Fe — Box 5280 NDCBU, Taos, NM 87571 **Voice:** 505-758-2793; 800-822-7183 **E-mail:** tia@taosnet.com **Web Site:** http://www.taosnet.com/TIA/ **Contact:** Judith Krull **Founded:** 1989 **Open:** Summer and fall **Admission:** Registration form **Deadlines:** First come, first served **Cost:** $250–$300 **Financial Aid:** Loans; Scholarship **Size-Class:** 12 **Handicapped Access**

AT THE TAOS INSTITUTE of Arts (TIA), the staff believe that by mixing artistic disciplines more creativity can emerge. A panoply of weeklong workshops in painting, weaving, dyeing, drawing, drum making, jewelry, photography and writing stretch out through the summer and into the fall. For writers there are workshops in fiction, writing fundamentals, poetry, mysteries and writing for children.

Workshops meet at various locations in Taos; there is no campus. Participants arrange their own housing. TIA staff can provide suggestions, and there are some places that offer discounts to students.

Award-winning writers—who are often college teachers as well—teach the writing and literature workshops. "Death in the Desert: Mysteries by New Mexican Writers" featured 2 local authors as guests.

Taos has become a center for artists. Home for centuries to the Pueblo Indians, later the Spanish explorers, and more recently waves of Anglos attracted to the Sangre de Cristo mountains, the high-desert landscape and the mix of cultures, Taos continues to inspire creative endeavors.

Taos School of Writing

For fiction and nonfiction writers Thunderbird Lodge, 23 mi. N of Taos — P.O. Box 20496, Albuquerque, NM 87154 **Voice:** 505-294-4601 **E-mail:** spletzer@swcp.com **Contact:** Suzanne Spletzer, Admin. **Founded:** 1993 **Open:** 1 week in July **Admission:** Application form ($20), manuscript **Deadlines:** Mid-May **Cost:** $995 (room and board incl.) **Size-Class:** 12

THOSE IMPRESSIVE mountains that give Taos Ski Valley its national reputation are the setting for the Taos School of Writing. Workshops, panels and one-on-one manuscript reviews may be why you choose to attend, but the 9,000-foot elevation with wildflowers, pines and southwestern light may be what you remember.

Mornings are structured, with the faculty rotating through the workshops to provide a variety of instruction styles. Afternoons and evenings include small- group and individual consultations, panels, talks, and time for reading and writing, hiking and relaxing.

Writers live, eat and study at the Thunderbird Lodge, 23 miles north of Taos. The brochure promotes the owner, declaring that "she is known internationally for setting 'the finest table in New Mexico.'" Even if it's not absolutely accurate, it gives you a sense of what she strives for—you ought to be fed well.

Nearby there are many attractions including the Mabel Dodge Luhan House, D. H. Lawrence Ranch and Shrine and Kit Carson's home.

Women's Wilderness Retreats: Hawk I'm Your Sister

For fiction and nonfiction writers, poets Heron Lake, NM; Missouri River, MT — P.O. Box 9109, Santa Fe, NM 87504 **Voice:** 505-984-2268 **Contact:** Beverly Antaeus **Founded:** 1992 **Open:** 1 week in June and/or July **Admission:** Registration form only **Cost:** $1,200 **Size-Class:** 14

A RIVER GUIDE, Beverly Antaeus founded Women's Wilderness Retreats to share her enthusiasm for the wilderness with other women. Two of the adventures are specifically designed for writers, especially those seeking a spiritual and feminist journey. One features poet Sharon Olds, who teaches at New York University and has taught at the Squaw Valley Writers' Workshop (see *California*). Olds and Antaeus take participants on a 46-mile paddle on the Missouri River in Montana. Participants work on their own poems, discuss poetry in groups, hear poems read and explore the river and its banks.

A second workshop, "The Rain of Fire You Dare: A Writing Retreat with Deena Metzger," takes participants to the shore of a cool high-desert lake in northern New Mexico. Days are filled with writing, reading, listening and canoeing. Metzger is a poet and psychotherapist. In her workshop serious attention is paid to each participant's internal and external experience.

Writing Today's Science

For nonfiction writers, journalists, scientists Plaza Resolana Study and Conference Center, downtown Santa Fe — 826 Camino de Monte Rey A-3, Santa Fe, NM 87505 **Voice:** 505-982-9301 **Fax:** 505-989-8608 **E-mail:** RECURSOS@aol.com **Web Site:** http:\\www.santafe.edu\~johnson\sciwrite.html **Contact:** Sandra Blakeslee and George Johnson, Dirs. **Founded:** 19 **Open:** Varies **Admission:** Application ($35), personal statement **Cost:** $355 **Size-Class:** 12 **Handicapped Access**

R ESPONDING TO THE increasing need for writers who can explain the universe in "clear and artistic prose," the Santa Fe Writers' Conference and the Santa Fe Institute initiated this conference in 1996. Here is where you can learn to explain scientific ideas in comprehensible and elegant prose, interact with scientists and reporters, and during breaks, explore the beauty of the high desert of New Mexico.

As with other conferences you can attend workshops and hear other writers describe their experiences, but the focus here is on how they translated scientific ideas, theories and discoveries into language for the lay audience. Writers participate in workshops with science reporters and editors, drawn for instance from the *New York Times,* may attend a special session on doing research on-line, and receive guidance on a manuscript brought to the conference.

Santa Fe Institute, the co-sponsor, "has devoted itself to creating a new kind of scientific community, pursuing emerging syntheses in science. ... [It] seeks to catalyze new collaborative research, to break down barriers between traditional disciplines, to spread its ideas and methodologies to other institutions, and to encourage the practical application of its results."

🏠 New Mexico Academic Programs

New Mexico State University, English Dept, Las Cruces, NM 88003; 505-646-3931; MA English (creative writing emphasis)
University of New Mexico, English Dept., Albuquerque, NM 87131; 505-277-6347; MA English (concentration in writing)

New York

92nd St. Y, Unterberg Poetry Center

📝 *For fiction and nonfiction writers, poets, and artists in selected other disciplines* Upper East Side, Manhattan — 1395 Lexington Ave., New York, NY 10128 **Voice:** 212-415-5760 **Contact:** Melissa Hammerle, Karl Kirchway, Co-Dirs. **Founded:** 1939 **Open:** Fall and spring **Admission:** Sample manuscripts, permission of the instructor **Deadlines:** Mid-Sept. for fall; Late Jan. for spring **Cost:** $60–$220 **Financial Aid:** Scholarship **Size-Class:** 25 maximum **Handicapped Access**

T HE STANDING JOKE is that New York is so big they had to name it twice. An adult education program on a truly grand scale is the 92nd St. YMHA's gift to the city. For writers the cornucopia includes numerous workshops in poetry, fiction and nonfiction. Given the city's inexhaustible supply of famous writers and fine teachers, almost any workshop or conference here is likely to offer contact with seasoned top-rank professionals.

Literary seminars of high intellectual caliber (such as "Horace and the Horatian Tradition") set the tone. Writing workshops often reflect the instructors' own professional or personal-development interests. For example, Hettie Jones's memoir class is rooted in her interracial 1960s Manhattan experience. Bonuses: the Y's "Reading Series," presenting many kinds of writers, often of Pulitzer or even Nobel Prize fame, offering peeks at their latest works-in-progress; and the "Biographers and Brunch" series. Unlike other equally good but different literary programs downtown, the 92nd St. Y attracts a somewhat older, less funky clientele.

NANCY CRAMPTON

Nobel Prize winner Saul Bellow reads at the 92nd St. Y, New York City

American Society of Journalists and Authors

🔁 **For all fiction and nonfiction writers** Hotel or university in New York City — 1501 Broadway, Suite 302, New York, NY 10036 **Voice:** 212-997-0947 **Fax:** 212-768-7414 **Contact:** Sandra Forsyth, Conf. Dir. **Founded:** 1948 **Open:** 1 weekend in spring **Admission:** Registration form only **Cost:** $260 full conference; $190 Sat. only; mentoring session $20 **Size-Attendees:** 700

YOU WOULD EXPECT as much from Broadway and New York: This conference is big, high-powered, expensive (when you add in a hotel room or even parking in the city) and intelligent. The conference is sponsored by and draws on the collective wisdom of one of the country's most important writers' organizations, the American Society of Journalists and Authors (see *Associations and Organizations*). ASJA provides a wide range of services to its members.

ASJA has offered this conference for over 25 years. A West Coast version was presented in the mid-'90s but its fate is currently uncertain. Recently the traditional East Coast rendition carried the title "Publish and Prosper in '96," and, the workshop sessions reflected an aggressively commercial orientation. There is little here for the strictly literary minded (indeed, poetry seems conspicuously absent, no doubt because it does not "sell"). For those who want to "sell," this is a cornucopia. "Fitness Sriting," "Hidden Bucks in Corporate Writing," "Humor Market," "Spiritual Markets"—the list goes on. There is scheduled time for mingling with editors and agents. The 25-minute "mentoring session" may be useful, but it strikes us as another Jiffy Lube approach to manuscript repairs. Then again, this is the town of the "New York minute."

ASJA also publishes useful books for writers (see *Bibliography*). Overall its program of services is commendable. Membership is not cheap, but if your writing is market-driven and you are climbing the professional ladder, you may well want to consider this conference as an investment.

There's a discount for early registration, and discounted hotel accommodations are offered; inquire early.

Attention medical and mental-health professional writers: ASJA has in the past offered special conferences for you. Inquire about future plans.

Blue Mountain Center

🏠 **For all writers, and artists in selected other disciplines** South central Adirondacks — Blue Mt. Lake, NY 12812 **Voice:** 518-352-7391 **Contact:** Harriet Barlow, Dir. **Founded:** 1981 **Open:** June–mid-Oct. **Admission:** Letter, biographical sketch, project description, writing sample, $20 fee **Deadlines:** Feb. 1 **Cost:** None **Size-Attendees:** 14 artists

THERE'S A LONG DIRT driveway, off a quiet mountain road, leading to the pristine woodland setting of Blue Mountain Center, an artists' retreat in the glorious Adirondacks. A handsome stone and shingle mansion (a throwback to prosperous Victorian times), with commodious common rooms and a library, houses the artists here, though the great outdoors is home to many visitors at BMC also. When you weary of writing, lakes, boats and hiking trails await your indulgence.

A writer friend of ours spent a productive, successful month at BMC, appreciating the financial support and the freedom. He had earned it, as have most BMC artists, who tend to be well credentialed, with writing that shows real promise. The center's philosophical mandate calls for supporting artists whose "work ... evinces social and ecological concern." No doubt the political struggle to preserve the Adirondack wilderness is an influence here.

Each artist at BMC has his or her own room; two meals are prepared each day (lunch is impromptu). Evenings may bring a formal reading or informal relaxation. On our October visit, it was popcorn, a video and a warming fire on the hearth.

Leave your cell phone at home. One pay phone serves all the artists here, and such deprivation is luxury. No interruptions or distractions; it's just you, the manuscript and the mountains.

Byrdcliffe Arts Colony

For all writers, and artists in selected other disciplines The Catskills, 90 mi. N of New York City — 34 Tinker St., Woodstock, NY 12498 **Voice:** 914-679-2079 **Fax:** 914-679-1529 **Contact:** Katherine Berger, Coord. **Founded:** 1902 **Open:** Early June–late Sept. **Admission:** Application, manuscript, project description **Deadlines:** Mid-April **Cost:** June & Sept., $400; July & Aug., $500 **Financial Aid:** Scholarship **Size-Attendees:** 10 artists in residence

ARTISTS IN residence at Byrdcliffe Arts Colony are standing on the shoulders of giants. Among writers who worked here is poet Wallace Stevens. Among dancers, Isadora Duncan. Among theater people, Viveca Lindfors. Nonetheless, it is evidence of one's serious commitment to a professional life in the arts, and not necessarily a host of prestigious professional accomplishments, that is most important to the panel of reviewers who consider applications to Byrdcliffe.

Residencies here last from 1 to 4 months. Each artist has a private room and appropriate studio space in the Viletta Inn, which houses the program. The inn, which is on the 600-acre Byrdcliffe estate, close to the Catskill nature preserves, includes common rooms and a library. Byrdcliffe is $1\frac{1}{2}$ miles from the busy town of Woodstock, a magnet for tourists and shoppers, mostly looking for crafts. Resident artists have abundant quiet at Byrdcliffe yet can enjoy the shops and cafes of the town as well.

There is history here, too. Byrdcliffe is now part of the Woodstock Guild, founded in 1940 to support study and practice in crafts, writing, theater and music. The guild itself is housed in an 18th-century mansion in the village, with the Kleinert Arts center (a performance space) next door. The Byrdcliffe estate, a National Register of Historic Places property, was inherited by the Woodstock Guild in 1975.

Catskill Poetry Workshop

For poets only The southern Catskills, 75 mi. from Albany — Office of Special Programs, Hartwick College, Oneonta, NY 13820 **Voice:** 607-431-4415 **Fax:** 607-431-4527 **Contact:** Carol Frost, Dir. **Open:** 1 week in late June **Admission:** Application form ($20), sample manuscript, resume **Deadlines:** May 1 **Cost:** $625 (room and board incl.); day visitor $55; college credit $75 extra **Financial Aid:** Scholarship

SUMMERTIME ON a college campus in a small country town, with 4,000-foot mountains rising nearby and a 20-mile Susquehanna Valley view: If this sounds good to you and you're a poet, apply immediately to the Catskill Poetry Workshop, based at Hartwick College in Oneonta. The 7-person faculty is consistently top-rate, with NEA Fellowship, Guggenheim and Pushcart Prize winners among them. Most are university teachers, too, suggesting competence at giving useful instruction in the craft of poetry.

Private conferences with the instructors make this workshop appealing for those who are ready for serious one-on-one critiques of their work. Daily classes get under the hood where the poetry engine really runs: meter, metaphor, free verse techniques, and more. Participants are expected, encouraged to revise, revise and ...

Housing (shared double rooms) is in a college dormitory; meals are in the dining hall. To compensate for these rigors, the college athletic facilities and art gallery are available.

Cave Canem

For African-American poets Southern Catskill Mountains — Mt. St. Alphonsus Retreat Center, P.O. Box 219, Esopus, NY 12429; 39 Jane St., Apt. GB, New York, NY 10014 **Voice:** 212-242-8646 **E-mail:** CEPoetry@ AOL.com **Contact:** Cornelius Eady, Dir. **Open:** 1 week in early June **Admission:** 6–8 poems **Deadlines:** Late Feb. **Cost:** No tuition; room and board $325 **Size-Attendees:** 20–24

AFRICAN-AMERICAN poets gather here—on a 400-acre estate overlooking the Hudson River in an idyllic setting—for a 1-week retreat devoted to developing their craft and to building camaraderie. The Mt. St. Alphonsus Retreat Center provides private rooms with plenty of quiet time for writing. There are daily workshops and readings as well. Directors Derricotte and Eady were joined by guest poets Elizabeth Alexander and Michael Weaver to make a 4-person faculty in 1996. The program's Latin name is pronounced *kay'-vay kay'-nem* and means "Beware of the dog."

Chautauqua Writers' Workshop

For all writers, and artists in selected other disciplines Extreme western NY — Chautauqua Institution, P.O. Box 1098, Chautauqua, NY 14722 **Voice:** 716-357-6200; off-season 716-357-6255 **Fax:** 716-357-9014 **Web Site:** http://www.chautauqua-inst.org **Contact:** Jack Voelker, Dir. **Founded:** 1946 **Open:** July and Aug. **Admission:** Registration form only **Deadlines:** Courses fill early; apply in winter or spring **Cost:** 1 week about $125; 2 weeks $225 **Size-Class:** About 15

CHAUTAUQUA Institution's summer catalogue consists of 64 pages of course descriptions in 10-point type. There is enough going on here, in the granddaddy of all American nonacademic intellectual and artistic education centers, to keep you busy for the rest of your life. No exaggeration. But if it's the writer in you that seeks training and contact with fellow artists, you can focus on either the Writer's Workshop or other shorter courses on special topics.

The 1996 program (marking CWW's 50th year) offered a general "Writer's Voice" workshop covering technique and marketing; a memoirs and fiction course; and "The Fiction Workout" for those who are blocked, unable to finish or to start writing. Each of these sessions ran for 2 weeks, meeting 2, 3, or 5 times weekly in 2-hour sessions. Plus there are personal manuscript consultations. And readings by the broadly experienced teachers, who are writers themselves (with serious literary and/ or commercial credits). A solid program to be sure.

Special-interest courses in writing at Chautauqua, outside CWW itself, can make a visit here worthwhile, too. Shakespeare's sonnets, haiku poetry, women's autobiography, selling freelance articles—the list goes on in true bonanza fashion. These classes are inexpensive (some under $75) and usually meet a few times during 1 week.

For many people, artists included, a Chautauqua visit is a holiday with a learning component. The concept is a venerable one by now. The institution, founded in the 1870s and now a National Historic Landmark, originally served as a vacation school for Protestant Sunday school teachers. Religion as a subject and as practice is still important here, but it's approached ecumenically nowadays. Seminars in this category range from Christian studies to Islam and Buddhism, with a substantial Jewish presence, too. The holiday element is just as important. With Chautauqua Lake, a resident symphony, theater, opera and many other stimulating entertainment options, the institution has become a family vacation center. Demand for lodgings, especially in the village's famed 19th-century houses, is intense. Some package deals are available, including a "gate pass" that gets you into almost all of the entertainment events. Inquire early.

Bring your laptop computer and your tennis racquet to this one!

Caveat: full payment is due with registration, and refunds are difficult.

Chenango Valley Writers' Conference

For all writers *Central upstate NY — Colgate University, 13 Oak Dr., Hamilton, NY 13346* **Voice:** 315-824-7267 **Fax:** 607-847-9921 **Contact:** Frederick Busch, Dir. **Open:** 1 week in late June **Admission:** Registration form ($50) **Cost:** $900 (room and board incl.); $600 tuition only (day students) **Financial Aid:** Fellowship

COLGATE UNIVERSITY may be small but it's academically strong, and its English department–based Chenango Valley Writers' Conference reflects these strengths. The conference schedule thoughtfully mixes writing time, private tutorials with experienced teachers, classroom discussions of student manuscripts, readings by visiting writers, a session or two about getting published, and a modicum of playtime to

enjoy the camaraderie of fellow writers and a lovely campus. It's a winning formula, with little wasted time in a full week of the writing life.

Instructors and visiting experts have included the editor of the *Georgia Review,* a W. W. Norton editor, a best-selling biographer, a PEN/Faulkner Award novelist, a literary agent, a consumer magazine editor and a TV scriptwriter. From such people any writer can learn. In our opinion, the staff here looks as good as at many a conference at bigger, flashier institutions.

Bonuses: (1) air conditioning in both the classrooms and the dormitory! and (2) great recreational opportunities in the nearby Finger Lakes region.

Cornell's Adult University Writing Workshops

For business writers, memoirists and other writers *Central upstate NY — 626 Thurston Ave., Ithaca, NY 14850* **Voice:** 607-255-6260 **Fax:** 607-254-4482 **E-mail:** cau@sce.cornell.edu **Web Site:** http://www. sce.cornell.edu/SCE/CAU/ **Contact:** Ralph Janis, Dir. **Open:** Apr.–Nov. **Admission:** Registration form only **Deadlines:** Vary **Cost:** $455 per week (commuter), $765 (dormitory), $825 (hotel); all include tuition, lodging, 16 meals **Size-Attendees:** About 150

FROM A WRITING programs viewpoint, Cornell's nonacademic offerings are few in number, but the university, and its location, ranks so high in our estimation that this is worth checking out. Run by Cornell's summer school, the "Adult University" season is actually spring through fall. Most workshops are likely to be scheduled in July and August, and most run for 1 week. Topics vary yearly, with business writing and memoir being the genres offered in 1996.

Around 75% of the attendees are Cornell grads, many of whom bring family or at least a spouse. Workshop sessions meet mornings and early afternoons most days of the week, but there is plenty of free time for family or personal vacation activities, which Cornell, Ithaca, Cayuga Lake and the Finger Lakes environs supply in abundance. While the teaching is stimulating, relatively few demands are placed on workshop participants. School without homework: now there's a winning formula.

Call for the catalogue early in the spring. The memoir course in 1996 filled early. Don't miss your chance if this westernmost Ivy League campus is where you'd like to work on your writing and spend some leisure time.

Feminist Women's Writing Workshops

For feminist women writers Central upstate NY — Hobart and William Smith Colleges, Geneva, P.O. Box 6583, Ithaca, NY 14851 **Contact:** Margo Gumosky and Kit Wainer, Dirs. **Founded:** 1974 **Open:** 1 week in mid-July **Admission:** Application form, writing sample (newcomers only) **Deadlines:** Apr. 25 for financial aid **Cost:** $535 (room and board incl.) **Financial Aid:** Scholarship **Size-Attendees:** 45

IF PAST BE PROLOGUE, then future Feminist Women's Writing Workshops promise to please their participants with useful instruction and supportive camaraderie. The emphasis here—aside from the obvious feminist leanings—is on inclusiveness and diversity. Attendees may be rank beginners or accomplished (a.k.a. published) writers. What's more, the program offers not only the standard fare of workshops, readings and tutorials but also an option to use the time for solitary work and reflection.

Hobart and William Smith Colleges (one combined campus) provide a convenient and handsome setting, with private (dormitory) rooms and dining hall,

your own Finger Lake (Geneva) and recreational facilities. While the faculty list at FWWW (or F3 as it's affectionately known) may not ring bells for many applicants, the results of the workshops seem indisputably positive. Former attendees praise FWWW to the skies, though in the participants' comments more attention was paid to inner psychological change than to improved writing per se.

One also gets the impression that there are a lot of beginners here, people still exploring to find their best genre. Indeed, attendees are encouraged to work in more than one genre. Evening programs range widely from erotica to children's books to publishing and multimedia writing/visual arts projects. All with the feminist political flavor.

Gell Writers Center of the Finger Lakes

For all writers Central upstate NY — Naples, NY; c/o Writers & Books, 740 University Ave., Rochester, NY 14607 **Voice:** 716-473-2590 **Contact:** Joseph Flaherty, Dir. **Open:** Year-round **Admission:** Application form, writing sample, references **Deadlines:** Revolving **Cost:** $35 per day ($25 for W&B members) **Size-Attendees:** 1 or 2 writers

KEEP AN EYE on Gell Writers Center, a writers' retreat: it's growing. Currently there is a house (of recent vintage), on spacious grounds but not a country estate like Yaddo or MacDowell, with 2 bedrooms accommodating 2 writers—that's it. Or even one writer (if he or she rents both rooms). Yes, it's a rental, and at $25 or $35 per night plus meals, the tab can grow quickly. But visits of both short and long duration are evidently welcome. You can make your own plan.

Perhaps more interesting is the newly built Gleason Lodge at the same location in Naples, serving as a literary conference center and eventually to

125

provide rooms for 16 more writers. Both Gell and Gleason are by-products of the generosity of Dr. and Mrs. Kenneth Gell, and both are linked to the Rochester-based literary association Writers & Books.

For writers based in the Finger Lakes region, including Rochester, a brief stay at Gell is an attractive possibility, offering seclusion and comfort. Remember, though, in this kind of setting, you're really on your own, both day and night.

Gotham Writers Workshop

For all writers *Manhattan, uptown and down — 1841 Broadway, New York, NY 10023* **Voice:** *212-974-8377* **Fax:** *212-307-6325* **Web Site:** *http://users.aol.com/ GOTHAMWW* **Contact:** *Jeff Fligelman, Co-Dir.* **Open:** Year-round **Admission:** Registration form only **Cost:** $395 for 10-wk. workshop; $145 1-day intensive workshops; discounts to returning GWW students **Size-Class:** maximum of 14 in 10-wk. workshops, 40 in 1-day sessions

WELL ORGANIZED, staffed and subscribed—this diverse program of workshops in numerous genres sets a high standard, as you would expect from a Manhattan literary outfit. From the Gotham catalogue: "Our aim is to demystify the writing process ..."; "We believe anybody can write. It's a craft, like being a carpenter." Clearly these are confident teachers, with success on their minds. A plethora of quotes in the catalogue, from workshop attendees, would seem to attest to the program's success, and a close, personal, no-nonsense friend of ours swears by it.

We like the emphasis on craft here, which is not to say that the writer's feelings or inspiration are ignored. In various ways, through writing exercises and

reading of short literary examples, the principles governing the workshop's literary genre are taught first, before students are set free to manipulate the "rules" in their own new work. An admirable traditionalism, we'd say, compared to many workshops that are entirely too touchy-feely. Workshops are offered in fiction and nonfiction, poetry, play- and screenwriting, and comedy. Small classes, basic and advanced levels, full season or 1-day only: GWW is ready to put the writer in you to work. Good enough to warrant a commute into the city if you have the time and inclination. And the price is entirely fair.

Highlights Foundation Writers Workshop

For children's book writers and illustrators *Extreme western NY — Chautauqua Institution, Chautauqua, NY 14722; 814 Court St., Honesdale, PA 18431* **Voice:** *717-253-1192* **Fax:** *717-253-0179* **Contact:** Jan Keen, Dir. **Founded:** 1984 **Open:** 1 week in mid-July **Admission:** Registration form only **Deadlines:** Around June 1 **Cost:** $1,700 ($415 discount for first-timers), meals included; housing $185–$475 per week **Financial Aid:** Scholarship **Size-Attendees:** About 200

THERE IS STRENGTH in numbers, or so the folks who sponsor and attend the Highlights children's writers workshop would say. What's the draw here that justifies the sizable price tag? *Highlights* magazine for kids has a large circulation and a sincere interest in promoting literacy. Learning to write for such a publication is a goal worth setting if you're a newcomer to the field. But *Highlights* aside, a week at Chautauqua, abuzz with artistic and intellectual activity to suit every taste, appeals to many as an ideal situation for a working holiday.

Highlights publisher Kent Brown has an evangelistic message for his workshop attendees. He wants them to believe their books may actually change someone's life forever. Brochure copy here tends toward the self-congratulatory and hyperbolic enthusiasm, but if that's your bent, you'll warm to it easily. Certainly the outline of skills and issues covered in daily workshop sessions is intelligent and comprehensive. Evidence of professionalism in writing and editing for kids is everywhere in this program. The basics of plot and character development are taught, of course, as are the basics of selling your work. But so, too, are research methods for those whose fiction requires credible factual backgrounds; and there's science writing for kids, photo research skills, even a session on how mainstream authors can write sensitively about minority cultures. HFWW faculty, though not in the echelon of a Maurice Sendak or Chris VanAlsburg, nonetheless include Newberry Award winners, National Council of Teachers of English poetry award winners, and many more admirable writers among them (the staff numbers about 30).

Evening entertainment at HFWW includes both workshop-related events (readings, a banquet, a cruise on the lake) and access to the vast array of temptations on the general Chautauqua summer program (opera, symphony, theater, lectures, films and sports galore). You may bring your spouse or partner (extra charge), but Jan Keen, conference director, warns, "Accommodations are severely limited, and the workshop itself is designed for immersion, not for partial attendance combined with a vacation for the family." The HFWW annual report is cheery and chatty, suggesting that camaraderie among attendees is intense and long lasting.

Reserve early, if only to get your pick of housing in crowded, popular Chautauqua.

Hofstra University Summer Writers' Conference

For all writers South shore of Long Island, 25 mi. from New York City — Continuing Education, Davison Hall, Rm. 205, Hofstra University, Hempstead, NY 11550 **Voice:** 516-463-5016 **Fax:** 516-463-4833 **Contact:** Lewis Shena, Ass't. Dean **Founded:** 1973 **Open:** 10 days in July **Admission:** Registration form **Cost:** Certificate students, about $600 plus registration fee; Graduate credit students, about $420 per credit plus registration fees; dorm housing about $455 **Financial Aid:** Scholarship **Degree or Certification:** Hofstra Writers' Conf. Certificate

PROXIMITY TO New York City, the publishing capital of the U.S., enriches the Hofstra conference year after year. Readers and/or teachers here have included James Baldwin, Saul Bellow, Erica Jong, Denise Levertov, Toni Morrison and Isaac Bashevis Singer, just for starters. The workshop leaders are not necessarily as prominent as these writers (often they are Hofstra faculty), but they're well qualified just the same. The convenient Long Island location means that city dwellers can commute to this conference, but dormitory housing is available for those who live farther afield.

Manuscript criticism is available to those who seek academic credit. Usually attendees choose 1 or 2 of the 5 workshops. Each workshop meets daily during the 10-day conference, amounting to 25 hours of contact. Evening sessions bring editors, agents and publishers to the campus, and special presentations cover both the business side of writing (negotiating the contract) and the more playful side (songwriting). Writing itself is squeezed into the busy schedule, which climaxes at a banquet with an address by a noted writer.

Institute of Publishing and Writing: Children's Books in the Marketplace

For children's book writers and illustrators Central Hudson Valley, 1 hr. N of New York City — Vassar College, Poughkeepsie, NY 12601 **Voice:** 914-437-5903 **Fax:** 914-437-7209 **Contact:** Maryann Bruno, Assoc. Dir. College Relations **Founded:** 1984 **Open:** 1 week in mid-June **Admission:** Registration form ($25); writing and art samples optional **Deadlines:** About 6 weeks in advance **Cost:** $525; room and board $275; student discount

SERIOUS, FOCUSED, productive, fun: the Institute of Publishing and Writing at Vassar College has served children's book authors and illustrators well for over a decade. The proximity to New York metro area publishing houses doesn't hurt when lining up faculty. The conference leader for some time has been Barbara Lucas of Lucas/Evans Books, a book packaging company specializing in children's titles.

The theme is how to get published and published well. Nuts-and-bolts workshops show authors and illustrators how to prepare a children's story in words and images and what editors expect at each stage of the book-building process. Selling your work is covered by agent Barbara Lucas and other visiting agents, including some who represent illustrators specifically. Even the marketing angle gets attention here, so that authors will understand what trends in the marketplace can be anticipated and addressed in books to come.

It's a tightly packed schedule. Participants live in dormitory rooms and take their meals on campus. And what a campus: Vassar, one of the famed "Seven Sisters" (the women's equivalent of the old Ivy League), is a great place for a stroll to clear your mind after a day full of book talk. There's more: as a Vassar guest, you'll have access to the library and the athletic facilities. Watch out. You may not want to go home.

International Women's Writing Guild Conferences

For all women writers Saratoga Springs, 1 hr. N of Albany — Box 810, Gracie Station, New York, NY 10028 **Voice:** 212-737-7536 **Fax:** 212-737-9469 **E-mail:** iwwg@iwwg.com **Web Site:** <http://www.iwwg.com> **Contact:** Hannelore Hahn, Dir. **Founded:** 1977 **Open:** 1 week in mid-Aug. **Admission:** Application form only **Cost:** $745 single room ($731 IWWG members); double room and commuter discounts **Financial Aid:** Scholarship **Size-Attendees:** 400 **Degree or Certification:** CEUs available

TWENTY YEARS of momentum and still growing nicely, thank you: the International Women's Writing Guild is one of this country's more impressive writers' organizations. (See *Associations and Organizations* for more about the membership and services of IWWG.)

Their annual 1-week conference is a lollapalooza, a virtual Wal-Mart of workshops, lectures and discussions on everything you can think of related to writing. (Attendees may opt for weekend sessions only.) From technique to (publishing) business, to cultural context, to mixed media, to New Age self-development: there is something here for nearly every woman writer. The tone of all the offshoot newsletters and commentary suggests a high degree of camaraderie and mutual support, perhaps to a fault. Those writers seeking a conference without all the hoopla and the just-add-water-and-stir cozy feelings of sisterhood might want to shop elsewhere. But for those who feel the need of sisterly support, welcome aboard. This is a top-notch program.

Director Hannelore Hahn gets our vote for most enterprising conference sponsor. Annually Hahn lines up interesting topics for workshops and well-qualified leaders. The backup support of the IWWG makes the conference even more impressive. There's a scholarship program, a newsletter, and a Web site with electronic bulletin boards, and shorter conferences (some of them subject-specific) at other times of the year in New York City and on the West Coast. There's a network of IWWG members and conference alumnae, and a certain lobbying effort on behalf of women writers' concerns (Hahn went to the International Women's Conference in Beijing in 1995 to help carry the banner for free speech and human rights).

During the weeklong event, at lovely Skidmore College in Saratoga Springs (taking advantage of college residences and dining halls), nearly 60 workshops are offered under the conference umbrella, each one of them repeating daily so that attendees can sample quite a few. The prospect may seem like a free ticket in a candy shop to some, dizzying and superficial to others. On the 1996 program, many of the nuts-and-bolts writing workshops emphasized getting your manuscript ready for the marketplace. Another group of workshops focused on memoir (and self-esteem issues). Still another group explored mythology and nonlinear knowledge (Goddesses, take note!). And the final cluster of sessions looked into "the arts and the body," a grab bag on voice, stage fright, puppet making, photography, dance, and more. Phew!

It (almost) goes without saying that such a conference can be a fine place for professional networking, and indeed at this event and others sponsored by IWWG, agents and editors do attend in search of publishable women writers. For beginning writers the door is open too, because IWWG invites all women writers to join or attend or both, "with or without portfolio."

Still not enough? Stick around for the retreat weekend following the summer conference: more talk, more sharing, watch grazing llamas and wallow in mineral baths on an 1890 country estate in Sharon Springs, NY.

just buffalo literary center

For all writers *Near old Univ. of Buffalo campus and Delaware Park area —* 2495 Main St., Buffalo, NY 14214 **Voice:** 716-832-5400 **Fax:** 716-832-5710 **Contact:** Deborah Kane, Marketing Dir. **Founded:** 1975 **Open:** Year-round **Admission:** Workshops: open to all; Residencies: letter of inquiry **Cost:** Residency, no cost; Workshops $55–$100 for members, slightly higher nonmembers **Size-Attendees:** 2 resident writers per month **Size-Class:** Varies

MUCH-MALIGNED Buffalo is in fact alive with arts and culture, despite its daunting snowfalls and seemingly endless winters. Perhaps it's because writing is largely an indoor sport. The "just buffalo literary center" (no CAPS, mind you) is not just for Buffalonians any more. Its writer-in-residence program operates mostly by invitation, bringing distinguished writers or rising stars to the city for a month at a time. While in residence, the writer has the bulk of his or her time free but is also expected to contribute to the literary community with readings and, sometimes, in workshops. The State University of New York at Buffalo, located nearby, has an unusually strong English department, including in recent years poet Robert Creeley and critic Leslie Fiedler. There is a close connection between "just buffalo," the university and the local bookstores, which help to sponsor programs. The Lannan Foundation underwrites the residency program, which, as of late 1996, is exploring plans for expansion with a house (in the Olmsted-designed Delaware Park section of the city) devoted to resident writers.

Workshops are offered year-round as well, for both adults and children. They vary from 1-day affairs to a series of 6 weekly sessions, covering travel writing, how to get published, women in literature and other topics. Ask for a current schedule.

Western New Yorkers with literary interests would do well to join the "just buffalo" association, taking advantage of its schedule of readings and other events. Regional literary organizations of this kind and caliber are too few and far between and thus deserve support.

Ledig House International Writers' Colony

🏠 *For all writers, including art critics, curators, art historians* Hudson Valley, 2½ hr. N of New York City — 43 Letter S Rd., Ghent, NY 12075 **Voice:** 518-392-7656 **Fax:** 518-392-2848 **Contact:** Elaine Smolin-Sruogis, Dir. **Founded:** 1922 **Open:** Apr.–Oct. **Admission:** Project description, biographical sketch, copy of latest published work, reference **Cost:** Transportation only **Financial Aid:** Scholarship **Size-Attendees:** About 10

F OR WRITERS WHOSE careers are well advanced, Ledig House offers residencies—from 2 weeks to 2 months—in an elegant Federal period house situated in Omi, near Ghent, a tiny Hudson Valley town between New York City and Albany. At Ledig House the conversation is likely to be cosmopolitan because residents are chosen from applicants around the world. In midsummer the resident writers are all art critics, curators or art historians. At other times from spring through fall, writers of any kind may be in residence here. As the application requirements suggest, this is a residency for those with a track record of published work and a serious new project underway.

Ledig House takes its name from the German publisher Heinrich Maria Ledig-Rowohlt, and its boards of directors and advisors include many people with German connections. Some of the stronger international publishers, such as Pen-

guin, are sponsors, as are several literary agents. The emphasis is decidedly on internationalism.

The Ledig House estate encompasses 130 acres on a hilltop overlooking the dramatic Catskill Mountains. Each writer has a private workroom/bedroom, and all costs are covered. Dinner is prepared; other meals are self-service. In extraordinary cases (usually visiting writers from overseas), travel grants are available.

While writers in all genres are welcome to apply, there is an emphasis on those whose work touches on the visual arts or whose expertise includes translation. The Ledig House brochure features a photo of Ledig-Rowohlt and William Faulkner, taken in 1949. One suspects that Ledig-Rowohlt may have been among those foreign publishers who helped rescue Faulkner from publishing obscurity (Faulkner had won the Nobel Prize for Literature but was virtually out of print in his native land).

Manhattanville College Writers' Week

✒️ *For writers and teachers of writing* 5 min. from White Plains, Westchester County; 45 min. from NYC — Office of Adult Programs, 2900 Purchase St., Purchase, NY 10577 **Voice:** 914-694-3425 **Fax:** 914-694-3488 **Contact:** Ruth Dowd, RSCJ, Dir. **Open:** 5 days in late June **Admission:** Registration form only; beginning writers submit short essay **Deadlines:** Early June **Cost:** $560; up to $1,100 for 3 graduate credits; dormitory housing $24 per night **Size-Class:** 15 maximum

B ASED AT A SMALL liberal arts college with a longstanding top-rank reputation, the Manhattanville Writers' Week of workshops is designed to serve everyone from nonacademic beginners to advanced graduate-level creative writing students, as well as professional writers. Tall order? Indeed, perhaps this good intention spreads things a bit too thin. Nonetheless, there's a welcome juxtaposition here of how-to writing workshops with seminars on how to teach writing. Among the faculty in 1996 was an award-winning junior high school English teacher. It's good to see writers and teachers of writing taken seriously in the same program.

When registering, choose your workshop wisely ("The Writer's Craft" is for beginners; the teaching methods seminar is for professionals). You can commute to this program (train service is good) or make it a residential program, using the inexpensive college dorm for your lodgings. Interesting add-ons include a tour of nearby publishing giant *Reader's Digest* and a session with editors and agents in which nuts-and-bolts business questions about writing can be raised. Manhattanville offers a Master's degree in writing, too.

Marymount Manhattan College Writers' Conference

For fiction and nonfiction writers
Upper East Side, Manhattan — *221 E. 71st St., New York, NY 10021* **Voice:** 212-517-0564 **Fax:** 212-628-4208 **Contact:** Lewis Burke Frumkes, Dir. **Founded:** 1992 **Open:** 1 day in mid-June **Admission:** Application form only **Cost:** $155 (lunch and reception incl.); discount for early registration

SHORT, SWEET AND well worth attending if you're in New York or nearby: the Marymount Manhattan College Writers' Conference offers a lineup of panelists who are savvy and articulate, some with national reputations as writers, editors or agents. The conference leans toward the practical issues of how to get published, how to survive as a freelancer and how to work with an agent. Genre-specific sessions are offered, however, ranging from memoir to sports, to humor, mystery and children's books.

In 1996 the conference keynote speakers were Grace Mirabella, "doyenne of the fashion industry," and Richard Lederer, an authority on the English language (1989 International Punster of the Year). Equally colorful were such panelists as Dan Okrent, Editor of Life and a baseball expert; Nan Talese, a senior editor at Doubleday; and Susan Cheever, the novelist-memoirist, Marymount's writer-in-residence.

All told, a good way to invest a day of listening and networking.

Millay Colony for the Arts

For all writers, and artists in selected other disciplines 30 mi. SE of Albany — P.O. Box 3, Austerlitz, NY 12017 **Voice:** 518-392-3103 **Fax:** 518-392-1234 **Contact:** Ann Ellen Lesser, Dir. **Founded:** 1973 **Open:** Year-round **Admission:** Application, writing samples, reference **Deadlines:** Feb. 1 for June–Sept.; May 1 for Oct.–Jan. **Cost:** No fees; contributions welcome **Financial Aid:** Stipend **Size-Attendees:** 6–10 per month **Handicapped Access**

WRITERS COMMUNE with their muses and with wildlife on this 600-acre woodland retreat in the Berkshire-Taconic Hills, hard on the New York-Massachusetts border.

Resident writer Ruth Knafo Setton in her studio at the Millay Colony

Writer Edna St. Vincent Millay and her husband bought Steepletop, a berry farm, in 1925, making it their country home. Edmund Wilson called Millay "a spokesperson for the human spirit." Visiting artists feed on her lingering influence. Now a National Historic Landmark, the homestead and outbuildings are well maintained but rustic.

Residencies run for 1 month and are available year-round. Up-and-comers predominate here; it's not a star showcase. Steepletop is a popular place: the ratio of applications to acceptances is 8 to 1. Ellis Studio, a combined work-living space, is ideal for any artist (perhaps best for visual artists, given its north-lit skylight). A porch overlooks a lovely stream and fields. The Barn provides studios (14' x 20') for 4 artists, with separate bedrooms. A new facility—accessible to the handicapped—is under design, promising 2 more studios, common areas, an expanded kitchen, a darkroom and offices. Social life at Millay is deliberately nil. Artists discuss and share their work informally. The focus is on self-discipline, with minimal distraction. Most meals are provided, with weeknight dinners prepared by staff and breakfast/lunch foods available for improvisation. Resident artists prepare weekend meals.

In sum, a beautiful mountain setting. An usually quiet place, the opposite of gregarious colonies like Yaddo. Convenient proximity to Albany airport and to the intense cultural life of neighboring Berkshire County, Massachusetts. Best suited for those who prefer solitude and focused work. The nearest store is 10 miles away.

Resident comment: "Everyone has remarked on the infinity of time one seems to have here, though contained paradoxically in four short weeks. This is not an art colony, a place created for art, it is a place created by art and existing partly in art's unbounded time." (A.R. Shapiro, 1977)

Millett Farm

⌂ ✎ *For women writers and visual artists* Hudson Valley, about 1 hr. N of New York City — RD 3, Old Overlook Rd., Poughkeepsie, NY 12603; 295 Bowery, New York, NY 10003, **Voice:** 914-473-9267 **Contact:** Kate Millett, Dir. **Founded:** 1981 **Open:** Spring–Fall **Admission:** Letter with self-description, interest in the farm, work samples **Cost:** Residency: "volunteer" farm work required, plus $70 per week for food; Workshop: $500 (room and board incl.)

SOMETIMES IDEALS do become reality, but rarely without hard work. Feminist writer Kate Millett (*Sexual Politics*) may list the Bowery as her residential address, but her heart and soul are on her farm near Poughkeepsie, where she has created a women writers' retreat and writing workshop. The retreat provides opportunities for stays as long as a whole summer, combining rigorous farm work (the main crop is Christmas trees, but there are vegetables, too); farm building (and studio) construction and maintenance; and writing. If you would like to come home from "summer camp" with memories of having worked in a community of women who are, as the brochure says, "strong and fast and proud of themselves with a tanned amazon assurance," then pull on your work boots and apply.

Visual artists join women writers on the farm. Residencies can be arranged for spring, summer or fall, and occasionally for shorter periods. The farm is self-supporting, with no outside funding (one wonders why not). Residents rise early to begin their 5-hour stint, weekdays, of farm work. Be prepared to learn new skills and to stretch old muscles. Afternoons and early evening are for writing. Weekends are free. To soothe sore muscles and enjoy the sunny pleasures of summer, there is a pond for swimming. Meals are communal, and there is a strong emphasis on the farm's continuity from year to year.

In 1995 Millett offered a 1-week writers' workshop (late July) and indicated availability again in 1996. Workshop attendees are not expected to work on the farm but rather to focus on their writing, with exercises and critiques directed by Millett.

The key words here are empowerment, community and women. And work. For those of the right persuasion, the setting and daily routine sound superb. Eat your spinach.

My Retreat

For all writers *Foothills of the Catskills, 90 mi. NW of New York City — P.O. Box 1077, Lincoln Rd., South Fallsburg, NY 12779* **Voice:** 914-436-7455 **Fax:** 914-436-6918 **Contact:** Cora Schwartz, Dir. **Founded:** 1994 **Open:** Year-round **Admission:** No application form **Cost:** Weekend, $110; week, $225; longer residencies negotiable **Size-Attendees:** 6 maximum

B ED AND BREAKFAST, your own cabin or a room in the main house, a quiet, unpretentious Catskill town, and little else to do but write. This is proprietor Cora Schwartz's formula for a small, noncompetitive writers' retreat. Her business is young, and the word is just now spreading. Low pressure is the key word here: no writing samples are required for admission (indeed, your reservation check is the admission ticket). And your time is your own, from a weekend to a week or longer. There are writing workshops on some weekends, directed by published writers Schwartz brings up from the city.

The retreat is dedicated to the memory of Olga Kobylianskaia, a forerunner of the women's liberation movement and a member of the Writers' Union of the (former) USSR. The town of South Fallsburg, as yet ungentrified, has a bargain-basement movie house and a Jewish bakery to recommend it. The nearby countryside is full of recreational opportunities year-round.

National Writers Union, Westchester/ Fairfield Chapter, Writers Conference

For all writers *The Bronx, New York City — Sarah Lawrence College, Bronxville, NY, 10708; c/o Lee Merritt, 105 Williamsburg Dr., Mahopac, NY 10541* **Voice:** 914-736-6308 **Contact:** Linda Simone, Dir. **Open:** 1 day in mid-Apr. **Admission:** Registration form only **Cost:** $75 (lunch incl.), $60 for NWU members

H ERE'S ONE OF several National Writers Union conferences around the country. Check your regional NWU office for pertinent local information (see NWU under *Unions & Other Labor Organizations*). The program is a happy jumble of options, from the technical/literary ("Finding the True Shape of the Story") to the nuts-and-bolts practical ("Yes, You Can Earn a Living as a Poet," "Writing for Corporate Video," "Secrets of Self Publishing"). An uncategorizable session on the 1996 program was our favorite: "What Your Characters Do in Bed (And How to Get Them There"). Workshop leaders have admirable credentials, many of them being business-of-publishing people, but others are strictly literary. The schedule permits attendance at 4 different sessions plus the "networking" luncheon (with a speaker). Schmooze on into the evening at the wine and cheese reception that wraps up the conference. NWU brings good people together at a fair price. Recommended.

New York State Summer Writers Institute, Skidmore

For fiction and nonfiction writers, poets *About 30 mi. N of Albany — Skidmore College, 815 North Broadway, Saratoga Springs, NY 12866* **Voice:** 518-584-5000 **Contact:** R. Boyers, Dir. **Founded:** 1984 **Open:** 4 weeks in July **Admission:** Application form ($30), letter, manuscript sample **Cost:** 4 weeks noncredit, $1,280; 2 weeks noncredit, $640; dorm housing with meals, 4 weeks $920, 2 weeks $460 **Financial Aid:** Scholarship; Work/Study

TOP-NOTCH PROGRAM, top-notch site. The NYS Summer Writers Institute at Skidmore College is a magnet for talented writers on the way up, as well as for teachers and practitioners of the craft who have achieved wide, well-deserved acclaim. Pulitzer Prize winners queue up for coffee with National Book Award winners, and with you. If this program appeals to you, apply early and send your best work.

If it were poetry alone, the regular and visiting faculty for 1996 would convince a writer to come here. Robert Pinsky and Carolyn Forche were joined by Robert Haas, U.S. Poet Laureate. In the other genres offered at Skidmore (fiction, nonfiction), the lineup is equally impressive. Options include 2- and 4-week sessions, and academic credit (extra charge). Classes meet for 3 hours, 3 days a week, plus there are writing tutors, special events (publishing symposia) and a schedule of readings.

Saratoga is an old spa town, long a popular summer resort offering crafts fairs, a giant outdoor performing arts center, and for those with money to burn, an elegant racetrack. Minutes away, Adirondack State Park beckons, as does nearby Lake George.

See also New York State Writers Institute at SUNY Albany.

New York State Writers Institute

For all writers *SUNY uptown and downtown campuses — SUNY at Albany, Humanities 355, Albany, NY 12222* **Voice:** 518-442-5620 **Fax:** 518-442-5621 **E-mail:** writers@poppa.fab.albany.edu **Web Site:** http://www.albany.edu/writers-inst/ **Contact:** William Kennedy, Dir. **Open:** Fall and spring semesters **Admission:** Open to the public **Cost:** Free

ALBANY'S CAMPUS of the State University of New York (SUNY) is the hub of a great academic system of colleges and universities spread throughout the Empire State. Its Writers Institute offers irresistible programs of readings, conferences, films and, starting in 1996, even an on-line magazine. Each fall and spring, internationally prominent writers visit SUNY at Albany to read from their work. Little known are the afternoon seminars preceding these well-attended evening (often crowded) readings. The seminars are free and open to the public.

Fall '96 offered a chance to interact with Robert Coover, Peter Matthiessen, Nicole Brossard (a Québecois writer), Philip Levine, Robert Stone and Stephen Jay Gould—among others. If you live near Albany, have a literary inclination,

and can steal away for an afternoon of delicious book talk, then head to SUNY. Check their handy Web site for details. Be sure to pin down which of the 2 campuses is hosting the event.

Can't get there in person? Tune in to *The Book Show* on Northeast Public Radio, hosted by novelist William Kennedy, who interviews authors and reviews new books.

See also New York State Summer Writers Institute, Skidmore.

Omega Institute for Holistic Studies

⌂ ✎ **For all writers, and artists in selected other disciplines** *Hudson Valley, 90 mi. N of New York City — 260 Lake Dr., Rhinebeck, NY 12572* **Voice:** *914-266-4444; 800-944-1001* **Fax:** *914-266-3769* **Web Site:** *http://omega-inst.org* **Contact:** *Andrea Johnson, Registrar* **Founded:** *1977* **Open:** *Spring–fall* **Admission:** *Varies* **Deadlines:** *2 weeks ahead* **Cost:** *$200–$600 per workshop* **Financial Aid:** *Scholarship; Work/Study* **Size-Class:** *Usually under 50*

MUCH LOVED (and respected), Omega is like summer camp for grownups. With a pronounced emphasis on health and healing, self-help and spiritual discovery, Omega's diverse workshops (from 2 to 9 days) attract a colorful crowd, often with therapists outnumbering everyone else. Some top-notch writer/teachers offer programs here every year. In 1996 poets Galway Kinnell and Andrei Codrescu joined nonfiction writer William Least Heat-Moon on the list. Workshops on writing and meditation stand beside those on writing and the natural world. The setting is rustic, spirits are high, and it's a great nearby escape from the city.

Meals, cafeteria-style, take place in a giant dining hall with a porch. Lodging options range from Spartan cabins (shared—bring earplugs) to camping (shared with critters—bring bug dope).

Robert Quackenbush's Children's Book Writing and Illustrating Workshops

✎ **For children's book writers and illustrators** *Upper East Side of Manhattan — 460 E 79th St., New York, NY 10021* **Voice:** *212-744-3822* **Fax:** *212-744-3822* **E-mail:** *NAA P95@aol.com* **Contact:** *Robert Quackenbush, Dir.* **Founded:** *1982* **Open:** *1 week in July* **Admission:** *Registration form only* **Cost:** *$650; $585 with early registration* **Size-Class:** *10 maximum* **Handicapped Access**

WHIRLWIND? Self-propelled vertically integrated one-man industry? He's something like that, Robert Quackenbush. With 150 children's books to his credit as either author or author-illustrator, this man is a leader in the field. Each summer Quackenbush offers an intensive 1-week workshop for writers and illustrators who want hands-on experience under the guidance of a master. The workshop meets in Quackenbush's Manhattan studio. Out-of-towners can get help from him concerning hotels in the neighborhood. The tab for a week in New York can be stiff, and applicants may well want to explore carefully what they can accomplish in this workshop by writing to the leader well ahead of time. The stated goal, and promise, is that each writer will leave the workshop with a project (usually an illustrated book) ready in dummy form to send to a publisher.

Quackenbush as printmaker has work in the collections at the Smithsonian and the Whitney. As a Simon & Schuster children's book author he qualifies for his own multi-title marketing flyer. One of Quackenbush's not-so-secret secrets for children's book authors: keep in close touch with kids, get them involved in your daily work (he offers illustration workshops for children, too) and let their energy and ideas replenish yours. Sounds good.

Romantic Times Booklovers Convention

For writers in the romance genre A different major city each year — 55 Bergen St., Brooklyn, NY 11201 **Voice:** 718-237-1097 **Fax:** 718-624-4231 **Contact:** Carol Stacy, President **Open:** Late Oct. **Admission:** Registration form only **Cost:** $350 (covers seminars, book fair, meals, social events)

UNDER THE HEADLINE "We're Havin' a Party," the convention invitation includes this teaser: "This is the year for readers and booksellers to pack their prettiest pajamas and niftiest nighties and head south for the Romance party of the decade!" We'd guess the prose style is appropriate. The workshops offered at the *Romantic Times* Booklovers Convention include one called "Writing the New Sensual Novel," emphasizing how to appeal to and stimulate a woman's sexual fantasies (sociobiologists were on the panel, presumably to put a fine point on what makes women tick).

Romance fiction is, of course, in the mass-market paperback genre, with many titles annually selling in the tens of thousands if not more. There is money to be made here, though for most romance writer wanna-bes, the payoff remains more hoped for than achieved. Many romance novels are written on the cheap, on work-for-hire contracts. The real profits go to the publisher, not the author.

This much said, it's also true that getting the gig you want as a romance writer may require a certain amount of partying with the appropriate editors and publishers. This convention may be the place to do this part of your work.

The workshops, however, are few (3 in 1996), and they address only the broadest of themes ("Basic Novel Writing Technique," "On the Road to Getting Published"). You might learn as much from some time well spent with a sympathetic agent who knows this genre and the relevant acquiring.

Tip: Most romance publishers have tightly defined formulas for character and plot development within each series. Try to get your hands on a "romance author's instruction memo" and follow it to a T. This is not a genre where creativity is highly rewarded.

Southampton Writers' Workshops

For fiction writers and poets Eastern end of Long Island — Summer Programs, Long Island University, Southampton College, Southampton, NY 11968 **Voice:** 516-287-8420 **Fax:** 516-283-4081 **E-mail:** Cagliot i@sand.liunet.edu **Web Site:** http://www. southampton.liunet.edu **Contact:** Michael Jody, Coord. **Founded:** 1975 **Open:** 1 week in late July **Admission:** Registration form only **Cost:** $402 per workshop; $423 for graduate credit; on-campus housing $200; meal plan $82 **Degree or Certification:** graduate and undergraduate credit available

SOME MAY COME for proximity to the fabulous beaches of the Hamptons (and the equally fabulous social life at beach houses owned and rented by scads of New York City publishing movers and shakers), but in fact the best reason to attend the Southampton Writers' Workshops is the caliber of the faculty. In 1996 essayist and poet Marvin Bell directed the poetry workshop. Bell has numerous books to his credit, several top awards (Guggenheim, NEA, Lamont) and a long record of distinguished teaching, primarily in the Writer's Workshop at the University of Iowa. Bell's fiction writing colleague in the SWW was Stewart O'Nan, himself a veteran of the SWW and more recently a successfully published novelist and prize winner.

Scheduling permits attendees to take 1 or both workshops and to see the instructors for private manuscript conferences. Every night during the workshop week, readings are offered either by the instructors or by other writers residing in eastern Long Island (expect the best here). Southampton College is a small campus (part of the giant Long Island University 6-campus system). Come for the writing, come for the sun: 2 equally good reasons to attend.

The Poetry Project

For poets and other writers Greenwich Village — 131 E. 10th St., New York, NY 10003 **Voice:** 212-674-0910 **Fax:** 212-529-2318 **Contact:** Ed Friedman, Dir. **Founded:** 1966 **Open:** Year-round **Admission:** Membership form only **Cost:** Workshop $150

THE EPICENTER of poets and poetry in the U.S. if there is one, The Poetry Project has long been a sponsor of readings and publications offering a venue for the innovators and bold voices in this least commercial of all the genres. No doubt it takes a great city to spawn and support a center devoted only to poetry. Kudos to New York. About 6 multi-session poetry workshops per year constitute the teaching component here, fall through spring. Readings occur year-round. Writers from all genres are welcome in the workshops, and the fee for 1 workshop admits you to others as well.

Each workshop reflects the personal enthusiasms of the leader—poetry and performance art here, poetic forms there. Ask for details about current offerings. Workshop leaders and participants are likely to include those with publishing credits in some of America's most colorful noncommercial literary journals and magazines. Although many of the avant garde's biggest names have crossed the portals at St. Mark's Church to read or teach at The Poetry Project (Allen Ginsberg, Gregory Corso, Amiri Baraka, Adrienne Rich), this is also home to the as yet unknown, unpublished and uncelebrated poet. The spirit here is defined by inclusiveness. If you're a New York writer, join up and get involved. As former Manhattanite Walt Whitman wrote, "I hear America singing."

The Writers Room

For all writers Greenwich Village — 10 Astor Pl., New York, NY 10003 **Voice:** 212-254-6995 **Fax:** 212-533-6059 **Contact:** Andrew VanDusen, Dir. **Founded:** 1978 **Open:** Year-round **Admission:** Letter, resume, 3 references **Cost:** $175 per quarter **Size-Attendees:** 185 members

PROBABLY NOWHERE else in the country has the problem of "a room of one's own" been solved as successfully as at The Writers Room. This is a good idea. No doubt the sheer abundance of writers in New York City, especially in the artsy and university-dominated lower Manhattan area, and the sheer dearth of quiet, inexpensive places to work in the same neighborhood conspired to make this success story get going. But kudos to the writers who in 1978 had the vision and to all those who have helped sustain The Writers Room since then. We call the WR a "Residential Program" because it's a place writers go to do their work, though it's not a sleepover camp like an artists' colony.

The idea is simple: $175 per quarter buys you access to the room where, on a first-come, first-served basis, you may choose among 35 desks in partitioned spaces. 'Round the clock, every day of the year, whenever the muse calls or a deadline approaches. Director Andrew VanDusen says that the room is frequently busy but rarely full, and waiting for a seat is not a problem. About 260 writers per year participate. Waiting to join the club, however, is another story. This may take 3 to 6 months.

Although the ergonomically correct furniture (inherited from Conran's, a home furnishings company that went bust) may make you wish you could move in here permanently, do not expect to set up a full-time office at the WR. Only 4 of the desks can be reserved (at twice the normal fee). No incoming phone calls (limited outgoing calls, too). Limited storage space, and you must clean your desk for the next writer to follow. Still, the fact that coming here tends to focus one's attention on the work itself is a big plus. Another bonus is a well-stocked writers' reference library on site.

On the social side, the WR encourages helpful professional chat among writers, and some of those who have published extensively are free with time and advice for others just beginning the journey toward fame and fortune. In 1995, 18 WR residents had a book of some sort published. Writers of all kinds—except students—are welcome. About 9 times per year (fall through spring) the WR sponsors 1-day seminars (call them workshops) on the practical side of writing and publishing: writers and taxes, how to recover hidden royalties, writing grant proposals, care and feeding of agents, public speaking for writers, and the like.

The Writers Studio

For fiction writers and poets Greenwich Village — 78 Charles St., Apt. 2R, New York, NY 10014 **Voice:** 212-255-7075 **Contact:** Philip Schultz, Dir. **Open:** Year-round **Cost:** Introductory classes $210, advanced classes $370, various levels in between

TALENT ABOUNDS in the Big Apple, and here's one of its well-staffed, well-conceived writing programs, unattached to an academic institution or YMCA. Director Philip Schultz of The Writers Studio, a lower Manhattan affair, was founder and director of the writing program at New York University. He won the Lamont Prize for his poetry, which has appeared in *The New Yorker* and various small, prestigious literary journals. His 9 colleagues have if not

equally impressive credits then certainly admirable backgrounds and lots of teaching experience. Tutorials are available and would appear to be a potentially good investment here for a writer with a major project underway.

Classes (8 or 10 weeks) run in all seasons, at several levels of sophistication, in the novel, short story and poetry. The emphasis is on the craft (not the business) of writing and on "developing a greater range of critical self-awareness." Sounds like a good weekly workout at the literary gymnasium. Do those sit-ups while you contemplate your next rhymed couplet.

William Flanagan Memorial Creative Persons Center / Edward Albee Foundation

For all writers, and artists in selected other disciplines Eastern tip of Long Is. — Fairview Ave., Montauk, NY 11954; Applications to 14 Harrison St., New York, NY 10013 **Voice:** 212-226-2020 **Contact:** Director **Open:** June–Sept. **Admission:** Application form, project outline, resume, manuscript sample, references **Deadlines:** Apr. 1 **Cost:** Food and transportation **Size-Attendees:** 5 resident artists

CONTEMPORARY American playwright Edward Albee helped make this residential program a reality by endowing it with funds and inspiration. The setting would have been inspiration enough. At the eastern end of Long Island, beaches and dunes meet the sea in a constantly evolving drama, and the light is interesting every day. Offshore scores of boats, from catboats to oil tankers, negotiate the passage around Montauk Point, famous for its lighthouse. Expect to hear the foghorn as you write through the night.

Facilities here are simple. The "Creative Persons Center," a.k.a. "The Barn," is named after the late William Flanagan (composer, collaborator and friend of Edward Albee) and serves a variety of artists. The idea is to bring together people of disparate talents in hopes of cross-fertilization. Residencies are 4

The Art of Critique

The Writer's Voice Workshops program is designed to be constructive, not destructive; to be supportive while providing serious writing critique. While the works of other writers may espouse philosophies you do not share, no critique should engage in *personal* criticism, nor should critiques attempt to limit writers by their ethnicity. Everyone's role in the workshop is that of peer. And everyone's responsibility to their peers is to help them write their story better. Following is an adaptation of "The Art of Critique" by Writer's Voice instructor Carol Dixon. Please read it and refer to it regularly.

The ability to critique well is a skill. It involves the ability to give constructive criticism. In most workshop environments, writers who are very close in skill level usually vary greatly when it comes to critiquing. The following is a basic guideline for participants to use to begin to develop good critiquing skills.

In order to give a constructive critique, you must first realize that the purpose of critique is to *help* the Writer. It should give the Writer some idea about how his/her work is received. The aim of the critique is not to destroy a work, but to give the Writer some ideas about where the problems are in the piece, as well as which parts work well.

Your critique should not be structured to try to convince the Writer to write the story *you would write* or the one you would like to see written.

Your critique should help the writer to best tell the story s/he is writing.

What to Look for When Critiquing

1. What is the story being told? Does the story have a discernible beginning, middle and end? Does the story begin/end where you feel it should? Is there a sense of completeness to the story?
2. What is the Writer trying to say to you? What is the message? Is the Writer's premise true to the story's logic?
3. Is the language used authentic? Is it true to time, place, region and background?
4. Is the writing poetic? Does it have rhythm, does it have a beat? Is it rich with images, metaphors, similes?
5. Is the story dramatic? Does it contain conflict at its essence?
6. Is the language tension-oriented, energizing? Does it move the story along? How is it paced?
7. Are there words, phrases that seem to jump out at you? Are there parts of the story that seem out of place? Not needed?
8. Is the story easy to follow? Are there places where you seem lost? Where you drift?
9. What are the strengths of the story? What character/situation holds your interest?
10. Are there places where you feel more information is needed? Too much information is given?

WEST SIDE YMCA

weeks in length. Your colleagues will be few, perhaps only 3 or 4 others. This is the opposite of the socially busy Mac-Dowell or Yaddo colonies. In fact, this is hardly a colony at all but rather a retreat for a select few.

The Albee Foundation resists codifying its admission standards, relying instead on their instincts about talent and need. They have, however, codified their application process (requiring even mailing labels of applicants, refusing to accept hand-delivered materials, on penalty of your application being returned unprocessed). Fair warning, then: follow the instructions.

Unlike the bigger artists' colonies, there is no program here of readings or lectures or presentations or banquets. This is a work-hard-on-your-own kind of residency, tempered by contact with a few fellow artists and, it is hoped, inspired by the sea.

Reminder: Use the New York City address for applications.

Writer's Voice of the West Side Y

For fiction and nonfiction writers, poets, screenwriters, and artists in selected other disciplines Upper West Side, Manhattan — 5 W 63rd St., New York, NY 10023 **Voice:** 212-875-4124 **Fax:** 212-875-4176 **E-mail:** WtrsVoice@aol.com **Contact:** Glenda Pleasants, Dir. **Founded:** 1981 **Open:** Year-round **Admission:** Varies — see catalogue; $25 registration fee **Cost:** $185–$330 **Financial Aid:** Work/Study **Size-Class:** 15 maximum

A LIVELIER URBAN neighborhood would be hard to find. The Upper West Side swarms with writers, bookstores, filmmakers, dancers, musicians and more. Lincoln Center is the hub, with the Juilliard School. On the literary scene, New Yorkers gravitate to the West Side Y for everything from aerobics to poetry.

Workshops here serve beginners and advanced writers in a multitude of genres within genres. "Writing the Thriller," "The Unconscious and the Writer's Imagination" and "Writing the One-Person Show" are only a few of the course titles in the Y's cornucopia-catalogue. Regular workshops run about 9 weeks; there are weekend intensives, too. Most classes are open to anyone. Advanced workshops require substantial manuscript submissions, and competition is, like everything else in New York, aggressive.

The Y offers electronic manuscript submission, was planning a Web site in 1996, and throws in a freebie to registered participants: swimming privileges 1 day per week. A colorful Reading Series features an open mike for emerging (and brave) writers seeking exposure. In several genres the Writer's Voice provides an "Agent's Evaluation" service (the Y's writing instructors review student manuscripts for potential submission to a literary agent). A nice bonus, with no fee.

Writers Forum Summer Writing Workshops

For fiction and nonfiction writers, poets Western NY, 15 mi. E of Rochester — SUNY College at Brockport, 350 New Campus Dr., Brockport, NY 14420 **Voice:** 716-395-5713 **Contact:** Stanley Rubin, Dir. **Founded:** 1967 **Open:** 5 days in mid-July **Admission:** Registration form, manuscript sample **Cost:** About $450 **Size-Attendees:** About 80

B ROCKPORT STATE College gets an A + for creating and sustaining— over 30 years—one of the more colorful conference/workshop programs on college campuses in the U.S. You may not have heard of Brockport itself, but you will certainly recognize the names of many visiting writers who have read or taught here in the Summer Writing Workshops or at other times during the academic year. Nobel Laureate Wole Soyinka. Soviet poet Andrei Voznesensky. South African novelist Nadine Gordimer. Another Nobel Laureate, Isaac Bashevis Singer. And a host of comparable American writers.

Teachers in the summer workshops are a mix of Brockport faculty and others with literary credentials, such as Hilda Raz, editor of the literary journal *Prairie Schooner*. The Writers Forum has built an extensive videotape library of writer interviews, a resource worth checking out.

What to expect at Brockport? It's the standard package: morning workshops, afternoon lectures and discussions, evening readings. The emphasis is on accessibility and the chance to mingle with other writers. Attendees may be mostly from the nearby area but by no means exclusively so. Many states are represented here. Graduate credit is available; inquire about costs.

Housing and meals on campus can be arranged. Brockport is a small college town of 8,700 people, pretty but not a tourist destination. If this is your first

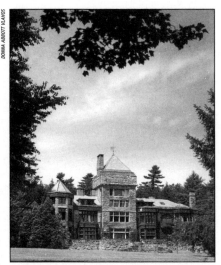

Yaddo Mansion, Yaddo Artists Colony, Saratoga Springs

visit to western New York, you might explore either the Lake Ontario shore or nearby Rochester with its Eastman (Kodak) House photography museum, or even Buffalo for its Albright Knox Art Gallery and summer theaters.

Yaddo

For all writers, and artists in selected other disciplines Foothills of the Adirondacks, less than 1 hr. N of Albany — P.O. Box 395, Union Ave., Saratoga Springs, NY 12866 **Voice:** 518-584-0746 **Fax:** to come **E-mail:** to come **Contact:** Candace Wait, Program Coord. **Founded:** 1926 **Open:** Year-round except certain weeks in Sept. **Admission:** Application form ($20), resume, work sample, references **Deadlines:** Aug. 1 for residencies from late Oct. to May; mid-Jan. for mid-May through Feb. **Cost:** Voluntary $20 contribution per day **Size-Attendees:** 35 summer, 15 winter **Handicapped Access:** Partial

ROBERT TOWERS, retired writing program chairman at Columbia University, said one colony (MacDowell) is Henry David Thoreau and the other (Yaddo) is Henry James. No matter how you slice it, Yaddo, in Saratoga Springs, and MacDowell, in Peterborough, NH, vie for the title of "most powerful, most coveted, most beloved of artists' colonies."

Start with Yaddo's quirks. The main house: a 55-room Victorian mansion which is itself something of a jumble of architectural styles and tastes. Plus outbuildings, some of which serve as artists' studios. Throw in the requisite tennis court, pool, a few lakes, 400 acres of woods and fields, a distinguished neighbor or two (John Jay Whitney estate, Saratoga Race Track), and you get the (Gilded Age) picture.

The origins: New York financier Spencer Trask and his poet wife, Katrina, built the mansion in 1893. Their small daughter named it "Yaddo," which rhymes with "shadow." The Trasks established a tradition here of literary salons, elegant lawn parties, the high life. Mrs. Trask envisioned artists here "creating, creating, creating." The doors opened as arts colony in 1926, and one director, Elizabeth Ames, was at the helm for several decades.

Add some further tradition: for 70-plus years Yaddo has welcomed, and some would say nurtured, artists of an enormous variety of tastes and styles (writers, composers, visual artists, choreographers and more recently, film- and videomakers). Critic Alfred Kazin exclaimed, "What a galaxy." Just for starters there were Saul Bellow, Truman Capote, Raymond Carver, James T. Farrell, Langston Hughes, Robert Lowell, Carson McCullers, Dorothy Parker, Katherine Anne Porter, Phillip Roth, Eudora Welty, William Carlos Williams, and the composers Aaron Copland, Virgil Thompson and Leonard Bernstein. And we haven't even touched the current generation of younger but significant writers. Nor have we mentioned visual artists, choreographers or film and video people.

While it's true that one's work needs to be of superior quality for the panel of professional reviewers to give a thumbs-up report on an application for a residency, it is not true that one must already be published by a major New York house. Talent, promise and seriousness of purpose—testified to by references from the writing field—are the passwords at the gatehouse here. Maybe a bit of personal quirkiness helps, too. Here's novelist John Cheever, a Yaddo alum, on whom Yaddo attracts: "all kinds—lushes down on their luck, men and women at the top of their powers, nervous breakdowns, thieves, geniuses, cranky noblemen and poets who ate their peas off a knife."

A residency (2 weeks to 2 months, averaging 5 weeks) can be spent snoozing by the pool, but there are strict rules about the structure of the day. Communal breakfast at 8; work without visitors from 9 to 4 (lunch goes with you to the studio or desk in a lunch box, sandwich of your choice); social time from 4 on; dinner at 6:30; no visitors after 10.

No spouses, no children, no pets. No evening readings or lectures except impromptu ones by the artists themselves. Yaddo, the sanctum sanctorum.

Then again, Yaddo has something of a reputation as a playground for those with a yen for extracurricular sex (probably sex more than romance). The age of AIDS may have toned things down a bit, and in the end the rumored sex at Yaddo, to outsiders anyway, is largely a bore. Perhaps novelist Jay McInerney's trenchant comment is enough said (he's a witness): "Any group of laboratory rats locked together is eventually going to start eyeing each other lasciviously. But I think there's more talk than tactile reality."

First-time applicants may request a residency period, but to be realistic, one ought to be ready to go whenever the call comes. One tends to see a residency here, or at MacDowell, as a kind of required way-station on the road to artistic and financial success. Yaddo is not for everyone, but the record shows that it is for those who, knowingly or not, are headed for Pulitzer Prize land, for NEA grants, for National Book Awards and Guggenheim fellowships, and, yes, for contracts with the major publishers of fine literature. Finally, writers and other artists from abroad are warmly welcomed at Yaddo, which prides itself on a certain international flavor.

New York Academic Programs

Brooklyn College, English Dept., 2308 Boylan Hall, Bedford Ave. & Ave. H, Brooklyn, NY 11210; 718-951-5195; MFA Creative Writing

Columbia University, Writing Division, School of the Arts, 305 Dodge Hall, New York, NY 10027; 212-854-2134; MFA Creative Writing

Cornell University, English Dept., 250 Goldwin Smith Hall, Ithaca, NY 14853; 607-255-7989; MFA Creative Writing

New York University, English Dept., Graduate Program in Creative Writing, 19 University Pl., New

York, NY 10003; 212-998-8816; MA Concentration in Creative Writing, MFA Creative Writing

Sarah Lawrence College, Graduate Studies, Writing Program, 1 Mead Way, Bronxville, NY 10708; 914-395-2373; MFA Writing

State University of New York at Albany, English Dept., Humanities Bldg. 333, Albany, NY 12222; 518-442-4055; MA English, Writing Sequence

Syracuse University, English Dept., 401 Hall of Languages, Syracuse, NY 13244; 315-443-2174; MFA Creative Writing

The New School for Social Research, Graduate Writing Program, 66 West 12th St., New York, NY 10011; 212-229-5630; MFA Creative Writing (new Fall 1996)

North Carolina

Asheville Poetry Festival

For poets, teachers UNC-Asheville campus — P.O. Box 9643, Asheville, NC 28815 **Voice:** 704-298-4927; 800-476-8172 **Fax:** 704-298-5491 **Founded:** 1994 **Open:** 3 days in July **Admission:** Registration ($10) **Cost:** $50 for full festival, or $10 per poetry reading at the door; $5–$35 for single workshops, $40 for manuscript reading **Size-Attendees:** 500 **Size-Class:** 15–30

POETRY—VIBRANT, shocking, scintillating, melodious, sensual, quiet. That's what the Asheville Poetry Festival celebrates through readings, performances and workshops. Poetry readings and performances by acclaimed poets are the highlight at this extravaganza, which takes place on a college campus in the beautiful Blue Ridge mountains. Pulitzer Prize-winning

poets are among the faculty—such as James Tate and Henry Taylor in 1996.

Writing and performance workshops have included "Using Metaphor: Telling the Truth But Telling It Slant," "Making Music with Words" and "The Art of Performing Poetry." Special-interest sessions focus on specifics, such as "Establishing Writing Workshops for Underserved Populations" and "Self-Publishing: What You Need to Know." "Special Talks" have provided an overview of the Naropa approach (see Jack Kerouac School of Disembodied Poetics) and a slide show on the making of a picture book.

College credit is available. The Blue Ridge mountains and Great Smoky Mountains National Park, a short drive east, offer great hiking possibilities. This event is co-sponsored by Poetry Alive!, a group of poets known for their performances and poetry slams.

Duke University Writers' Workshop

For fiction and nonfiction writers, poets Duke's West Campus—Box 90703, Duke University, Durham, NC 27708 **Voice:** 919-684-5375 **Contact:** Georgann Eubanks **Founded:** 1980 **Open:** 1 week in early June **Admission:** Registration form only **Deadlines:** First come, first served **Cost:** $350 **Size-Class:** 10–15 per workshop

DUKE'S CONTINUING Education Department sponsors this week of small workshops for both beginning and experienced authors in writing novels, short stories, creative nonfiction and children's books. The workshop titles and teachers may change from year to year, but the emphasis remains the same: providing a nurturing, noncompetitive environment. Teachers are drawn primarily from North Carolina campuses. Workshops have included "How the Poem Is Made," "Your Novel-in-Progress" and "(Un)Covering Stories: Bringing Color and Clarity to Narrative Writing."

Short story writer Robin Hemley describes his 1996 Duke workshop, which

143

borrowed its name from his book *Turning Life Into Fiction*, this way: "Good fiction, like life, is in the details. In some ways, writers are spies, observing, taking notes, eavesdropping on conversations. In this workshop, we'll be emphasizing this kind of intense observation and scrutiny of life—the stories that already surround your life, but are waiting to be noticed and recorded: stories from your family, anecdotes, the newspaper. ... "

North Carolina Writers' Network Conference and Workshops

For fiction and nonfiction writers, poets, playwrights *Various locations throughout the state* — *P.O. Box 954, Carrboro, NC 27510* **Voice:** 919-967-9540 **Fax:** 919-929-0535 **E-mail:** nc_writers@unc.edu **Open:** 1 weekend in Nov., 1 day in spring (workshops year-round) **Cost:** Conference $100–$125, Workshop $30–$40 **Financial Aid:** Scholarship **Size-Attendees:** 400 per conference **Size-Class:** 15 per workshop

LITERARY CULTURE thrives in North Carolina, thanks to the efforts of individuals, informal groups, bookstores, schools and organizations such as the North Carolina Writers' Network. NCWN offers a wealth of resources, including an annual weekend conference in November, a 1-day spring conference and "Writers Outreach Workshops" throughout the year.

NCWN's annual conference attracts over 400 writers to its concurrent workshops in fiction, poetry, journalism, screenwriting and marketing. Well-known writers read, consult and teach. Past faculty include novelist William Styron and Pulitzer Prize–winning poet Rita Dove. The lectures and panel discussions at both the annual and the spring conference focus on the craft as well as the business of writing. NCWN's spring conference is a full day of panels, workshops and readings in the Triangle area.

NCWN serves over 1,600 writers, editors, teachers, publishers, librarians and bookstore owners across North Carolina. While its annual conference moves around the state, workshops tend to take place in Chapel Hill at the NCWN Resource Center & Library.

From reports in *The Network News*, NCWN's bimonthly, it seems that almost everyone in the state is writing (or at least reading). The newsletter lists a dazzling array of writers' groups and classes, in bookstores and at schools, plus readings by well-known authors at public libraries throughout the state.

NCWN helps emerging writers find mentors, offers a manuscript critiquing service, and sponsors outreach programs in schools, prisons and senior centers.

Weymouth Center

For writers from North Carolina *Mid-state, W of Fayetteville* — *P.O. Box 939, Southern Pines, NC 28388* **Voice:** 910-692-6261 **Contact:** Sam Ragan **Founded:** 1979 **Open:** Year-round **Admission:** Application, project description **Cost:** Food **Size-Attendees:** 2–3 at a time

A RETREAT EXCLUSIVELY for North Carolina writers, Weymouth Center is a Georgian-style home, surrounded by gardens, in one of the oldest and loveliest neighborhoods in Southern Pines, a town in the middle of the state. Only 2 or 3 writers are residents at a time, which gives everyone ample space and enough quiet in this large 5-bedroom, 3-bath historic home, parts of which are open to the public. Writers design their own schedules during their residencies, which range from a weekend to 2 weeks. Most concentrate on a specific project during that time. Residents provide and prepare their own meals.

The Weymouth Center was once novelist James Boyd's private residence. Boyd and his wife invited writers and musicians to visit, turning Weymouth into a cultural and social center. After their deaths, the Friends of Weymouth incorporated in 1977 to create a regional cultural center for the arts and humanities and to protect the house and the land. Much of the Boyds' estate is now Weymouth Woods Sandhills Nature Preserve.

The Friends are responsible for the house and outbuildings and 24 acres of forest land. Besides the writers-in-residence program, they also sponsor lectures, workshops and the annual North Carolina Poetry Festival, which attracts 150 poets to readings, discussions and workshops.

Wildacres Writers Workshop

For fiction and nonfiction writers, poets, playwrights, screenwriters Mountains 50 mi. NE of Asheville — 233 S. Elm St., Greensboro, NC 27401 **Voice:** 910-273-4044 **Fax:** 910-273-4044 **E-mail:** judihill@aol.com **Contact:** Judith Hill, Dir. **Open:** Early July **Admission:** Application, writing sample **Deadlines:** Early May **Cost:** Workshop $410, retreat $170 (room and meals incl. for both) **Size-Attendees:** 90 **Size-Class:** 10 **Handicapped Access**

WILDACRES RETREAT, near Little Switzerland in the Blue Ridge, is the site for a 4-day retreat followed by a week of workshops. Participants may attend both the retreat and the workshop, or choose to come for only one. Fewer attend the retreat, which offers unscheduled days to write, meet with other writers, and relax in a beautiful mountain setting. The workshop week brings award-winning authors and 90 participants together to write and socialize. Individual workshops are limited to 10 members; manuscripts are the focus. Participants may request specific workshop leaders, who are assigned on a first come, first served basis; so register early. However, if you don't get your first choice, you may audit the session you requested.

Participants live in a lodge-type building, sharing bedrooms (each with a private bath), and eating meals together family-style. The workshop is designed to be a retreat. There are no phones, TVs, or radios in the rooms, though a pay phone is available in the lobby. Some writers come more for the socializing and rejuvenation of the retreat than for the workshops. There are ample opportunities for hiking, golf and tennis.

North Carolina Academic Programs

University of North Carolina at Greensboro, English Dept., Greensboro, NC 27412; 910-334-5459; MFA Creative Writing
University of North Carolina at Wilmington, English Dept., Wilmington, NC 28403; 910-962-3320; MFA English
Warren Wilson College, MFA Program for Writers, P.O. Box 9000, Asheville, NC 28815; 704-298-3325; MFA Creative Writing

North Dakota

University of North Dakota Writers' Conference

For all writers UND campus — Dept. of English, UND, P.O. Box 7209, Grand Forks, ND 58202 **Voice:** 701-777-3984 **Fax:** 701-777-3650 **Contact:** John Little **Founded:** 1970 **Open:** 4–5 days in spring **Admission:** Open to all **Size-Attendees:** 500

A CELEBRATION OF literature featuring a lively and distinguished group of visiting authors who give readings, participate on panels and sign books. There are no workshops, no manuscript consultations, no sessions on how to market your writing. The UND Writers' Conference offers writers a chance to listen, to hear the language as it sounds when used and spoken by talented writers. Come to be inspired.

The readings and panels focus on a theme, such as "La Literatura: Contemporary Latino/Latina Writing," which brought authors from Buenos Aires, Texas and New Mexico to share their work in 1993. The emphasis is on lively, forceful writing. Featured writers have included poet Sharon Olds and novelists Tim O'Brien and Bharati Mukherjee.

The readings, book signings and panel discussions are open to the public.

North Dakota Academic Programs

University of North Dakota, English Dept., Box 8237, Grand Forks, ND 58202; 701-777-3321; MA and PhD English (creative thesis/dissertation option)

Ohio

Antioch Writers' Workshop

For fiction and nonfiction writers, poets Antioch College campus, 30 min. E of Dayton—P.O. Box 494, Yellow Springs, OH 45387 **Voice:** 513-767-9112 **Contact:** July DaPolito, Dir. **Founded:** 1986 **Open:** 1 week in July **Admission:** Registration form ($50) for workshop; manuscript and personal statement for intensive seminars **Deadlines:** Early June for seminars and reduced tuition **Cost:** $375–$450 (discount for early registration) **Financial Aid:** Scholarship **Size-Attendees:** 80–110 per workshop **Size-Class:** 12 per seminar

AT THE ANTIOCH Writers' Workshop, interaction between faculty and students is paramount. The faculty not only give readings and lead seminars; they eat and socialize with the students. This is not a hierarchical workshop with those who are "stars" maintaining their distance from the "peons."

At the core of the workshop experience are the optional "intensive seminars" in fiction, poetry and nonfiction, each limited to 12 students. Apply early for these. Beginning writers, or those undecided about their genre, may sign up for "Finding Your Voice."

In the evenings there are readings, lectures and special events with authors and editors from literary magazines, such as *Story,* and book publishing companies, such as Warner Books. Course credit is available through Antioch or Wright State University. For an additional fee, manuscript readings and one-on-one consultations with faculty are offered.

While the workshop is based on the campus of Antioch College, it is an independent project, administered by the Yellow Springs Writers' Workshop, supported in part by Poets & Writers, Inc.

There are hiking trails, rocky streams and an old forest nearby.

Columbus Writers Conference

For fiction and nonfiction writers P.O. Box 20548, Columbus, OH 43220 **Voice:** 614-451-3075 **Contact:** Angela Palazzolo, Dir. **Founded:** 1993 **Open:** 1 day in Sept. **Admission:** Registration form only **Cost:** $75–$90 **Size-Attendees:** 200

PRACTICAL WORKSHOPS in a variety of commercial genres are the emphasis at the Columbus Writers Conference. There are workshops on cookbooks, mysteries, science fiction, humor and travel writing. At past events, a children's book writer discussed the 2 different markets in this genre: kids and adults. A greeting cards specialist gave an overview of this field, sharing her experience on everything from brainstorming to marketing the final copy.

If a writer needs to become more familiar with legal issues or how to sell his or her services in the corporate market, or simply wants to get a foot "inside the publisher's door," this conference addresses the issues.

Imagination

For fiction writers, poets *CSU campus — Dept. of English, Cleveland State University, 3100 Chester Ave., Cleveland, OH 44114* **Voice:** 216-687-4522 **Fax:** 216-687-6943 **E-mail:** nchandler@csuohio.edu **Contact:** Dr. Neal Chandler, Dir. **Founded:** 1991 **Open:** 1 week in early July **Admission:** Registration form; for workshop, manuscript and $10 reader's fee **Deadlines:** Workshop, early June; conference and colloquium, first come, first served **Cost:** Workshop, $400; conference and colloquium, $225; colloquium alone, $105 **Financial Aid:** Scholarship **Size-Attendees:** 80–90 **Size-Class:** 10

WHERE WOULD WRITING be without imagination? So how can one resist a weeklong conference and workshops that promote "strong, imaginative writing from minimal to magical realism, from mainstream to science fiction, from poetry to the novel"? The practical question is, how much time do you have to participate? There are 3 options: the workshops, the conference and the colloquium, or the colloquium alone.

If you want to work on a manuscript, apply for a workshop. This option is the most comprehensive; it includes the conference and colloquium. But admission is selective, based on the quality of the manuscript submitted. The small workshops meet each morning throughout the 5-day conference. The faculty rotates so that participants may benefit from a variety of instructors. In addition, students meet individually with 1 faculty member to go over their manu-

script a second time. Classes, lectures and discussion groups, open to all conference participants, are scheduled during the afternoons. These sessions focus on the craft as well as the "practice, the theory and the politics of writing."

For the others, there are 2 less demanding options. The Saturday "Colloquium on the Business of Writing" can stand alone. Or sign up for the conference, which includes everything—colloquium, panels, discussions, classes, readings—except the workshops.

The "Colloquium on the Business of Writing" brings in lecturers to discuss practical questions, such as finding and working with an agent, the economics of publishing, the logistics of manuscript submissions, and the politics of publishing in the U.S. Guests have included prize-winning authors and editors with experience at Pantheon, Vintage, Morrow and Harcourt Brace.

Midwest Writers' Conference

For fiction and nonfiction writers, poets *KSU Stark Campus — Kent State University Stark Campus, 6000 Frank Ave., Canton, OH 44720* **Voice:** 330-499-9600 **Founded:** 1968 **Open:** 1½ days in early Oct. **Admission:** Registration form only **Cost:** $65 (box lunch and manuscript entry fee incl.) **Size-Attendees:** 350

CONFERENCE PLANNERS begin this literary event with a bang by inviting a well-known writer, such as novelist Tom Wolfe (1995) or NPR commentator Alan Cheuse (1996), to give the keynote address on Friday evening. There is also a dialogue with the guest speaker the next morning. Following that, concurrent workshops in several genres are offered—for example, "How to Write and Sell a Children's Book in Today's Market," "Writing the Narrative Sports Story for Newspapers and Magazines," "Plotting is Murder: Every Good Mystery Starts with a Skeleton."

Workshops on the commercial aspects of writing have included "How to Sell Your Novel," "You and Your Agent: How to Get, Work With, and Keep One" and an editors' roundtable on "What Do Editors Want?" with representatives from Bottom Dog Press, Pudding House Press, Wick Chapbook Series at Kent State University, and Cleveland State University Poetry Center.

Note: there is a "Midwest Writers Conference" in Indiana as well.

Thurber House Residencies

For fiction writers, playwrights, journalists Near downtown — 77 Jefferson Ave., Columbus, OH 43215 **Voice:** 614-464-1032 **Contact:** Michael Rosen, Literary Dir. **Founded:** 1984 **Admission:** Application, writing sample (see below) **Deadlines:** Dec. 15 for letter of inquiry, Jan. 1 for applications **Financial Aid:** Stipend **Size-Attendees:** 1 at a time

WRITERS WITH experience and interest in teaching will appreciate the residencies offered by the Thurber House, named for writer and cartoonist James Thurber (1894–1961). Each year a journalist, a fiction writer and a playwright are selected as the journalist- (fiction writer-, playwright-) in-residence. Each resident lives in an apartment on the third floor of Thurber House for 1 academic quarter, receives a $5,000 stipend, and is responsible for teaching 1 class at Ohio State University. Aside from the 2 afternoons a week reserved for teaching, the resident is free to concentrate on his or her own work. For writers who are energized by teaching but do not want a full class load, this arrangement offers an appealing balance.

Call for details about current openings. Usually the residency is available for 1 quarter, sometimes 2. Writers sub-mit a letter of interest along with their resume, and then on the basis of these submissions an advisory panel invites a select group to submit an application and writing sample.

Thurber House is a restored 19th-century dwelling (the author's home during his college years) that has become a literary center. It houses the Thurber archives, a bookstore, a children's writing academy, a gallery, and a garden with 5 limestone Thurber dog sculptures (probably worth a visit with a camera).

Columbus, the largest city in Ohio, offers a mix of old and new urban delights, including diverse eateries, micro breweries, galleries, bookstores, funky cafes, great coffee and cappuccino, alternative newspapers, a farmers' market, music clubs, a symphony, an art museum and BalletMet Columbus.

Western Reserve Writers Conferences

For fiction and nonfiction writers, poets Lakeland Community College — 34200 Ridge Rd. #110, Willoughby, OH 44094 **Voice:** 216-943-3047; 800-653-4261 **Fax:** 216-943-3047 **E-mail:** fa837@cleveland. freenet.edu **Contact:** Lea Leever Oldham, Coord. **Open:** ½ day in Mar., 1 day in Sept. **Admission:** Registration form only **Cost:** $30–$50 **Financial Aid:** Scholarship **Size-Attendees:** 125 -150

BEGINNING WRITERS with an interest in writing for the mass market will find the Western Reserve Writers Conferences of particular interest. These nuts-and-bolts sessions meet on the campus of Lakeland Community College. The mini-conference is a half-day springtime event. The full-day conference occurs annually in early September. Freelance writers, sports writers, children's book authors, and mystery and romance novelists have been instructors recently.

Several workshops take place simultaneously, with sessions such as "Surviving as a Freelancer," "Writing and Selling Science Fiction," and "Inspirational Writing." For the business-minded writer, there are information sessions on copyright laws, taxes, manuscript preparation and syndication.

Writer's Digest Novel Writing Workshop

For fiction writers In your home — 1507 Dana Ave., Cincinnati, OH 45207 **Voice:** 800-759-0963 **Contact:** Mert Ransdell, Book Club Dir. **Open:** Year-round **Admission:** Application form only **Cost:** $389 **Size-Class:** Tutorial by mail

THE WRITER'S DIGEST Book Club, from whom you can order the helpful reference book *Writer's Market* (and its clones concerning specific genres), also sponsors an at-home tutorial novel writing workshop. Some writers (beginners, we imagine) may find this useful, especially if they are located in isolated rural places and cannot travel to workshops at universities or urban literary centers. But caveat emptor: this is a for-profit operation, geared primarily to selling books. That much said, consider the details.

Participants indicate what kind of novel they hope to write (mainstream/literary, mystery, sci-fi, romance, horror, action, historical, or other). WD assigns an instructor. The 3 instructors described in the brochure had reasonable credentials as writers, but their teaching credentials were harder to gauge. A package of instructional booklets and exercises arrives in the mail, including the latest *Novel and Short Story Writer's Market*, which, presumably, will help you target your submissions to publishers. As your manuscript progresses, individualized feedback from the instructor helps you along.

Interestingly, this is the same process used by some of the better academic programs where "low residency" is the plan and student-teacher correspondence is the method of guidance.

We can't testify to the results, and we wonder about the price tag. For writers who use the tutorial relationship extensively, the money may be reasonable. For those who do not, $389 is a lot to pay for a few books and pamphlets, even good ones, some of which are available at most libraries. Clearly the burden is on the consumer to make the investment worthwhile. Writer's Digest is careful to offer an escape clause for anyone who is dissatisfied. The program certainly looks clean.

A monthly payment plan is available, and the workshop can last up to 2 years. If your version of the great American novel isn't out of the oven by then, perhaps you should trim it down to a short story, send it off to some magazines, and start something new.

Writers Workshop

For fiction writers, poets NE of Columbus — The Kenyon Review, Sunset Cottage, Gambier, OH 43022 **Voice:** 614-427-5208 **Fax:** 614-427-5417 **Contact:** David Lynn, Ed. **Founded:** 1995 **Open:** 10 days in late June **Admission:** Application, writing sample **Cost:** $1,450 (room and board incl.) **Size-Attendees:** 36 **Size-Class:** 12

THE EDITORS OF THE *Kenyon Review* invite distinguished poets and fiction writers to teach and visit their 10-day summer Writers Workshop. There are 3 workshops—poetry, fiction and crime fiction—with 12 participants each. The emphasis is on writing and on serious dialogue between participants and the skilled writers/teachers. Afternoons are deliberately left free to encourage participants to write and to meet individually with instructors.

The *Kenyon Review* has attracted celebrated and ambitious young writers to the village of Gambier for decades. While Kenyon is the oldest private college in Ohio, and many of its buildings, gravel pathways and mature old oaks reflect these historic roots, workshop participants live in renovated modern campus apartments, with comfortable places to work and access to the latest computer technology.

Ohio Academic Programs

Antioch University, McGregor School, 800 Livermore St., Yellow Springs, OH 45387; 513-767-6321; Individualized MA (IMA)

Bowling Green State University, Creative Writing Program, English Dept., Bowling Green, OH 43403; 419-372-8370; MFA Creative Writing

Ohio State University, Creative Writing Program, English Dept., 164 W. 17th Ave., Columbus, OH 43210; 614-292-6065; MFA Creative Writing

University of Cincinnati, English Dept., Cincinnati, OH 45221; 513-3906; MA and PhD English (creative writing option/dissertation)

Ohio University, English Dept., Athens, OH 45701; 614-593-2838; MA and PhD English (creative thesis/critical creative dissertation)

Oklahoma

Oklahoma Fall Arts Institutes Writing Weekend

For fiction and nonfiction writers, poets Lone Wolf, 2½ hr. SW of Oklahoma City — P.O. Box 18154, 720 NW 50th, Oklahoma City, OK 73154 **Voice:** 405-842-0890 **Fax:** 405-848-4538 **E-mail:** okarts@okartsinst.org **Contact:** Linda DeBerry **Founded:** 1983 **Open:** 1 weekend in Oct. **Admission:** Registration form only **Cost:** $450 (room and board incl.) **Financial Aid:** Loans; Scholarship **Size-Attendees:** 100 per institute **Size-Class:** 20 **Handicapped Access**

SET IN QUARTZ Mountain State Park in the beautiful Wichita Mountains, in a lodge overlooking a lake, these workshops vary in subject from year to year. What remains constant is that you live in a small intimate community for a long weekend and concentrate on your writing in a workshop with a noted teacher/writer. The emphasis is on artistic self-renewal.

Distinguished writer/teachers lead workshops on fiction, poetry, writing for children and screenwriting. In 1995, Diane Middlebrook, noted for her biography of poet Anne Sexton, led the workshop on biography and autobiography.

Living is casual at the Quartz Mountain Arts and Conference Center. People eat buffet style; share double-occupancy dorms, cabins, or duplexes; and support each individual's independent artistic endeavors.

The Institute is supported by a broad partnership of individuals, businesses, corporations and foundations, as well as the State Arts Council and Department of Education. In addition to retreats for writers, the Institute offers weekends for musicians, visual artists, photographers and teachers.

🏠 Oklahoma Academic Programs

Oklahoma State University, English Dept., 205 Morrill Hall, Stillwater, OK 74078; 405-744-9469; MA and PhD English (concentration in creative writing)

Oregon

Arts at Menucha

For poets, and artists in selected other disciplines Overlooking the Columbia River Gorge, 20 min. E of Portland — The Creative Arts Community, P.O. Box 4958, Portland, OR 97208 **Voice:** 503-760-5837 **Open:** 1 week in Aug. **Admission:** Application **Deadlines:** First come, first served (July 1 for scholarships) **Cost:** $475 (room and board incl.) **Financial Aid:** Loans; Scholarship **Size-Class:** 10

THE CREATIVE ARTS Community at Menucha primarily offers workshops in pottery, sculpture, woodcuts, ceramics, maskmaking, drawing and other arts, with occasional writing workshops. Participants live, eat and study on a 96-acre retreat, 20 minutes east of Portland. Call to find out what is on the schedule for this year.

Free verse, tanka (lyrical 5-line poems), haibun (prose/poetry), senryu (short humorous poems) and haiku were the focus of the 1996 poetry workshop. Poet/teacher Maggie Chula began each day with "a meditative reading," followed by discussion and exercises in the form of the poem read. Walks around the retreat took place in the afternoon for "heightening your senses and refreshing your spirit."

Coos Bay Writers' Workshop

For fiction and nonfiction writers, poets Charleston, on the coast — P.O. Box 4022, Coos Bay, OR 97420 **Voice:** 541-756-7906 **Contact:** Mary Scheirman **Founded:** 1989 **Open:** 1 week in Aug. **Admission:** Registration form only **Cost:** $400

THIS ANNUAL CONFERENCE brings poets, fiction writers and nonfiction writers together for 5 days of workshops. The schedule is flexible, promoting time for relaxation, reading, writing and exploring the local area. Housing in student dorms is available. Evenings are for socializing and readings.

Set at the Oregon Institute of Marine Biology, many of the workshop events take place in the "boathouse" auditorium, which offers floor-to-ceiling views of the bay. Not far from the conference site is a wonderful slough for watching wildlife and tides. Even in the frequent fog, the coast and slough provide a multitude of visual treats.

Fishtrap Gathering: Writing and the West

For fiction and nonfiction writers, poets, journalists Wallowa Mountains, NE OR, over 200 mi. E of Portland, near ID and WA borders — P.O. Box 38, Enterprise, OR 97828 **Voice:** 541-426-3623 **Contact:** Rich Wandschneider, Dir **Founded:** 1987 **Open:** 1 week in early July, 1 week in Feb. **Admission:** Application **Cost:** Gathering, $170; Workshops, $210; housing and meals, $28 a day; meals only, $23 a day **Financial Aid:** Loans; Scholarship **Size-Attendees:** 90 in the summer, 50 in the winter **Size-Class:** 12 **Handicapped Access**

FISHTRAP ATTRACTS writers from across the West, as well as rural and urban westerners, ranchers and environmentalists, government workers and private citizens. The Gathering, an annual summer event, is designed somewhat like the old Chautauquas. Writers, historians, teachers, publishers, editors and readers gather for a long weekend to discuss a theme, such as "Eros and Nature," "Language and Politics," or "Family." The Writing Workshops take place during the 4 days preceding the Gathering.

Workshops such as "The First Chapter," which focuses on "how to draw a reader in," and "Listening to the Land's Heart," which asks participants to respond to a sensory universe, are available. Evenings offer an open mike for readings as well as scheduled Fellow's Readings, musical events and informal socializing. At Wallowa Lake Camp offers rustic dorm-style housing. RV spaces, tent sites and other accommodations are nearby.

Fishtrap sees itself as "a cross between a writers' organization and a Western think tank." It also publishes an annual *Anthology*, offers a Winter Fishtrap, and sponsors Fishtrap Currents, which is a series of lectures and short workshops.

Flight of the Mind Summer Writing Workshop for Women

For fiction and nonfiction writers, poets Rustic retreat center on McKenzie River, 50 mi. E of Eugene — 622 SE 29th Ave., Portland, OR 97214 **Voice:** 503-236-9862 **Fax:** 503-233-0774 **E-mail:** women-write@aol.com **Contact:** Judith Barrington **Founded:** 1984 **Open:** June **Admission:** Application, writing sample **Deadlines:** Apr. **Cost:** $700–$800 (room and board incl.) **Financial Aid:** Loans; Scholarship **Size-Attendees:** 65 per session **Size-Class:** 13 **Handicapped Access**

SOME WOMEN FEEL more creative, competent and able to concentrate on their writing in a community of women. If this suits you, here are 2 weeklong sessions of 5 workshops each, set in the foothills of the Cascade mountain range. Distinguished writers, such as Ursula Le Guin and Valerie Miner, teach the workshops. Participants range in age from 20 to 80. Admission is based on manuscript submissions and the applicant's self-description. Workshop leaders put together a group that mixes cultural backgrounds, races and levels of experience.

Workshops meet for 3 hours daily. Each session includes workshops on poetry, nonfiction, memoir and fiction writing. In 1966, "Writing Nonfiction" underscored a feminist approach to the subject matter, "emphasizing the validity of all women's real and imaginary life experiences." In "Reclaiming Eden: Writing About Animals," techniques were taught for conveying "the animals' personalities and the unique connections that some women seek with other species."

In between classes and evening readings, take a soak in the nearby hot springs, or explore waterfalls and lava beds, or river raft, swim and hike. The rustic retreat center is a camplike setting. Bathrooms are shared. One luxury: cooks prepare the meals for you.

Getting It Write

For fiction and nonfiction writers, poets S central OR, 78 mi E of Medford — P.O. Box 8113, Klamath Falls, OR 97602 **Voice:** 541-883-1266 **Fax:** 541-884-6916 **Founded:** 1995 **Open:** 3 days in Oct. **Admission:** Registration form only **Deadlines:** First come, first served **Cost:** $110 (breakfast incl.) **Financial Aid:** Loans; Scholarship **Size-Attendees:** 175

THERE IS AN ENERGY behind this conference that reflects its founders' enthusiasm. Begun in 1995 and co-sponsored by the Klamath Writers' Guild and the Department of Extended Studies at Oregon Institute of Technology, the conference brings writers, publishers and agents together for "interactive workshops."

Both the craft and the business of writing are covered. The 1996 workshops included "Rejecting Rejection by Redirection," "Outlining a Book in an Hour" and "Who's Telling This Story Anyway? An Exploration Into Point of View."

Klamath Falls, the site of the conference, is on the edge of Klamath Lake, near the southern edge of the state, where there are conifers and rolling hills, and sun—this is not the rainy region of the state. The striking Crater Lake National Park is only 60 miles to the north.

Haystack Program in the Arts & Sciences

For fiction and nonfiction writers, poets Cannon Beach, 80 mi. W of Portland — Portland State University School of Extended Studies, 1633 SW Park Ave., P.O. Box 1393, Portland, OR 97207 **Voice:** 503-725-8500 (info); 503-725-4832 (to register); 800-547-8887 (outside Portland) **Fax:** 503-725-4840 **Founded:** 1968 **Open:** Late June–mid-Aug. **Admission:** Registration form only on **Deadlines:** First come, first served **Cost:** $145–$360 **Size-Class:** 15 **Handicapped Access**

SITUATED ON THE dramatic Oregon coast, Portland State University's School of Extended Studies' summer series of workshops includes a range of courses for writers. Classes have included "Fiction Writing for the Restless," "Strange Landscapes: The Inner and Outer Spaces of Science Fiction" and "Reading Their Writes: True Crime for the Writer." Workshops cover poetry, fiction, mysteries, essays and memoirs, and children's books.

Six hours a day are given to writing in the 5-day workshops. But then you are free to explore the rocky, often foggy coast, and to attend readings, concerts, art exhibits and lectures. Camping is available. Courses in theater, art, music, gardening, film and the environment are also offered.

Neahkahnie Institute

For fiction and nonfiction writers Nehalem Bay, 25 mi. N of Tillamook on the coast — P.O. Box 447, Manzanita, OR 97130 **Voice:** 503-368-7878 **Contact:** Lisa D. Norton **Admission:** Registration form ($50) **Cost:** $190 (breakfast incl.) **Financial Aid:** Loans; Scholarship **Size-Class:** 25

LISA NORTON, whose story of her return to the Sandhills of Nebraska formed the basis of a memoir, *Hawk Flies Above,* began offering workshops for women in 1996. "Writing Memoir" and "Writing the Landscape: Honoring Women's Voices Through Poetry and Prose" are open exclusively to women. "Writing & the Natural World," with Norton, writer Robin Cody, and biologist Peter Walczak, is open to all writers.

Oregon Writers Colony

For fiction and nonfiction writers, poets Newport, on the coast — P.O. Box 15200, Portland, OR 97215 **Voice:** 503-621-3534 **Contact:** Elizabeth Bolton, Pres. **Open:** Year-round **Admission:** Registration **Cost:** Conference, $170–$255 (room and board incl., discount for Newport residents); Colonyhouse retreat, $150–$450

FOUNDED IN 1981 by 5 writers who wanted a place on the beach, the Oregon Writers Colony provides a wide variety of workshops throughout the year and puts on an annual conference in April; housed at the Sylvia Beach Hotel, a writers' haven in Newport (no phones or televisions). Each of the rooms there is decorated in the style of a particular writer, including the choice of books by the bed.

Writers can join OWC for $25 and receive its newsletter, *Colonygram.* For a weekend or a week, members may also rent Colonyhouse, a retreat in Rockaway, on the dramatic and enchanting Oregon coast.

Sitka Center for Art and Ecology

Fiction and nonfiction writers, poets *Cascade Head Ranch in Otis, on the coast, just N of Lincoln City — P.O. Box 65, Otis, OR 97368* **Voice:** 541-994-5485 **Founded:** 1971 **Open:** Residencies: Fall (Oct. 1–Jan. 15), Spring (Feb. 1–May 21). Workshops: June–Sept. **Admission:** Residencies: application, project description (preference given to research on the OR coast environment), writing sample, references. Workshops: registration form only. **Deadlines:** Residencies: June 20. Workshops: first come, first served **Cost:** Residencies: Meals, transportation, materials. Workshops: $60–$175 **Size-Attendees:** 2 residents per session **Handicapped Access**

SITKA CENTER PROMOTES the "expression of the strong relationship between art and nature." Workshops in a wide range of arts, crafts and the natural sciences are scheduled year-round, with approximately 50 occurring during the summer. For writers, the emphasis has been on poetry and memoir or journal writing.

Think about towering conifers, a foggy, rocky coast and the ebb and flow of the tides, and you will begin to glimpse this location. The Center borders a Nature Conservancy preserve, the Salmon River Estuary and the Siuslaw National Experimental Forest. Many workshops concern the ecology of the area; some involve using a sea kayak to explore the estuary.

In addition there are two 4-month-long residencies available in the fall, and two in the spring. Residents live in their own rustic self-contained house with sleeping loft. However, the emphasis is on interaction with the community. Twenty hours of community service are expected. For those whose work focuses on the northwestern coastal environment, this residency offers terrific opportunities. Writers, artists and natural scientists are encouraged to apply at varying phases of their professional life—emerging, mid-career or on sabbatical.

Walden Residency for Oregon Writers

For fiction and nonfiction writers, poets, playwrights *SW Oregon — Extended Campus Programs, Southern Oregon State College, Ashland, OR 97520* **Voice:** 541-552-6901 **Fax:** 541-552-6047 **Founded:** 1987 **Open:** Mar.–Aug. **Admission:** Application, writing sample, project description **Deadlines:** Nov. 30 **Cost:** Transportation, some meals **Size-Attendees:** 3 residents per year

FOR SOMEONE WHO appreciates solitude, here is a fully furnished cabin on a beautiful mountain farm called Walden Farm, located in southern Oregon. The cabin is available for 3 consecutive 6-week residencies; only nonsmoking Oregon residents qualify. Partial board is also provided. This residency is sponsored by a private citizen and coordinated through the Extended Campus Programs at Southern Oregon State College.

The cottage "opens on a meadow surrounded by forest." A phone is nearby. Walden Farm is 10 minutes from Gold Hill and 40 minutes from Ashland, home of the summer Oregon Shakespeare Festival.

Willamette Writers' Conference

For fiction and nonfiction writers *Hotel at Portland Airport — 9045 SW Barbur Blvd., Suite 5A, Portland, OR 97219* **Voice:** 503-452-1592 **Founded:** 1965 **Open:** 2 days in Aug. **Admission:** Registration form only **Cost:** $200 **Size-Attendees:** 200 per conference **Size-Class:** 15

A PRAGMATIC ORIENTATION characterizes the Willamette Writers' Conference. Representatives from many established publishing houses in New York attend this 2-day event, making it possible for writers in the Northwest to gain essential information and skills without leaving the region. Workshops and one-on-one and group consultations with editors and agents aim at helping participants craft a salable proposal.

Looking for another reason to travel to Portland? Try Powell's, a book lover's paradise—a city block of used, remaindered and new books. There is a map to help you find your way around this incredible bookstore. When your energy flags, or you find you are lost, head for the in-store coffee bar. There you will also find a multitude of magazines, handy for researching your next article or book project.

🏠 Oregon Academic Programs

University of Oregon, Creative Writing Program, Eugene, OR 97403; 503-346-3944; MFA Creative Writing

Pennsylvania

Bouchercon: The World Mystery Convention

For mystery writers *Varies — 507 S. 8th St., Philadelphia, PA 19147* **Voice:** 215-923-0211 **Fax:** 215-923-1789 **Contact:** Deen Kogan **Founded:** 1970 **Open:** 1 weekend in the fall **Admission:** Registration form only **Cost:** Membership dues $50 (covers convention); $30 for writing seminars **Size-Attendees:** 2,000

B OUCHERCON IS MORE than workshops; it is a celebration of mysteries in all genres. Yes, writers come and there are workshops, but there are oodles of attendees, from authors, editors, publishers and booksellers to many, many devotees. There are readings and a steady stream of discussions. Every aspect of mystery and suspense writing is part of the unending conversation. And the focus is not just on fiction or books; attention is also paid to works of nonfiction and films.

Well-known authors lead workshops. Book (and assorted other) dealers are on site selling mystery-related items. There is a large awards banquet honoring the best in crime and mystery writing. There are meetings of groups such as Sisters in Crime and Private Eye Writers of America.

The convention's title, Bouchercon (rhymes with voucher), honors the late mystery reviewer and critic for the *New York Times,* William Anthony Parker White, who used the pseudonym Anthony Boucher.

This large gathering moves around annually, and its chair also changes. The contact listed above will know where and when the big event will occur this year, and will know how you can register for it.

Celebration of Black Writing

For fiction and nonfiction writers, poets *Moonstone Inc., 110 S. 13th St., Philadelphia, PA 19107* **Voice:** 215-735-9598 **Fax:** 215-735-2670 **Founded:** 1985 **Open:** Presidents' Day Weekend in Feb. **Admission:** Registration form only **Deadlines:** Early Feb. **Cost:** Free **Size-Attendees:** 1,000

E XCITEMENT PROBABLY peaks on Sunday afternoon, when the book fair takes place at the annual Celebration of Black Writing. Fifty authors representing a wide variety of genres and philosophical, political and literary perspectives take part in a mass autographing session. Thought-provoking readings punctuate the event and have featured writers such as Darius James, the controversial author of *Negrophobia,* and the Dark Room Collective, an ensemble composed of "unabashed disciples of James Baldwin." Readings, discussions and networking are at the heart of it all.

This Celebration is on the cutting edge of the culture, highlighting the work of recently published writers, often before they have become famous. Poet Rita Dove is among the many authors who participated before becoming well known. The conference sponsors follow no political or literary line or dogma; they produce the event to celebrate and to promote the extraordinary diversity and richness of black writing.

Workshops take place on Saturday, led by such distinguished writers as Pulitzer Prize-winning poet Yusef Komunyakaa, and focus on fiction, nonfiction, poetry, children's books and drama. A panel discussion on "The State of Black Writing" features authors from most genres. A meeting of the Union of Writers of the African Peoples has taken place at this conference to encourage younger writers to join.

And the whole celebration is free, made possible by grants from numerous sources. It takes place in various locations in Philadelphia.

Confluence: Pittsburgh Science Fiction Conference

For science fiction writers P.O. Box 3681, Pittsburgh, PA 15230 **Founded:** 1988 **Open:** 1 weekend in July **Admission:** Registration form for conference, manuscript for workshop **Cost:** $35 **Size-Class:** 10

CONFLUENCE, THE science fiction conference, takes place annually. However, the fate of its related writers' workshop (as of late 1996) is unknown. Numerous authors appear at the Confluence conference, which means that if you are interested in science fiction you might want to attend, even if it does not offer writers' workshops. There will be lots of talk, books on display, informal discussions, public presentations. Confluence is an event for anyone interested in science fiction.

Cumberland Valley Fiction Writers Workshop

For fiction writers Dickinson College campus — Dept. of English, Dickinson College, P.O. Box 1773, Carlisle, PA 17013 **Voice:** 717-245-1291 **Fax:** 717-245-1942 **E-mail:** gill@dickinson.edu **Contact:** Judy Gill, Dir. **Founded:** 1990 **Open:** 6 days in June **Admission:** Application, manuscript, $10 readers fee, SASE **Deadlines:** End of May **Cost:** $325; dorm room, $130 **Size-Attendees:** 50 **Size-Class:** 10

SERIOUS FICTION WRITERS are attracted to the small summer workshops and top-notch faculty at the Cumberland Valley Fiction Writers' Workshop. Each faculty member is a published author, most are also teachers, many are prize winners, and some have been Pulitzer Prize nominees as well as Guggenheim and NEA Fellowship recipients.

Workshops meet for 5 days, supplemented by faculty readings and roundtable discussions. For breaks, participants hike on the Appalachian Trail to a nearby lake for swimming, canoe on the Juniata River, visit Civil War sites in Gettysburg or go fly fishing. The workshop takes place on the 58-acre campus of Dickinson College, in Carlisle (pop. 25,000), in the Cumberland Valley. There are athletic facilities, computer labs, a student union and a library for participants to use.

Ligonier Valley Writers Conference

📝 ♻️ **For fiction and nonfiction writers, poets** Ligonier Town Hall — RR #4, Box 8, Ligonier, PA 15658 **Voice:** 412-238-5749 **Fax:** 412-238-5190 **Contact:** Dr. Tina Thoburn, Dir. **Founded:** 1985 **Open:** 3-day weekend in July **Admission:** Registration form only **Cost:** $180–$200; 1-day rates available **Size-Attendees:** 75

ROOTED IN ITS LOCALE, the Ligonier Valley Writers Conference takes advantage of authors and teachers of southwestern Pennsylvania to staff its weekend of workshops. The sessions and panels take place in Ligonier's Town Hall, and the town's galleries, restaurants and shops play a role by hosting special conference events, such as faculty book signings and buffets.

The workshops focus on fiction, nonfiction, poetry and writing for children. One evening features a country picnic and faculty reading at the conference director's 150-year-old-brick home, just south of Fort Ligonier. For the second evening many of Ligonier's shops sponsor "Twilight in the Garden Readings." More towns should do this!

Mid-Atlantic Mystery Book Fair and Convention

📝 ♻️ **For mystery writers** Holiday Inn at Independence Mall — Detecto-Mysterioso Books, Society Hill Playhouse, 507 S. 8th St., Philadelphia, PA 19147 **Voice:** 215-923-0211 **Fax:** 215-923-1789 **Contact:** Deen Kogan **Founded:** 1991 **Open:** 1 weekend in early Nov. **Admission:** Registration form only **Cost:** $50 **Size-Attendees:** 450

WHAT MAKES THE annual Mid-Atlantic Mystery Book Fair and Convention so much fun is that it is a book fair as well as a series of workshops. Writers meet and mingle with other writers, agents, editors and fans. Writing workshops on most mystery genres—from police procedural to hard-boiled detective to cozy—are available. Panel discussions featuring authors, agents and editors provide useful information for beginning and more experienced suspense fiction writers.

And then there is the book fair. Book signings. Book selling. Book dealers. It offers an opportunity to meet authors and to find books you've been searching for in the Mystery Book Room. Fans are as welcome as would-be writers here in Philadelphia's Independence Mall. Discussions among writers, readers and editors are encouraged.

Pennwriters Conference

📝 ♻️ **For fiction and nonfiction writers** Hotel — P.O. Box 339, Edinboro, PA 16412 **Voice:** 814-734-5189 **Contact:** Jamie Saloff **Founded:** 1989 **Open:** 2 days in May **Admission:** Registration form only **Deadlines:** Early Apr. **Cost:** $95–$130 (some meals incl.) **Size-Attendees:** 150–200

HOW TO MARKET popular writing is the focus of this jam-packed 2-day conference sponsored by Pennwriters, a nonprofit organization that represents over 500 published and aspiring writers in Pennsylvania. Many sessions focus on the basics, from "Secrets of the Sale" and "Writing as a Business" to "Understanding Copyright."

Published writers from a variety of popular genres—mysteries, horror, romance, children's books, science fiction, young adult—serve on panels. Literary agents and editors are available for individual appointments on a first-come, first-served basis.

The conference coordinator, who is the contact for this conference, changes annually, but the mailing address remains constant. In addition to the annual conference, Pennwriters sponsors regional mini-conferences, workshops and meetings throughout the year. It offers manuscript critiques for its members and maintains a library.

Philadelphia Writers' Conference

🖉 ⓔ *For fiction and nonfiction writers, poets* Holiday Inn at Independence Mall — P.O. Box 7171, Elkins Park, PA 19027 **Voice:** 215-782-1059 **Contact:** William Delamar **Founded:** 1949 **Open:** 1 weekend in June **Admission:** Registration form only **Deadlines:** Late Apr. for manuscripts **Cost:** $140–$150; $25 each for buffet and banquet **Financial Aid:** Scholarship **Size-Attendees:** 200

FOUNDED IN 1949, the Philadelphia Writers' Conference is one of the oldest conferences in the country to be established by a group of local writers who joined together to benefit from each other's experience. Professionals—published authors, editors, literary agents—were invited to the very first conference and continue to participate as speakers. But much of what happens occurs among fellow writers—amateurs and professionals—sharing their experiences in workshops.

Workshops meet each of the 3 days and focus on various genres, including the popular short story, literary short story, poetry, novel, nonfiction book, mystery, juvenile, magazine articles and reviews. Manuscript critiques are available in the workshops. Often there are special panels and lectures, such as "Local Interest for Local Freelance Writers" with the editor of *Pennsylvania Magazine,* and "Chapbook Magic: The Necessary Thread" with the poetry editor from a small press.

🏠 Pennsylvania Academic Programs

Pennsylvania State University, English Dept., 119 Burrowes Bldg, University Park, PA 19802; 814-865-6381; MFA Creative Writing

Temple University, Creative Writing Dept., Anderson Hall 022-29, Philadelphia, PA 19122; 215-204-1796; MA English (creative writing)

University of Pennsylvania, English Dept., Philadelphia, PA 19104; 215-898-7341; MA Literature and Writing

University of Pittsburgh, English Dept., 4200 Fifth Ave., Pittsburgh, PA 15260; 412-624-2976; MFA Creative Writing

Rhode Island

Newport Writers Conference

🖉 ⓔ *For fiction and nonfiction writers, poets, screenwriters, playwrights* Varies — Newport Community Writers Association, P.O. Box 12, Newport, RI 02840 **Voice:** 401-846-9884 **E-mail:** ascreengem@ aol.com **Contact:** Eleyne Austen Sharp, Exec. Dir. **Founded:** 1992 **Open:** 1 weekend in Sept. or Oct. **Admission:** Application **Cost:** $250–$295 **Financial Aid:** Scholarship **Size-Attendees:** 150 **Size-Class:** 10

SMALL WORKSHOPS in fiction, poetry, writing for children and screenwriting are at the heart of the fall Newport Writers Conference. The emphasis is on craft rather than marketing. Authors, screenwriters and members of the publishing industry serve as faculty, actively participating on panels and in workshops. Authors' readings and book signings are on the schedule, and consultations with a literary agent are available.

In 1994 the Community Writers Association was established to sponsor the conference and other activities that promote writing. Besides the conference, CWA sponsors 6-week writing workshops throughout the year in Providence and Newport. CWA also offers a literary service that provides manuscript critiques, an annual literary contest and a newsletter.

⌂ Rhode Island Academic Programs

Brown University, Creative Writing Grad. Program, Box 1852, Providence, RI 02912; 401-863-3260; MFA Creative Writing

South Carolina

Charleston Writers' Conference

📝📂 *For fiction and nonfiction writers, poets* College of Charleston campus — Lightsey Conference Center, College of Charleston, Charleston, SC 29424 **Voice:** 803-953-5822 **Fax:** 803-953-1454 **Contact:** Paul Allen, Dir. **Founded:** 1990 **Open:** 4 days in Mar. **Admission:** Registration form only **Cost:** $140, manuscript evaluation $50, banquet $30 **Size-Attendees:** 160

THE SOUTH IS FAMOUS for its literary culture, and southern authors are read closely, emulated and adored. No surprise then that Charleston hosts a distinguished faculty of writers at the Charleston Writers' Conference. Here, the love of literature is strong. A featured writer reads one evening and answers questions the next morning (Joyce Carol Oates in 1996). Panels and workshops explore a multitude of complex literary issues. Under the topic "Art and the Writing Life," discussions may focus on: "serious art" vs. "popular art," exploring the unknown, inspiration vs. discipline, arrogance vs. individuality, and the artist's responsibility to society and to him- or herself.

Sessions on the craft of writing cover the basics, from research and generating ideas to rewriting, narration, character and conflict. Manuscript evaluations are available on a first-come, first-served basis prior to the conference. Participants may choose to read their work during the scheduled open-mike sessions.

With easy access to beautiful downtown Charleston, attendees may take advantage of breaks to explore the colorful shops, restaurants and historic sites.

⌂ South Carolina Academic Programs

University of South Carolina, Columbia, English Dept., Columbia, SC 29208; 803-777-5063; MFA Creative Writing

South Dakota

⌂ South Dakota Academic Programs

University of South Dakota, English Dept., 414 E. Clark St., Vermillion, SD 57069; 605-677-5229; MA English

Tennessee

Sewanee Writers' Conference

📝📂 *For fiction writers, poets, playwrights* University of the South campus — University of the South, Sewanee, TN 37383 **Voice:** 615-598-1141 **Contact:** Cheri Peters **Founded:** 1990 **Open:** 12 days in July **Admission:** Application ($20), manuscript **Deadlines:** Rolling through early summer **Cost:** $750; room and board $450 **Financial Aid:** Scholarship; Fellowship **Size-Class:** 12–15

GIVE THANKS TO Tennessee Williams, for he left money to the University of the South, along with explicit directions that those funds be used to encourage creative writers. Sewanee is a result, one of the most popular conferences in the country for serious fiction writers, playwrights and poets. Competition is stiff. A remarkable faculty, including Pulitzer Prize winners and nominees, lead workshops and discussions and give readings.

Williams's legacy includes fellowships, one named for his grandfather, Reverend Walter E. Dakin, who studied at Sewanee and inspired Williams to choose Sewanee as the recipient of his support.

Poet Juan Delgado, the Walter E. Dakin Fellow in 1995, wrote about his experience at Sewanee: "Like most people, I get to know a book first, then I wonder about the personality behind the words, so it was a joy finally to meet Ellen Douglas, Horton Foote, Anthony Hecht, and others. At Sewanee I also found myself getting to know writers first, then their books or manuscripts. This reversal made for an interesting way to be exposed to literature. As writers and readers we are part of a community of memory, bound by the books that have helped shape us."

Each participant meets in a small workshop with 2 faculty members 5 times during the 12-day conference. In addition, there are one-on-one consultations with faculty and lectures by visiting editors, critics and literary agents. For breaks, there are squash and tennis courts, a swimming pool, golf course, library, and 10,000 acres to explore on foot, bicycle or horseback.

Fiction workshop at Sewanee Writers Conference, Sewanee

🏠 Tennessee Academic Programs

University of Memphis, Creative Writing Director, English Dept., Memphis, TN 38152; 901-678-3602; MFA Creative Writing

Texas

Austin Writers' League Workshops and Seminars

📝 ♻️ *For fiction and nonfiction writers, poets* 1501 West Fifth St., Suite E-2, Austin, TX 78703 **Voice:** 512-499-8914 **Fax:** 512-499-0441 **E-mail:** asmith1411@ aol.com **Contact:** Angela Smith, Exec. Dir. **Founded:** 1981 **Open:** Year-round **Admission:** Registration form only **Deadlines:** Varies **Cost:** Classes $35–$75; Workshops $35–$170 **Size-Class:** 15–30

BOASTING 1,600 members from age 8 to 102, the Austin Writers' League offers a wide variety of classes, weekend workshops and study groups. Practical skills are stressed in the classes, which have included "Getting and Working with an Agent" and "A Legal Primer for Writers." The workshops are more craft oriented, such as "Character and Conflict" for writers with works in progress and "Finding Your Voice as a Writer" for beginning writers.

Members qualify for reduced rates on classes and workshops, receive the *Austin Writer,* the monthly newsletter, and may use the resource library and job bank. For more amusement, you can attend special events such as the "Molly's Follies," a fund-raising event featuring nationally syndicated political columnist and author Molly Ivins, or participate in the Texas Literary Touring Program.

Craft of Writing Conference

For fiction and nonfiction writers, poets, screenwriters Hotel in Richardson, near UT Dallas, N of downtown Dallas — University of Texas at Dallas, Center for Continuing Educ., P.O. Box 830688, CN1.1, Richardson, TX 75083 **Voice:** 214-883-2204 **E-mail:** janeth@utdallas.edu **Contact:** Janet Harris **Founded:** 1983 **Open:** 2 days in Sept. **Admission:** Registration form only **Deadlines:** Sept. 1 if you need special accommodations **Cost:** $195 (1 lunch and banquet incl.) **Handicapped Access**

THE CRAFT OF Writing Conference emphasizes the business and technical side of writing. "Make Their Hearts Race: Using Suspense in Fiction," "Can I Say That?—A Writer's Guide to Copyright and Defamation Laws," and "Show and Tell: How to Balance and Pace Your Fiction" were some of the 28 workshops offered in 1996. Editors, agents and authors sit on panels, give workshops and can be approached in between scheduled events. There is a banquet, and a prize is given for the best unpublished manuscripts in a variety of genres. Co-sponsored by the Greater Dallas Writers' Association and the University of Texas at Dallas Center for Continuing Education.

Creative Writing Retreats

For fiction and nonfiction writers, poets Varies — 2340 Guadalupe St., Austin, TX 78705 **Voice:** 512-479-8575 **Contact:** Pat Lee Lewis **Founded:** 1995 **Open:** Year-round **Admission:** Registration form only **Cost:** $55–$100 **Size-Class:** 7

CERTIFIED BY Amherst Writers & Artists, Pat Lee Lewis offers a variety of 1-and 2-day retreats in Texas and Massachusetts throughout the year. The emphasis is on writing—participants write for most of the day, with some time off for discussion, lunch and walking.

Some of the retreats are exclusively for women. Some mix writing and yoga. In each of them you will become inspired by this charismatic, caring, intelligent woman. "Joseph Campbell said: 'Where there is a path, it is someone else's way.' You are the only one who can write your truth. Your voice is the only voice that is perfect for your story, your poem, your thoughts."

Dobie Paisano Fellowships at University of Texas at Austin

For all writers Just outside Austin — Office of Graduate Studies, Univ. of Texas at Austin, Main Bldg. 101, Austin, TX 78712 **Voice:** 512-471-7213 **Fax:** 512-471-7620 **E-mail:** GSANS@UTXDP.DP.UTEXAS.EDU **Contact:** Audrey Slate, Dir. **Founded:** 1967 **Open:** Feb.–July, Aug.–Jan. **Admission:** Application ($10), project outline, writing sample **Deadlines:** Mid Jan. **Cost:** Transportation, meals **Financial Aid:** Stipend **Size-Attendees:** 2 per year

CALLING ALL TEXANS! Here is a fellowship that offers you a place to live and a stipend; the catch is that you have to either live in or write about Texas. Those who apply must be either native Texans, or have lived in Texas for at least 2 years, or have published work that has been substantially identified with Texas. The lodgings are a "simply furnished house" on the late J. Frank Dobie's 265-acre ranch. That's plenty of room to think.

Just west of Austin, the location provides easy access to the lively and stimulating environment of that university city for those times when you want to get away from the isolation of your writing.

North East Texas Writers' Conference

For fiction and nonfiction writers
NTCC campus — Continuing Education, Northeast Texas Community College, P.O. Box 1307, Mount Pleasant, TX 75456 **Voice:** 903-537-4292 **Founded:** 1995 **Open:** 1 Sat. in May **Admission:** Registration form only **Cost:** $45

C O-SPONSORED BY the North East Writer's Organization and the continuing education department of Northeast Texas Community College, this 1-day event attracts local writers. In 1996 four writers shared personal experiences, passing on tips about how to understand what editors want. One spoke on "Telling Tales about East Texas Neighbors," a discussion of developing "characters from your own backyard." Another spoke on "the difficult art of balancing humor and pain in mystery novels."

Rice University Writers' Conference

For fiction and nonfiction writers, poets, playwrights, screenwriters *Downtown Houston — Rice University, School of Continuing Studies, MS 550, 6100 Main St., Houston, TX 77005* **Voice:** 713-527-4803 **Fax:** 713-527-285-5213 **E-mail:** scs@rice.edu **Open:** 2 days in early June **Admission:** Registration form only **Cost:** $215 (luncheons extra) **Size-Attendees:** 300

P RACTICAL MATTERS dominate in these workshops, which are organized by genres: mysteries, children's and young adult books, poetry, fiction, short stories and screenplays/plays. Participants can follow one track and attend 5 workshops per day in that genre, or attend workshops on a variety of genres.

The panels highlight topical and infrequently discussed subjects, such as trends in African-American and Hispanic publishing. Over 40 speakers make presentations, including such best-selling writers as Rita Mae Brown and both local and New York-based editors and agents. Houston's Council of Writers invites writers to bring works-in-progress to their "informal Critique Corners" for evaluation and guidance. The emphasis at this event is definitely on career development, especially for the beginning writer.

Romance Writers of America National Conference

For romance writers *Hotels in various cities — 13700 Veterans Memorial Dr., Suite 315, Houston, TX 77014* **Voice:** 713-440-6885 **Fax:** 713-440-7510 **Founded:** 1980 **Open:** July 30–Aug. 3, 1997; July 29–Aug. 2, 1998 **Admission:** Registration form only **Deadlines:** June 1 **Cost:** $300–$350 (some meals incl.) **Size-Attendees:** 2,000 per conference

R OMANCE NOVELS, according to Romance Writers of America account for 49% of all mass-market sales, racking up $885 million annually sales. Mostly females writing for females, romance writers gather annually for a gigantic conference that attracts over 2,000 people. The meeting will take place in Orlando, Florida, in 1997 and in Anaheim, California, in 1998. That means you can attend the conference and visit the Disneyland cosmos, too!

The brochure for the 1996 conference, "Deep in the Heart ... RWA '96," wins the prize for the most user-friendly guide to a conference. Along with a list of nearly 100 agents and editors who will attend, there is an article with tips to help you through those potentially high-pressured editor and/or agent appointments. There is also a letter welcoming first-timers with information on how to get from the airport to the conference site, as well as providing advice on what clothes to bring. While some may scoff at such detail, it is critical information if you intend to do serious, effective networking.

There are at least 2 tracks for participants. The Basic Skills track serves newcomers. The workshops in advanced writing techniques and career enhancement are designed for members of the Professional Authors Network (PAN) to serve the pro. In addition, there are exclusive sessions for PAN members to meet with editors from the various presses in attendance, including such houses as: Bantam, Dutton, Harper, Warner, Harlequin, St. Martin's, Avon.

Special events include a "Welcome Reception" and a "Literacy Reception." The Literacy Reception is one of the first events during the conference. Published authors gather, autograph their books and are available to the press for interviews. The autographed books are then sold to conference attendees and the public, and the money raised goes to support literacy projects.

In addition to the writing workshops, conference "EXTRA!" workshops range far and wide: "Guns: Contemporary and Historical," "Native American Spirituality," "The Lure of Medieval London, 1100–1400."

RWA is a network of over 7,800 writers, with regional chapters throughout the country. Its monthly magazine includes news on contests and conferences, as well as articles on writers, books and the business side of writing.

Each of the chapters is an independent organization, and many schedule their own conferences throughout the year.

Texas Academic Programs

University of Houston, Creative Writing Program, English Dept., Houston, TX 77204; 713-743-3015; MFA Creative Writing

University of North Texas, English Dept., UNT Box 13827, Denton, TX 76203; 817-565-2114; MA English (creative thesis)

Southwest Texas State University, English Dept., 601 University Dr., San Marcos, TX 78666; 512-245-2163; MFA Creative Writing

Texas Tech University, English Dept., Box 43091, Lubbock, TX 79409; 806-742-2501; MA and PhD English (creative writing emphasis/specialization and dissertation)

University of Texas at Austin, English Dept., Austin, TX 78712; 512-471-4991; MA English (creative writing concentration)

University of Texas at Austin, Texas Center for Writers, Austin, TX 78713; 512-471-1601; MFA Creative Writing

University of Texas, Dallas, Humanities Dept., Box 830688, Richardson, TX 75083; 214-883-2756; MA and PhD Humanities (creative writing concentration)

University of Texas, El Paso, English Dept., El Paso, TX 79968; 915-747-5731; MFA Creative Writing (with bilingual option)

Utah

Desert Writers Workshop

For fiction and creative nonfiction writers, poets Ranch retreat 13 mi. S of Moab — Canyonlands Field Institute, P.O. Box 68, Moab, UT 84532 **Voice:** 801-259-7750 **Fax:** 801-259-2335 **Open:** 4 days in Oct. or Nov. **Admission:** Application **Cost:** $400 (lodging and meals incl.) **Financial Aid:** Loans; Scholarship **Size-Attendees:** 30 per conference **Size-Class:** 10

WHEN YOU FIRST arrive at Pack Creek Ranch, the palpable western character of the place is striking, for what is now an inn was once a working ranch. During the workshop participants live, eat and work at the ranch.

The three genres offered in workshops here are fiction, creative nonfiction and poetry. While there are opportunities to meet the other faculty and participants, your writing efforts are concentrated in a single workshop with 1 faculty member. A panel featuring all 3 writer/workshop leaders focuses on a theme; in 1996, "Humor and Beauty."

Because there are only 30 participants in the program, it can be a more intimate experience than most conferences and increases the possibility that you will receive close attention from the faculty. There has usually been an optional naturalist-guided hike one day to introduce you to the striking landscape.

Make time for visits to Arches and Canyonlands National Parks.

Canyonlands Field Institute "encourages writers, as important record-keepers and influencers of civilization ... to think creatively about their own relationship to Nature, to explore the vital connections between human communities and the environment, and to

The Lodge at Pack Creek Ranch, Moab

"Humor and Beauty"

Poet Karen Chamberlain, literary advisor to Canyonlands Field Institute and former director of the Aspen Writers' Workshop, describes the theme for the panel discussion at the Desert Writers Workshop in 1996: "We're sometimes so concerned to protect what we perceive as the 'fragile' desert landscape that we forget that up until recently it was quite well-equipped to protect itself, thank you. The desert has a humor and absurdity all its own, well but not solely conveyed by Coyote tales and more macabre spirit-stories. There is a lightness, or perhaps a 'rightness' about some of the desert's evolutionary adaptations that makes them seem designed by a jokester, prankster, or at least a cartoonist. "We're fortunate to have with us this year three faculty members whose writing reflects the unabashed, robust, sometimes frolicsome, sometimes fatalistic spirit of the land. We'll explore such questions as 'How does humor open us to the world around us?' or 'Is there a type of humor that makes us more receptive to landscape and living beings? Is there a type that distances us?'"

identify ways their own writing can promote awareness, respect and effective actions to sustain the earth."

Four Corners School of Outdoor Education

For nature and natural history writers, poets, and artists in selected other disciplines San Juan River, SE Utah — P.O. Box 1029, Monticello, UT 84535 **Voice:** 801-587-2156 **Fax:** 801-587-2193 **E-mail:** <fcs@igc. apc.org> **Contact:** Janet Ross, Dir. **Founded:** 1984 **Open:** May–Oct. **Admission:** Registration form only **Cost:** $800–$1,050 (meals and lodging incl.) **Financial Aid:** Scholarship

THE FOUR CORNERS School of Outdoor Education combines river rafting, camping and hiking trips with a wide range of workshops, including studies in archaeology, environmental studies, natural history and wilderness advocacy. The good news is that there are several trips designed especially for writers.

The school's mission is to use the Colorado Plateau as an outdoor classroom, to educate "people of all ages and backgrounds about the need to preserve the natural and cultural treasure" that the Southwest offers. If you have never been to the Four Corners area—where Utah, New Mexico, Colorado and Arizona come together—you can look forward to experiencing its strange and awe-inspiring beauty. This is a desert landscape, marked by huge structures that give Monument Valley, with its Valley of the Gods, its name. These are monuments created by the earth. They force you to think about geology, the universe, time, space and our place in the Big Picture.

If you are drawn to the Southwest and are intrigued by the idea of mixing river running and writing, you can order a briefing packet for $12 for each trip that interests you.

In 1996 there were weeklong trips during June, July and September on the San Juan River, led by writers and photographers. Journal writing, pho-

tography and drawing were emphasized. "Coming Home: Reading and Writing the San Juan River," as 1 example, combined the study of natural history and writing with an 80-mile float on the river.

Writers at Work Conference

For fiction and nonfiction writers, poets, screenwriters, playwrights Park City, E of Salt Lake City — P.O. Box 1146, Centerville, UT 84014 **Voice:** 801-292-9285 **Web Site:** http://www.ihienv.com/w@ w.html **Founded:** 1985 **Open:** 1 week in July **Admission:** Application **Deadlines:** First come, first served **Cost:** $410; $40 for an afternoon session **Size-Attendees:** 300 per conference **Size-Class:** 16 maximum **Handicapped Access**

NOVELIST AMY TAN commented on this event: "I loved being part of Writers at Work. ... I'd encourage any serious writer to go there, because it's all there—the art of writing, the pragmatics of getting published, and a mountain setting that inspires the writer in all of us."

Writers at Work—this bland literal title may be accurate, but it hardly indicates the buzz of excitement that emanates from this annual event. Mornings are reserved for small workshops, each led by an accomplished writer in one of a variety of genres. Afternoons and evenings are for readings, panels, lectures and discussions.

Park City is an exceptional setting. At 7,000 feet in the Wasatch Mountains, there are numerous possibilities for outdoor adventures, but you may see an occasional thundershower. Try a walk to an alpine lake, or mountain-bike, play golf or go horseback riding.

One attraction of a conference featuring well-known members of the literati is that it fuels the fantasy, ever present, that you just might meet someone who takes a fancy to your writing and then, who knows ... doors open, and "the rest is history." According to the grapevine, this was the conference where Rick Bass and Pam Houston were "quite literally discovered." Perhaps this will be your year.

🏠 Utah
Academic Programs

University of Utah, English Dept., Salt Lake City, UT 84112; 801-581-6168; MFA Creative Writing

Vermont

Bread Loaf Writers' Conference

🏠 ✏️ ♻️ **For fiction and literary nonfiction writers, and poets** *Ripton, 7 mi. SE of Middlebury, central VT — Middlebury College, Middlebury, VT 05753* **Voice:** 802-388-3711; during conference: 802-388-7945 **E-mail:** BLWC@mail.middlebury.edu **Web Site:** http://www.middlebury.edu/~blwc **Contact:** Carol Knauss, Admin. **Founded:** 1926 **Open:** 2 weeks in Aug. **Admission:** Contributors, application and sample manuscript; Auditors, application only **Deadlines:** June 15; Apr. 1 for financial aid **Cost:** Contributors, $1,600; Auditors, $1,535; room and board incl. **Financial Aid:** Scholarship; Fellowship; Work/Study **Size-Attendees:** 230 maximum **Size-Class:** 10 maximum

H ALLOWED GROUND here. If you believe the woods and walls can speak, at Bread Loaf you may hear great voices. None other than poet Robert Frost got the ball rolling by convincing Middlebury College to dedicate the farmhouse and cottages on the nearby Battell estate to the purpose of en-

couraging new writing. A young editor, John Farrar (later of Farrar, Straus and Giroux), organized the first session. Bread Loaf never looked back.

A subsequent Bread Loaf director, poet John Ciardi, commented, "No great writer ever became one in isolation. Somewhere and some time, if only at the beginning, he had to experience the excitement and intellectual ferment of a group something like this." Indeed, Bread Loaf became the model for scores of other conferences.

Participants are either "Contributors" or "Auditors." The former submit manuscripts for rigorous private and group discussion. The latter attend all classes and readings but do not bring their own work for discussion at the conference. Either way it's a heady environment, made all the more inspiring by a gorgeous setting—Vermont's green hills and national forest. The college town of Middlebury is fully civilized (espresso, bookshops, boutiques), but attendees have an intense literary schedule at the conference. This is not a holiday outing.

While classes focus on the craft of writing, lectures take up special topics ("The Role of Place in Literature," "Good Messiness"). Panels of editors, agents

Students at Bread Loaf Writers' Conference

and publishers visit in order to discuss the publishing business and how to submit your work.

Serious networking ensues. The roll call of well-known writer/teachers at Bread Loaf is impressive. Do the names Benet, Frost, Ransom, Stegner, MacLeish and Auden ring any bells? Among those who came here as young writers and then climbed to the stars are Welty, Roethke, Sexton, Didion and Morrison. If you want to be the next Bread Loafer, apply early, expect to be wait-listed, and in any case be sure to submit only your most polished work in fiction, nonfiction or poetry. Children's book writers and other specialty genres are not welcome here.

Fellowships and scholarships are available to those who have previously published. Competition is stiff. Work-study scholarships (dining-room labor...) are a possibility for first-time participants and as-yet-unpublished writers.

On Working Alone

Some love it. Some hate it. Every writer has to face it. Workshops, conferences and some artists' colonies provide opportunities to schmooze, but the real work happens when you're alone. How to make the best of it?

Set a regular time, each day, each week, when your writing and nothing else gets undivided attention. Give family and friends fair warning: You're not answering the phone or going out for coffee.

Choose a high-energy and fertile-imagination period for your work—top of the day, late at night, right after a jog ... whatever suits you best. Least likely periods are just after meals or when tightly scheduled appointments may encroach.

Establish a regular writing place where you, your muse and your computer or typewriter can convene without having to shuffle other papers (keep the bills out of sight!) or shoo the kids or housemates away. Your setup needn't be expensive or elegant, but a few totemic items (I use my grandfather's fountain pen) may lend comfort or serve to get the juices flowing.

Always draft at least a paragraph, or a verse or two, even though you may not finish much else in this session. If the time goes into plotting, outlining, background reading, spell-checking or whatever, that is okay—it's all part of the job.

Keep the business side of your writing separate from the creative side. During sacred writing time, no query letters, mailing-list maintenance, or office-supplies ordering!

Tempt yourself with rewards. We all want them and need them, and often the promise of even a little one goes a long way toward spurring us on. Reward yourself with a late-afternoon walk, a treat from the bakery, an unnecessary call to a friend ... but only after you've put your sacred writing time to full and good use.

Dorothy Canfield Fisher Writers' Conference

⬚ ⬚ **For fiction and nonfiction writers** Sheraton Hotel, Burlington — P.O. Box 1058, Waitsfield, VT 05673 **Voice:** 802-496-3271 **Fax:** 802-496-7271 **Contact:** Kitty Werner **Founded:** 1989 **Open:** 1 weekend in late June **Admission:** Open **Cost:** $160 conference and workshops (meals incl.); $340 with hotel); discounts for League of Vermont Writers members

EMPHASIZING commercial fiction and nonfiction, including the romance novel, this 2-day workshop brings in editors and agents who actually buy the kinds of material discussed here. Among the bright lights are young, upwardly mobile agent Sheree Bykofsky and Pulitzer Prize-winning memoirist Ron Powers. Alas, manuscript review is not permitted, but schmoozing and networking are encouraged.

Dorset Colony House

⬚ **For all writers** SE Vermont—P.O. Box 519, Dorset, VT 05251 **Voice:** 802-867-2223 **Contact:** John Nassivera, Dir. **Founded:** 1980 **Open:** Late Mar.–late May; mid-Sept.–late Nov. **Admission:** Application letter, project description, resume **Cost:** $95 per week (minimum $60), plus food **Size-Attendees:** 8 resident artists

HOW DOES AN 1880s railroad executive's mansion in a small town (on the National Register of Historic Places) with a population of 550 sound as a writers' retreat? DCH provides quiet, unstructured writing time in a quintessentially rural New England setting—although only minutes down the road is Manchester Center, with enough upscale boutiques (including a superior bookstore) to quench any shopper's thirst.

No more than 8 writers (most often playwrights, reflecting the linkage to the Dorset Playhouse) or other artists are in residence at one time, most for about a month (longer stays are feasible). DCH welcomes new writers as well as Pulitzer Prize and Academy Award winners. Residents prepare their own meals in a common kitchen, and a handsome library with fireplace is the focal point for evening conversation. When you put down your pen, the surrounding Green Mts. beckon for recreation year-round.

Olders' Travel Writing Workshop

⬚ **For travel writers** Various resorts in VT — Box 163, Albany, VT 05820 **Voice:** 802-755-6774 **Fax:** 802-755-6216 **Contact:** Jules and Effin Older, Dirs. **Open:** 1-day events throughout the year **Cost:** $175 (lunch incl.) **Size-Class:** 16

PARTICIPANTS write rave reviews of these seasonal 1-day travel writing workshops, praising the how-to handouts and encouragement offered by veteran travel writers Jules and Effin Older. Emphasing how to get the gig and maximize the ancillary benefits (free airline fares, lodging, etc.), the Olders bring a colorful array of writing and other work experiences to their teaching. They are especially strong on writing for the winter sports market. In 1 intensive daylong session, expect to hear about travel computers, ethical dilemmas in travel writing, electronic rights, hot contacts and other useful information. Unabashedly commercial.

Discount lodging packages are available for participants.

Summer Writing Program, University of Vermont

🏠 📝 *For fiction and nonfiction writers, and poets* NW VT, on Lake Champlain — Continuing Education, UVM, 322 S. Prospect St., Burlington, VT 05401 **Voice:** 802-656-5796; 800-639-3210 **Fax:** 802-656-0306 **E-mail:** summer.writing.prog@moose.uvm.edu **Web Site:** http://uvmce.edu:443/sumwrite.htm **Contact:** Cara Worthley, Coord. **Founded:** 1994 **Open:** May - July **Admission:** Application form ($25), manuscript sample, brief bio, personal statement **Cost:** VT residents $790 credit or non-credit; nonresidents $790 noncredit, $1,595 credit; university housing $675 for 2 weeks, $950 for 3 weeks (available July only) **Size-Class:** 12 **Handicapped Access**

AMONG THE newer and more attractive university-based summer workshops, UVM's program is well thought out and well staffed, and couldn't be situated in a lovelier place. The campus is fine enough, but the city of Burlington and its spectacular Lake Champlain waterfront (with an Adirondack Mountains panorama) go over the top.

Introductory and advanced workshops in several genres provide avenues for all varieties of writers here, including those with publications to their credit. Two standout nonfiction writers offered workshops at UVM in 1996: journalist Tom Wicker (writing about politics) and memoirist/travel writer William Least Heat-Moon (writing about "people and places"). Other staff have equally colorful credentials. While the program serves more Vermonters than outlanders, all are welcome. Graduate and undergraduate credit available.

University of Vermont, Church Street Center

📝 *For fiction and nonfiction writers, and poets* NE VT, about 4 mi. N of Burlington — 30 S. Park Dr., Colchester, VT 05446 **Voice:** 802-656-5800; 800-639-3188 **Fax:** 802-656-3891 **Contact:** Carol Fournier-Gunter, Program Mgr. **Open:** Year-round **Admission:** Registration form only **Cost:** $75–$100 per course **Size-Class:** Small groups **Degree or Certification:** Some classes may be taken for credit. **Handicapped Access**

BEAUTIFULLY situated Burlington doesn't need it, but this program is proof that the quality of life is as high as the mountains near this thriving Vermont university city. One of the more colorful adult (continuing) education programs we've seen, CSC's cornucopia covers everything from arts and crafts to writing. Classes for writers on nuts and bolts ("Grammar for Adults"), "Poet Aerobics" (beginners practicing many styles of writing) and "Writing as a Path to Personal Depth" suggest the breadth of opportunities.

Serving generally a local population, and generally those who do not seek academic credit.

Vermont Studio Center

🏠 *For fiction and nonfiction writers, and poets* N central VT, about 40 mi. from Burlington—Box 613, Johnson, VT 05656 **Voice:** 802-635-2727 **Fax:** 802-635-2730 **Contact:** Neil Shepard, Coord. **Founded:** 1984 **Open:** Year-round **Admission:** Application form ($25), portfolio, resume, references **Cost:** Studio Session, $1,200; Residencies, $750 for 2 weeks, $1,400 for 4 weeks (room and board incl.) **Financial Aid:** Loans; Fellowship; Work/Study **Size-Attendees:** 500 per year

THERE SHOULD BE more like this one. Either of Vermont Studio Center's 2 programs for emerging and mid-career writers is well worth the dollars and the trip to isolated northern Vermont.

Writing "Studio Sessions" are 2-week intensive retreats with distraction-free time and access to 2 resident writers, who lead workshops, critique new work, and offer private conferences. Evening readings by resident writers and by participants alternate with slide shows by the visual artists (painters, sculptors) who share VSC. In 1996 among the numerous skilled and seasoned resident writers (1 week each) were nonfiction master Noel Perrin (*First Person Rural*) and poet/translator Robert Pinsky.

Writing residencies here run for 1 month year-round and are basically unstructured: you make the best use of your own time.

Accommodations are in several Victorian homes in tiny Johnson (VSC's brochure says pop. 2,500; Rand McNally shrinks it to 1,470), where linens, lamps, writing tables and meals (drawing on an organic garden) are all provided.

Residents have access to the Studio Session workshops and conferences, and also to the facilities at Johnson State College.

Caveat: Be sure you want small-town life before venturing north here. Although the local college is lively, and VSC itself offers warm collegiality, and Montreal is "only" 2 hours away, this is decidedly *not* Soho.

Wildbranch Workshop

✏️ *For fiction writers, essayists, journalists* N central VT, 1½ hr. from Burlington—Sterling College, Craftsbury Common, VT 05827 **Voice:** 802-586-7711; 800-648-3591 **Fax:** 802-586-2596 **Contact:** David Brown, Dir. **Founded:** 1987 **Open:** 1 week in June **Admission:** Aplication form, writing samples **Deadlines:** Mid-May **Cost:** $625; room and board $150 (dormitory) **Financial Aid:** Scholarship **Size-Attendees:** 30 maximum

BRING YOUR binoculars and butterfly net to this one. Emphasizing environmental writing—fiction or nonfiction—Wildbranch offers sessions in journalism, natural history, conservation and publisher/editor perspectives. If you're a (politically) green writer or love writing about the green world, this is your locale.

The staff includes residential and visiting faculty, all with substantial environmental writing and/or editing credentials, some with field biology experience, too. Their wide familiarity with freelancing opportunities is beneficial to workshop participants, who can discuss manuscripts in conference with selected faculty.

Wildbranch uses the campus of lovely Sterling College, in a town popular as an outdoor recreation destination.

🏠 Vermont Academic Programs

Bennington College, Bennington Writing Seminars, Bennington, VT 05201; MA, MFA Writing and Literature

Goddard College, Plainfield, VT 05667; MFA Creative Writing

Vermont College of Norwich University, Montpelier, VT 05602; MFA in Creative Writing

Virginia

Associated Writing Programs

For all writers and teachers of writing Changes annually—Tallwood House, Mailstop 1E3, George Mason University, Fairfax, VA 22030 **Voice:** 703-993-4301 **Fax:** 703-993-4302 **E-mail:** awp@gmu.edu **Web Site:** http://web.gmu.edu/departments/AWP **Contact:** Markham Johnson, Dir. **Founded:** 1967 **Open:** Apr. **Admission:** Registration form only **Cost:** $135; $115 for AWP members **Size-Attendees:** 1,000

THIS WELL-PLANNED and -executed conference, which has grown exponentially over the last few years, shifts its site each year and changes its theme as well. In 1996 the theme was "Writers of the South," including tributes to the major players: Faulkner, O'Connor, Dickey, (Alice) Walker and others. Seminar leaders and plenary session speakers are published writers and experienced teachers, though to our eyes the names did not suggest world class, as is the case at some other similar conferences. Nonetheless, AWP is itself a top-notch writers' service organization. You can't go wrong investing some time here, and how could a conference that schedules a Saturday night dance-blowout with a band named "Yuppie Scum" be all bad?

AWP proudly asserts that it serves 16,000 writers and 285 college and university writing programs, providing people with creative writing programs, opportunities for publishing, a job search service, and occasions for exchanging ideas on the professions of writing and the teaching of writing. The annual conference is but one such event. You can also check out the *AWP Chronicle* (a bimonthly magazine); the *AWP Official Guide to Writing Programs* (which lists more academic programs than we could include in this book, though it does not evaluate them); the

AWP professional standards lobbying and advocacy work; and the AWP awards series.

All services are available to AWP members; some entail an additional fee.

Another admirable offshoot of AWP is IWC, the International Writers Center (at Old Dominion University, 1411 West 49th St., Norfolk, VA 23529; 804-683-3839). IWC finds international writers for U.S. events and plans to sponsor a readings series; several publications may intrigue or assist those hoping to work abroad (*IWC Journal, IWC Guide to International Literary Opportunities*).

For writers who feel the need to connect with others in the profession, especially those in the university circuit, AWP (like Poets & Writers in New York) is a good place to look. The conference has grown so large, however, that those who seek a quiet, intimate setting for manuscript discussion may want to shop elsewhere.

Highland Summer Conference

For all writers VA highlands, 36 mi. SW of Roanoke — Box 7014, Radford University, Radford, VA 24142 **Voice:** 540-831-5366 **Contact:** Jo Ann Asbury, Dir. **Founded:** 1977 **Open:** 1 week in mid-June **Admission:** Registration form only **Deadlines:** June 1 **Cost:** $25 **Size-Attendees:** 20 **Degree or Certification:** Undergraduate and graduate credit available

VIRGINIA'S Highland Conference has the theme "Appalachian Culture and Writing," and that's a big umbrella. Seminars and evening presentations may range from traditional literary events to music or folktales. Instructors here are themselves steeped in the regional culture of the southern Appalachian mountains. It's refreshing to see a conference staffed by people whose day jobs may not be at Ivy League campuses or New York publishing houses but whose publishing credits in the smaller, high-quality literary journals are substantial. One leader at the 1996 conference (Bill Brown) is a high-school writing teacher whose innovative work with his students has led them into print many times over. Elizabeth McCommon (an Appalachian singer, musician and actress) offers a seminar on performance skills.

Housing is inexpensive, in college dorms. The conference fee is bargain basement (unless you want academic credit). Highland offers a rare chance for some immersion in writing and the regional culture without spending a fortune. Radford University offers an academic program in Appalachian Studies.

Concurrent with Highland is the Selu Writer's Retreat, an opportunity to use the college facilities as a haven from worldly distractions during a 1- or 2-week stay. Ask for details.

Shenandoah International Playwrights Retreat

For playwrights *Shenandoah Valley, NE VA Pennyroyal Farm — Box 167-F, Staunton, VA 24401* **Voice:** 703-248-1868 **Contact:** Robert Small, Dir. **Founded:** 1977 **Open:** Mid- to late summer **Admission:** Bio, draft of play **Deadlines:** Feb. 1 **Financial Aid:** Fellowship **Size-Attendees:** 15

THERE MAY BE nothing else like this in the U.S., and more's the pity. Driven by an idealistic sense that the arts are a bridge among all world cultures, SIPR brings together playwrights (screenwriters welcome) from the U.S. and far-flung countries to develop their own works and to cross-fertilize with one another. A resident acting company (with a director and dramaturge) helps the playwrights see their work take shape on a daily basis. This is a rare opportunity for writers of drama, who often wait years to see or hear their words embodied on the stage.

After several weeks of work at the Shenandoah site, the entire troupe travels to the Big Apple for performances (staged readings) of each writer's new play in the Festival of New Works for a New World. Visiting foreign playwrights have come from 16 countries and 6 con-

tinents, U.S. writers from 38 states. A heady brew.

All writers here are on full fellowship, including room, board and transportation. Competition is stiff. This is a program for mature writers. Rewards are commensurate.

Virginia Center for the Creative Arts

For all writers, and artists in selected other disciplines *SW VA, 160 mi. from Washington, DC — Admissions Committee, Box VCCA, Sweet Briar, VA 24595* **Voice:** 804-946-7236 **Contact:** William Smart, Dir. **Founded:** 1971 **Open:** Year-round **Admission:** Application form ($20), resume, work samples, references **Cost:** $35 suggested daily fee for 2-week residencies; $30 for longer residencies **Financial Aid:** Fellowship **Size-Attendees:** 24 resident artists

THOUGH VCCA is not nearly as old nor as steeped in legend as the MacDowell Colony or Yaddo—indeed it's the young stepchild of both, a mere quarter century of age—it has become the biggest year-round artists' colony in the U.S. and without doubt one of the finest. Serving a variety of artists including writers, VCCA offers its residents that rare chance to commingle with artists in other disciplines while at the same time focusing intensely on their own. The results are often sparkling, and the VCCA correspondence file shows that residents here are amazed at how much work they accomplish while holed up in their private studio at the VCCA's Mt. San Angelo estate. Books finished, stories and poems published, readings given and awards won seem to be the standard aftermath of a writer's stay at VCCA.

Competition for a residency here is tough. The application hurdles are high. Call for details, and anticipate pulling together a full portfolio, which will be reviewed by an external committee of professional artists. Expect also that you may not get in the first time you apply and may not get the residency period you asked for. These caveats aside, the news from VCCA is all good.

Residential "Fellows" here set their own schedules, and many keep their nose to the grindstone for 12 hours and 7 days at a stretch. The writers' and other artists' studios (converted barns in the Norman fieldstone style) are sanctum sanctorums: No visitors allowed. As at MacDowell, lunch appears magically in a basket at the studio doorstep, with no interruption, thank you. During an average residency of 5 weeks, it's no wonder a lot gets done.

After a manor house burned down some years ago, VCCA built a state-of-the-art residence for its Fellows, with individually heated (passive solar) and cooled bedrooms, and common rooms including a library and dining hall. While readings, concerts and the like are frequent here, they are impromptu; there is no program of distracting public events. For a breath of fresh air, how do 12 acres of lawns with boxwood hedges and a swimming pool sound? Or wander farther afield while waiting for the muse to call you—over the entire 450-acre estate in the foothills of the Blue Ridge Mts.

Nearby Sweet Briar College (for women) owns the property, leasing it to VCCA and also providing valuable access to the college library and athletic facilities, plus a ready-made audience for VCCA artists' presentations.

Studio complex, Virginia Center for the Creative Arts, Sweet Briar

Quality of credentials and seriousness of purpose determine who gets into VCCA, not one's capacity to pay. The suggested daily fees for those who can pay are modest and well worth the investment for the freedom to work that's part of the exchange. Try to buy this freedom elsewhere and you'll see what we mean.

VCCA also sponsors international programs for artists, including residencies in Germany and Ireland.

🏠 Virginia Academic Programs

George Mason University, Dept. of English, Fairfax, VA 22030; MFA Creative Writing

Old Dominion University, Dept. of English, Norfolk, VA 23529; MFA Creative Writing

University of Virginia, Dept. of English, 115 Wilson Hall, Charlottesville, VA 22903; MFA Creative Writing

Virginia Commonwealth University, Dept. of English, Richmond, VA 23284; MFA Creative Writing

Washington

Centrum Artist Residency Program

🏠 📝 *For all writers, and artists in selected other disciplines* Fort Worden State Park, 2 mi. from Port Townsend — P.O. Box 1158, Port Townsend, WA 98368 **Voice:** 360-385-3102 **Fax:** 360-385-2470 **Founded:** 1978 **Open:** Sept.–May **Admission:** Application ($10), project description, copy of your most recent publication **Deadlines:** Oct. 1 **Cost:** Transportation, meals **Financial Aid:** Stipend **Size-Attendees:** 15–20 per year

HERE IS A WAY TO work on your writing while living in on the northwestern tip of the spectacular Olympic Peninsula. The Centrum Artists Residency Program provides a month-long stay in a cottage overlooking the Strait of Juan de Fuca, on land that was once used as a military fort and is now a 445-acre state park . There are beaches and walking trails. When the sky is clear you can see islands, the shipping lanes and 2 different mountain ranges.

And although you are located in an immense park, you are only 2 miles from picturesque and arty Port Townsend. So when it's time to see people, just walk out your door, stretch your legs and make your way to town. The cottage has no phone, no television, no radio.

Centrum—A Center for the Arts and Education initiated the Port Townsend Writers Conference and offers workshops, festivals and concerts in the summer; silence, solitude and space for writers and artists are its mission the rest of the year. (See also Port Townsend Writers' Conference.)

Clarion West Science Fiction and Fantasy Writers Workshop

For science fiction and fantasy writers Seattle Central Community College — 340 15th Ave. E., Suite 350, Seattle, WA 98112 **Voice:** 206-322-9083 **Founded:** 1984 **Open:** 6 weeks in June–July **Admission:** Application ($25), manuscript, personal statement **Deadlines:** Apr. 1 **Cost:** $1,300; dorm room $750 **Financial Aid:** Scholarship **Size-Class:** 20

HERE IS A PROGRAM specially designed for the science fiction and fantasy writer by Clarion West, an association of writers in these genres. The workshop admits only 20 people, each of whom must want to become a professional writer. Workshops, readings, informal discussions and gatherings fill the 6 weeks. In 1996 the 6 instructors included 5 authors and an editor of science fiction, each with an impressive background in the field.

The organizers recommend that you stay in the dorms on campus, where the workshop occurs. College credit is available for an additional fee. There aren't too many writers' workshops for science fiction writers, so even if this particular one does not fit your needs, it may be worth a call to the organizers at Clarion West to discover what else might be available in the field.

Cottages at Hedgebrook, A Retreat for Women

For novelists, playwrights, poets, journalists, essayists, short story writers screenwriters On Whidbey Island, about 1½ hr. N of Seattle — 2197 E. Millman Rd., Langley, WA 98260 **Voice:** 360-321-4786 **Founded:** 1988 **Open:** Mid-Jan. to mid-June, July to mid-Dec. **Admission:** Application ($15), writing sample, project description **Deadlines:** Oct. 1 for Jan.–June; Apr. 1 for July–mid-Dec. **Cost:** Transportation **Financial Aid:** Scholarship **Size-Attendees:** 6 at a time

THIS IS A DREAM residency for women writers: For up to 3 months, your own timber-frame cottage set amidst woods and meadows on an island. Gardens you can work in. Ponds, waterfall, brook, forest. You are pam-

At work in a corner of a cottage at Hedgebrook writers' colony, Langley

pered. Fed nightly at a communal meal in the farmhouse. Brought lunch in a basket to your door. Given supplies so that you can make your own breakfast.

Once, only the rich, very lucky or extremely talented had access to such places. But at Hedgebrook diversity is highly valued and reflected in the residents, the board and the selection committee. Generally half of the residents are women of color.

The most compelling reasons for coming to this retreat are expressed by prior residents: "At Hedgebrook I felt, truly for the first time, alive with my ideas—friendly with them. Time took on an unnatural shimmer, in which I could wake up and not write and still feel connected to my work or I could work late into the enormous night and feel the pulse of the natural world around me, sensing its place in my own writing. I laughed and ate well, I took long walks along hilly roads, I gobbled blackberries till I thought I might burst, I cried hard bitter tears at the fear of my own work and the terror I had in telling the truth, my truth." (Karyn Kiyoko Kusama)

ple," "Women's Voices in the Wild" and "Art & Poetry in the Wild" were among the 1996 workshops sponsored by NCI. The program changes annually. Academic credit is available.

Accommodations for the various workshops vary widely, from Brown's Farm B & B, which sleeps 13 in 3 separate cabins, each with its own kitchen; to a lodge with hot tub; to camping under the stars. Prices reflect the differences in amenities.

"There is no such thing as bad weather, only inappropriate clothing"—a quote from the NCI catalogue. At NCI there is a deep affinity for the Northwest; they know how to live in—and appreciate—this wet and glorious environment.

NCI, a nonprofit educational organization, cooperates with various other organizations, such as Elderhostel, to sponsor sessions for adults over 55; NCI also works with the U.S. Forest Service to train eagle watchers. Every year NCI joins with the National Park Service and a wide number of teachers, naturalists and other professionals to develop programs to increase the understanding and appreciation of the Pacific Northwest.

North Cascades Institute

For nature writers, poets, environmental journalists, and artists in selected other disciplines North Cascades, from Puget Sound to the Columbia River — 2105 State Route 20, Sedro-Woolley, WA 98284 **Voice:** 360-856-5700 **Fax:** 360-856-1934 **E-mail:** ncascades@igc.apc.org **Contact:** Saul Weisberg, Exec. Dir. **Open:** Mar.–Oct. **Admission:** Registration form only **Deadlines:** First come, first served **Cost:** $95–$175 (food and lodging incl.) **Financial Aid:** Scholarship **Size-Class:** 8–15

AT NORTH CASCADES Institute, the emphasis is on natural history field seminars focusing on the Northwest. Leaders for the 3- to 5-day workshops include poets, writers and naturalists. "Exploring a Sense of Place," "Writing in the Wilderness for Busy Peo-

Olympic Field Seminars

For fiction and nonfiction writers, poets, and artists in selected other disciplines Olympic National Park — Olympic Park Institute, 111 Barnes Point Rd., Port Angeles, WA 98363 **Voice:** 360-928-3720; 800-775-3720 **Fax:** 360-928-3046 **Web Site:** http://www.olympus.net/opi/ **Contact:** Anna Manildi, Dir. **Founded:** 1984 **Open:** Apr.–Oct. **Admission:** Registration form only **Deadlines:** First come, first served **Cost:** $75–$285 (some include meals, lodging) **Financial Aid:** Scholarship **Size-Class:** 8–18

IMAGINE backpacking with poet and naturalist Tim McNulty, who co-authored *Olympic National Park, Where the Mountain Meets the Sea* for a weekend workshop called "Poetry in the

Wild." Or if you are not a backpacker, you could choose a prose writing workshop based at Rosemary Inn, the Olympic Park Institute's main campus. Take your meals while looking out at Lake Crescent. Explore the rugged beauty of the Northwest. Read, write, talk. Listen, look, write some more.

OPI's many workshops were established to serve a mission: "to inspire environmental stewardship through education."

Naturalist, butterfly expert and author Robert Michael Pyle taught "Writing From Home" in 1996, a weekend workshop set on Pyle's home turf. In his workshop, he shares his insights while leading a walk on a wild beach and through an old-growth spruce forest.

In addition to OPI's writing workshops, there are seminars on birds, intertidal life, the ecology of the Olympic lowlands, Pacific Northwest culture, history and crafts. Call to find out what's scheduled this year.

Pacific Northwest Writers Conference

📝 ♻️ *For fiction and nonfiction writers* Downtown Seattle — 2033 Sixth Ave., #804, Seattle, WA 98121 **Voice:** 206-443-3807 **Founded:** 1956 **Open:** Summer **Admission:** Registration form only **Cost:** $290–$310 (day rates available) **Size-Attendees:** Nearly 1,000

WITH AROUND 1,000 writers attending, the Pacific Northwest Writers Conference is one of those huge events held in a hotel, with simultaneous workshops scheduled mornings and afternoons, and panels, speakers and appointments squeezed around these sessions. A glamorous awards dinner attracts the crowds. Some writers thrive on these giant events; others run from them. If you live in the Northwest and don't plan on going to New York this year but want to make some literary contacts, this may be the place to do it.

The emphasis is on marketing and other business-related skills; numerous representatives from literary agencies, magazines and publishing houses attend. "Meet the Publishing World!" is a headline for 2 pages of pictures and descriptions in the conference schedule. Simon & Schuster, Putnam, Berkley, Sasquatch Books, Coffee House Press, Norton, Penguin and Blue Heron Press were all present in 1996, as were reps from *Writer's Digest, Redbook,* and *Bicycling.* The conference schedule tells you how to schedule an individual appointment with an editor and/or agent.

Port Townsend Writers' Conference

📝 ♻️ *For fiction and nonfiction writers, poets* Fort Worden State Park, at the tip of the Olympic Peninsula — P.O. Box 1158, Port Townsend, WA 98368 **Voice:** 360-385-3102 **Fax:** 360-385-2470 **Contact:** Carol Bangs, Dir. **Founded:** 1973 **Open:** 10 days in July **Admission:** Registration form, writing sample for manuscript workshop **Deadlines:** July 1 **Cost:** $300–$425 **Financial Aid:** Fellowship **Size-Attendees:** 180 per conference **Size-Class:** 16

THERE ARE 2 different ways to attend the Port Townsend Writers' conference. The more strenuous Manuscript Workshop requires daily 2-hour sessions with an assigned faculty member, in addition to the full range of panels, classes, special events and readings. This option requires that you submit a writing sample and be accepted into one of the workshops. The faculty includes distinguished poets and fiction and creative nonfiction writers, such as novelists Percival Everett and Ursula Hegi.

The Open Enrollment path enables you to attend every event *except* the daily manuscript workshops. There are classes in poetry and/or fiction techniques, journal writing and other topics. With Open Enrollment, you have more free time, which suits those who want to relax, work on their own projects, benefit from the presence of others, but not be tied down to a 2-hour morning workshop. Both beginning and experienced writers may choose this option.

The conference takes place at Fort Worden State Park, on the edge of the Olympic Peninsula, where you can enjoy views of snow-capped mountains, woods, and the Strait of Juan de Fuca. Stroll down to sandy beaches or drive 2 miles to Port Townsend, an historic seaport, popular for its Victorian-style buildings, restaurants, galleries and arts and crafts stores. Olympic National Park and Vancouver Island are 2 outstanding places nearby.

SBPI Writers' Conference

For fiction and nonfiction writers, poets College campus in the Northwest — P.O. Box 2197, Redmond, WA 98073 **Voice:** 206-836-8634; 800-881-4008 **Fax:** 206-868-4022 **Web Site:** http://www. stephenbrunopublishing.com **Contact:** Stephen Bruno **Founded:** 1995 **Open:** 1 weekend in Apr. **Admission:** Registration form only **Cost:** $225, plus $35 per workshop **Financial Aid:** Scholarship **Size-Class:** 30 **Handicapped Access**

WHAT DIFFERENTIATES this conference from almost every other writers' conference is its Interactive Trade Show. Software companies that specialize in supplies for writers participate, demonstrating and even giving away some of their products. If you have been longing to learn how to create your own Web page, here's your chance. There will be step-by-step instruction at the conference so that by the time you leave, you'll have the knowledge and skills you've been seeking.

The conference site moves around, so call to find out where it will be this year. The first year it took place at the University of Oregon in Eugene; the second year at Lake Washington Technical College in Kirkland, just east of Seattle. During 1996 there were workshops focusing on a variety of genres, including "Vampires, Werewolves and Ghosts: Creating Genre Fiction from Literary Lore," "Writing about the Natural World," "Writing for Children" and "Travel Writing." An unusual workshop called "Poetography: brings together photographers and writers in collaborative efforts.

There is a hum of extra energy emanating from (the SB of SBPI). This conference is his dream, and he wants it to serve writers well. Financial support is offered to approximately a third of the participants. There are giveaways, storytelling, music and nightly readings at nearby coffeehouses.

Write On Sound Writers Conference

For fiction and nonfiction writers, poets, screenwriters, playwrights On Puget Sound, 20 min. N of Seattle — Edmonds Arts Commission, 700 Main St., Edmonds, WA 98020 **Voice:** 206-771-0228 **Fax:** 206-771-0253 **Contact:** Christine Weed, Dir. **Founded:** 1985 **Open:** 2 days in Oct. **Admission:** Registration form only **Cost:** $75; $40 for 1 day **Size-Attendees:** 160 **Handicapped Access**

THE EMPHASIS IS on practical advice at the Write On Sound Writers Conference. From "How to Build a Plot" to "Taxes for Writers," these workshops are designed to make you a more savvy, effective writer.

The Edmonds Arts Commission supports this effort. At the 10th-anniversary conference Anne Lamott (*Bird by Bird*) gave the keynote address. Pulitzer Prize-winning journalist William Dietrich and best-selling author Robert Ferrigno were among the speakers.

Writer's Weekend at the Beach

🖊 *For fiction and nonfiction writers,* **poets** *Ocean Park Methodist Retreat Center, 3½ hr. SW of Seattle* — *P.O. Box 877, Ocean Park, WA 98640* **Voice:** 360-665-6576 **Contact:** Birdie Etchison **Founded:** 1991 **Open:** 1 weekend in Feb. **Admission:** Registration form ($35) **Cost:** $110–$125 (room and board incl.)

T HE LONG BEACH Peninsula on the southwest coast is well worth exploring for the way the land and sea meet, and for what each element brings to mind, body and spirit. This weekend brings together an assortment of writers, mostly from the region, to network, share stories and learn from each other. There are 3 consecutive sessions of workshops on Saturday, covering a variety of genres including romance, mystery, poetry, short story, journalism, writing for children and playwriting. The topics scheduled depend on the writers who have been invited to teach the sessions. Sunday morning is reserved for manuscript critiques.

🏠 Washington Academic Programs

Eastern Washington University, Creative Writing Program, English Dept., MS 25, Cheney, WA 99004; 509-359-7064; MFA Creative Writing

University of Washington, Creative Writing Program, English Dept., Box 354330, Seattle, WA 98195; 206-543-9865; MFA Creative Writing

West Virginia

GoldenRod Writers Conference

♻ *For all writers* N central WV — 219 Kingwood St., Morgantown, WV 26505 **Voice:** 304-296-9132 **Fax:** 304-293-6957 **Contact:** George Lies, Dir. **Open:** 1 weekend in mid-Oct. **Admission:** Registration form only **Deadlines:** Early Sept. for manuscript submissions **Cost:** $35 for 1 day, $55 for 3 days; manuscript review $15

P OTPOURRI: a little of this and some of that in a variety of genres makes the schedule of workshops at the GoldenRod Writers Conference attractive to a broad spectrum of writers—most of whom come from the surrounding West Virginia and Pennsylvania area. The instructors here are recruited from the ranks of the region's universities, with the exception of the occasional visiting New Yorker with publishing experience. In 1996 that was Peter Rubie, former fiction editor at Walker and Co., who offered a workshop on fiction writing and on agents and markets.

For a short, smallish conference, the scope of offerings is broad here. Special sessions on historical fiction, feature articles and op-ed columns, young adult writing, and lyrics and music for ballads make the program quite colorful. The very brief (20-minute) manuscript review sessions fall into what we call the "Jiffy Lube" approach to teaching writing: not likely to be worth the time or the dollars. Nonetheless, this inexpensive conference (budget hotel deals available) seems worth investigating if you live within easy driving distance to Morgantown.

Symposium for Professional Food Writers

For food writers *Resort town in WV mountains — The Greenbrier, White Sulphur Springs, WV 24986* **Voice:** 707-963-0777; 800-624-6070 **Fax:** 304-536-7834 **Contact:** Antonia Allegra, Dir. **Open:** 1 weekend in late Mar. **Admission:** Registration form only **Deadlines:** Mid-Feb. for manuscript analysis **Cost:** $350; $145 per person per night for room and 2 meals

GREEN ASPARAGUS stalks and a sharpened pencil poking up from a white chef's toque: the poster art says it all. This symposium attracts celebrity food writers like Julia Child and prominent food editors like Laurie Ochoa (*LA Times*). Writing coaches, agents and numerous top-rank professional chefs and specialty cooks round out the impressive team.

And that's only half the show. The setting is the other half. One year it was San Francisco's Nob Hill (The Stanford Court Hotel); in 1996, The Greenbrier, one of the grand old southern mountain resorts where luxury knows no bounds.

Master chefs and cookbook authors Julia Child and Anne Willan, Symposium for Professional Food Writers, The Greenbrier, White Sulphur Springs

No jeans in the dining room, please! Dine you will, and well, with demonstration meals prepared by prominent chefs.

If you're not comatose in a digestive stupor, the workshops can be valuable, too. Copyright and contract technicalities in one, use of narrative in another, how to sell to editors in a third. Many more. Useful, fun, a great schmooze, tax-deductible, and awesomely self-indulgent.

Wisconsin

Apostle Islands National Lakeshore Artist-in-Residence Program

For fiction and nonfiction writers, poets, and artists in selected other disciplines *Sand Island, in western Lake Superior, off the Bayfield Peninsula — Route 1, Box 4, Bayfield, WI 54814* **Voice:** 715-779-3397 **Contact:** Kate Miller **Open:** Late June–mid-Sept. **Admission:** Application, personal statement, resume, manuscript **Cost:** Food, transportation **Size-Attendees:** 3 per year

APOSTLE ISLANDS National Lakeshore includes 21 of the 22 Apostle Islands and a 12-mile stretch of mainland shoreline off western Lake Superior. This 2-to 3-week residency will appeal to the healthy artist who is in good shape and is eager to live the rustic life. No electricity, no running water, and the ranger is about 3 miles away by boat! All supplies—food and gear (and that includes typewriter!)—must be carried a half mile from the dock to the cabin.

If this sounds appealing, make sure you include with your application a personal statement that describes your ability to meet the challenges of living in a primitive environment, and engagingly explain what you hope to achieve from an island residency. Residents are chosen by a panel of professionals who evaluate not only artistic integrity but also the applicant's ability to live simply in a remote area. Each resident must be willing to relate to park visitors and to donate a finished piece of work that was inspired by their stay on the island.

Clearing

For fiction and nonfiction writers, poets, and artists in selected other disciplines 75 mi. NE of Green Bay, overlooking Lake Michigan — 12183 Garrett Bay Rd., P.O. Box 65, Ellison Bay, WI 54210 **Voice:** 414-854-4088 **Fax:** 414-854-9751 **E-mail:** buchholz@mail.wiscnet.net **Open:** May–Oct. **Admission:** Registration form only **Cost:** $535 (room and board incl.)

THIS "CLEARING" stands for a "clearing of the mind," not a clearing in the woods. Founded by Jens Jensen, a Chicago area architect who at age 75 decided to create a place for adults to withdraw from the man-made world, the Clearing is an independent school offering weeklong courses in writing, arts and nature studies. It was 1935 when Danish-born Jensen moved to the bluffs overlooking the Green Bay in northeastern Wisconsin and built the Clearing. Students still live in the handsome rustic log cabins that Jensen constructed by hand out of indigenous stone and wood. The care and craft that went into Jensen's buildings have been recognized; they have achieved a place on the National Register of Historic Places.

The workshops for writers include poetry, beginning and advanced writing, and creative personal journal writing. Sessions on arts, crafts, music, photography and nature studies—from "Mushrooms of Door County" to "Spring Birds of the Northern Woods and Waters"—are also available.

Trails wind through 100 acres of woods and meadows, and follow cliffs that overlook Lake Michigan.

Great Lakes Writers' Workshop

For fiction and nonfiction writers, poets Alverno College campus — Telesis Institute, Alverno College, 3401 S. 39th St., P.O. Box 343922, Milwaukee, WI 53234 **Voice:** 414-382-6200 **Fax:** 414-382-6354 **Contact:** Debra Pass, Dir. **Founded:** 1986 **Open:** 1 week in July **Admission:** Registration form only **Deadlines:** Early July **Cost:** $99 for complete program, or $20–$30 per workshop **Handicapped Access**

ALVERNO COLLEGE offers 1 week of evening workshops and a Saturday session during July for beginning to semi-professional writers. If you live in or near Milwaukee, this may be the most accessible writing workshop available. Sessions have focused on "Writing Lives: Biography, Autobiography and Writing Family Stories," "Turn Your Travels into Sales," and "Research for Writing—From Rumor to Databases." Instructors include published authors and teachers from Alverno College.

Guest House at New Light Studios

For all writers, and artists in selected other disciplines 1890 Turtle Town Hall Rd., Beloit, WI 53511 **Voice:** 608-362-1417 **E-mail:** blakeley@als.lib.wi.us **Contact:** Sharon Blakeley **Founded:** 1992 **Open:** Year-round **Admission:** Call for reservations **Cost:** $45 per night

POET AND FICTION writer Sharon Blakeley, sculptor David Lundahl and musician Rolf Lund rent out a guest house in the quiet southern Wisconsin countryside to artists, writers and musicians. Guests live in a 2-bedroom cottage with its own kitchen, bathroom and living room. There are readings, in which visiting writers may participate, at nearby New Light Studios. This is not an organized residency or communal experience. Rather it offers writers a way to find quiet and solitude in the Midwest, near other working artists.

School of the Arts at Rhinelander

For fiction and nonfiction writers, poets, screenwriters, playwrights University of Wisconsin-Madison, Continuing Education in the Arts, 715 Lowell Hall, 610 Langdon St., Madison, WI 53703 **Voice:** 608-263-7787 **Contact:** Harv Thompson, Dir. **Founded:** 1964 **Open:** 5 days in July **Admission:** Registration form ($30), manuscript for some workshops **Deadlines:** First come, first served; check on deadlines for manuscripts **Cost:** $130–$265 **Financial Aid:** Scholarship **Size-Attendees:** 384

SPONSORED BY THE University of Wisconsin-Madison Department of Continuing Education in the Arts, this week of workshops takes place in Wisconsin's north woods, providing families with an opportunity to combine a vacation with study. For beginning and semi-professional writers there are daily classes in poetry, playwriting, humor, journals, nonfiction, screenwriting, children's books and feature articles. Several classes have focused on reminiscences and writing one's own story. Some workshops require a manuscript for admission; most do not.

Writers are not restricted to the literary workshops. They may also register for theater and drama, photography, music, art and dance classes. Because the workshops take place during the tourist season and nearby campgrounds and resorts fill quickly; make your reservations early.

University of Wisconsin-Madison Annual Writers' Institute

For fiction and nonfiction writers, poets, screenwriters University campus — Communications Program, 610 Langdon St., Madison, WI 53703 **Voice:** 608-262-3447 **Fax:** 608-265-2329 **Contact:** Christine DeSmet, Dir. **Founded:** 1990 **Open:** 2 days in summer **Admission:** Registration form only **Deadlines:** Inquire for critique deadline **Cost:** $155 for 2 days; $85 for 1 day; $25–$75 for critique **Handicapped Access**

PRACTICAL ADVICE, with an emphasis on succeeding in the marketplace, characterizes the University of Wisconsin's Annual Writers' Institute. Participants may sign up for one or both days; one focuses on fiction, the other on nonfiction. Sessions feature guest speakers, such as a best-selling author, as well as a faculty of local teachers, authors and editors who provide concrete information on a range of subjects from "How to Make the Transition to Full-time Freelancing" to "How Authors Find Big Sales Through Regional Publishers."

Sessions on writing mysteries, science fiction, magazine articles, humor, novels, scripts, short stories and children's books take place concurrently, along with a few sessions on the process of writing, such as "Sustained Inspiration" and "'Sensory Magic' lab: jump-starting your imagination." Writers may send in manuscripts ahead of time for critiques by the faculty.

The Continuing Studies Division at the University of Wisconsin-Madison also offers writing workshops throughout the year, led by many of the same instructors. The Institute staff of writers will also continue to answer questions and consult with participants months after the event at no extra cost.

🏠 Wisconsin Academic Programs

University of Wisconsin-Milwaukee, Creative Writing Program, English Dept., P.O. Box 413, Milwaukee, WI 53201; 414-229-5913; MA and PhD English (creative writing concentration)

Wyoming

Snake River Institute

📝 🔄 *For fiction and nonfiction writers, poets, and artists in selected other disciplines* Jackson Hole — P.O. Box 128, Wilson, WY 83014 **Voice:** 307-733-2214 **Fax:** 307-739-1710 **E-mail:** snakeriverinst@ wyoming.com **Contact:** Samantha Strawbridge, Adult Prog. Dir. **Founded:** 1988 **Open:** June–Sept. **Admission:** Registration form only **Cost:** $300–$600 **Financial Aid:** Work/Study **Size-Class:** 15

B RING THE FAMILY, hike in the Grand Tetons, explore Yellowstone National Park, and then take a weekend to concentrate on your writing. The Snake River Institute offers "learning adventures" throughout the summer, generally with a focus on the West. "Native Americans in Greater Yellowstone," "The Straw Bale House," "Cheyenne Frontier Day: 100 Years of Rodeo" and "Art or Tradition? Native American Craft" were among the 1996 programs.

For fiction and nonfiction writers, short story writer Pam Houston (*Cowboys Are My Weakness*) offered a weekend workshop called "The Nature of the Western Character." Award-winning poet Pattiann Rogers led the "Natural Poet" workshop, 3 afternoons of exercises aimed at learning them how to express in poetic form what you see, hear and feel as you watch the light change on an autumn day. Workshops vary from year to year, with the emphasis on the history and culture of the West remaining constant.

Ucross Foundation Residency Program

🏠 *For all writers, and artists in selected other disciplines* E of Yellowstone National Park, 27 mi. SE of Sheridan — 2836 U.S. Hwy. 14–16 East, Clearmont, WY 82835 **Voice:** 307-737-2291 **Founded:** 1983 **Open:** 2–8 weeks in Feb.–June and Aug.–Dec. **Admission:** Application, recent writing sample, project description, references **Deadlines:** Oct. 1 for Feb.–June, Mar. 1 for Aug.–Dec. **Cost:** Transportation **Size-Attendees:** 8 at a time

W HEN YOU SEE photographs of this rural spot in Wyoming, you will probably feel tugged to be there, out under those big skies and wild cloud formations. It's a classic western landscape—wide open spaces, incredible vistas, 22,000 acres of High Plains.

The Ucross Foundation has been restoring the Clear Fork headquarters of the Pratt and Ferris Cattle Company for a number of years, using its remodeled buildings for its Artists' Residency Program and educational activities. The residency program can serve 4 writers and 4 visual artists at one time. The writers live and work during the 2- to 8-week residency at the Kocur Writers' Retreat on the bank of Clear Creek or in the remodeled Clearmont Depot. Communal meals are served daily in the remodeled School House, where writers and visual artists meet and mingle.

There is a competitive selection process; manuscripts are judged by a rotating panel of professionals. The Foundation is committed to supporting "exceptional creative work."

🏠 Wyoming Academic Programs

University of Wyoming, English Dept., P.O. Box 3353, Laramie, WY 82071; 307-766-6452; MA English (creative writing concentration)

PART THREE

The Business of Writing

Financial Aid—The Inside Scoop

THERE ARE ENTIRE REFERENCE BOOKS on the important subject of grants and awards for writers, and we won't pretend to have distilled all their information here. Rather, we want to help you become a little more savvy about what to expect if you need financial aid to attend one of the programs listed in this book. Those programs described as offering financial aid are indexed as such.

Many writing programs are nonprofit, and many are in need of financial aid themselves. Writers who can pay full tariff or can make donations should do so. Applying for financial aid should be done only after a conscientious effort to earn the tuition and travel money yourself.

At *Residential Programs* (artists' colonies), expect anything from no financial aid at all (and high costs) to full financial support. Often this depends on the E word: endowment. Some offer aid analogous to collegiate "work/study." This may be meaningful work or slave labor (bussing tables or scrubbing pots). If you think this builds character or will someday turn up in a short story of yours, go for it.

Writers' Conferences are frequently inexpensive (this includes some of the best of them). Yet sometimes conferences are organizational extravaganzas, with gaudy and gilded rented facilities, overpaid celebrity keynote speakers, and pricey "materials" fees for a lot of photocopied handouts with not much more than common sense printed on them but all bound up in a neatly labeled three-ring binder as a sort of souvenir of the conference itself. Beware these excesses. Indeed, there may even be an inverse ratio here, with the simpler affairs providing more direct contact between teachers and students, offering the better value. If you do apply for financial aid at a conference, expect only partial help, and don't be surprised if the financial aid that's available is restricted to selected groups (regional, ethnic, gender) who are presumed to be in need.

Financial aid for *Writing Workshops* is less common largely because so many workshops are inexpensive or meet only for short periods of time. At the bigger institutions (such as a YMCA writing program), prices may have risen to the point where asking for financial aid is reasonable. Not many of these programs offer work/study dollars, though, and scholarship money is generally very limited for any particular workshop in a broader program.

The subject of financial aid for graduate students in *Academic Programs* in creative writing is arcane and deep enough for its own book. See the bibliography at the end of this section. Most universities have both federal money and private money to hand out to qualified students. Make a careful reading of the catalogue to see if there are scholarships provided specifically for any ethnic, geographical or gender group to which you swear allegiance. If the catalogue is unclear, request an annotated list of all scholarships offered, and if the university is within easy reach, go there for an exploratory talk with a financial aid officer. Leave no stone unturned.

Are *loans* worth the risk? First, be aware that loans are generally not available for *Workshops* or *Conferences,* and only rarely for *Artists' Colonies* (where monthly charges can outstrip what you were paying to live at home in the city). By contrast, few people get through college or graduate school these days without taking on some debt for tuition. The theory is that the loan is an investment in your own future. If you won't bet on your own horse, why should anyone else? That's the rationalization; then there are the feelings. Some people simply hate to carry any debt, or hate the banks for charging usurious interest (though federally insured student loans have lower rates). Before you conclude that a loan is the right choice for you, take stock not only of your dollar resources but of your attitude toward borrowing in general. Recent graduates of medical school at least have a chance of earning back the investment they made to get their certificate. But people with an MFA in Creative Writing may be climbing a steeper slope to get out of debt. If the loan you are considering is substantial, be sure to take a good look at your overall financial needs now and expected in the years just after finishing the degree. Put the loan in context (mortgage, car payments, health insurance, kids, etc.) to see its relative value. If you believe you can handle it and really want that degree, by all means step up to the plate and swing away.

It's a true scandal that paying back student loans has become, in the words of Shakespeare's moody student, Hamlet, "a custom more honored in the breach than in the observance." No matter how unfair you may think the cold, cruel world out there may be to you and to your fellow writers, not paying back your federally or state insured loan(s) is hardly good citizenship, and what does it say to the even younger writers coming along behind you? Under the Clinton administration, new legislation has empowered the government to aggressively prosecute student loan deadbeats. We say, Here, Here! About time!

Finally, we recommend that you keep your day job, to borrow a phrase from the theater world. The best financial aid you can give to your writing habit is a paycheck. We dismiss the argument that a writing life and a paid working life are incompatible. Consider the precedents. T. S. Eliot worked in a bank. Wallace Stevens was an insurance executive. Ernest Hemingway, a reporter. William Carlos Williams, a medical doctor. Okay, you get one point for countering with, "Yes but they all had wives at home folding laundry and cooking dinner." Still, the job creates benefits that go beyond the immediate value of the paycheck. It gets you up and moving in the morning into a structured day. It takes you out into the world and out of yourself. It makes you appreciate (and put to better use) the time you do assign to your writing. Remember the old saying: "If you have all morning to write a letter, it will take you until eleven o'clock to find a pencil."

In sum, we'd say the best financial aid plan for a determined writer is to assume nothing, be open to anything, and learn to negotiate for a whopping good advance on your first novel!

See the Bibliography for more help, under *Financial Aid for Writers.*

Setting Up Shop

NLESS YOUR WRITING is entirely private or totally a hobby, you are, like it or not, in business. Part time or full time, making big bucks or pennies, there are business, legal and tax consequences of your writing habit. Here are some of the salient issues. See also the bibliography at the end of this section for books about managing your business affairs as a writer.

Marketing Your Skills
Self-Promotion or Working with an Agent

We believe that most imaginative, organized and determined writers can sell their own work. Nonetheless, there is a perennial writer's question: Should I get an agent? In our numerous years in the publishing business, we've heard scores of writers ask this question without having considered the necessarily preceding one: Why would an agent want to represent my work? Let's do some arithmetic.

You have written a short story and believe it is dynamite. You have heard that *The New Yorker* pays a dollar a word. At 3,800 words that amounts to more than pocket change, if the magazine buys it. But *The New Yorker* is probably the top of the line unless you score an even bigger hit with *Playboy* or *Redbook,* and of course what's suitable for one magazine isn't suitable for another. Still, even at $3,800, what's in it for your agent? Fifteen percent ($570) isn't pocket change either, and you tell him or her, that your file cabinet is full of other equally dynamite stories. Why, if this one sells, then the next one, and so on, we'll be raking in the dough.

But hold on there, pardner. What does it take in terms of labor and overhead to sell your story? If the agent is lucky and well connected (already known and respected at the magazine), one letter or phone call and a manuscript submission may do it. Much more likely is a protracted ordeal in which neither *The New Yorker* nor any other top-rank magazine says yes, and the weeks and months go by as the agent's inbox fills with rejection slips. Meanwhile the meter is running. Costs are mounting, and even if the story does sell, it will bring in at best the $570 you and the agent hoped for in commission. And that payment may not come until publication date, which could be many months after the acceptance.

Is this any way to run a battleship? Of course not. And so most agents turn down the short story writers and poets. Some will take on a few novelists. But more of them want nonfiction writers with "big" books on topics of contemporary interest, or they want fiction, novels that may have a chance to cross over to film or television. Fifteen percent of $35,000 ($5,250) or $350,000 ($52,500) will at least buy a cruise or a new Mercedes. The moral: Don't waste your time asking agents to do for you what you couldn't afford to do for other writers if you were an agent yourself.

An agent can sometimes provide good advice about developing your manuscript for commercial purposes. The better agents know what editors are looking for currently. Do not sign on with an agent unless you have had extensive conversations with him or her that convince you that the level of sensitivity to the literary qualities of your manuscript is high. Agents who are too busy to read or who just don't like good literature are not what you're looking for if you are a serious writer. If, on the other hand, you are cranking out potboiler westerns or mysteries, according to a formula an editor told you is a short route to success, then your agent's literary sensitivity rating is a moot point. Only the agent's Rolodex matters to you, and if the phone list has the right contacts on it, forge ahead.

Some literary agencies charge a "reading fee" just to look at your manuscript. Squadrons of underemployed graduate students at the University of East Kookamunga make their living writing reports on manuscripts they read about as carefully as one reads billboards on the highway. This is the factory model brought to bear on your product. The conveyor belt keeps moving, each unit is stamped from the same mold, and quantity is the name of the game. Form letters are waiting for you on the reader's word processor: *Dear Author, It has been a pleasure reading your work. While your manuscript has certain attractive aspects, overall we find that it needs more work, especially insofar as. ... Though we are unable to represent your work at this time, it would be our pleasure to read more of your writing at a future date. Please do contact us again. Sincerely...* We advise that you avoid such agencies unless there's a compelling reason to overlook this form of writer exploitation.

Selling your work by yourself is not easy either, and you may want to consider a middle path between agent and no agent. Sometimes, for a fee less than the fifteen percent the manuscript might earn if a sale goes through, an agent will act as consultant or advisor, reading your work, commenting, suggesting publishers to contact, and then stepping out of the way. If you expect to be sending material to a selected set of editors time and again (because you write for a niche market), it may be worthwhile to buy an agent's or editorial consultant's services to help you set up your own Rolodex and network of contacts. Former editors for the larger publishing houses can sometimes provide this service.

The How-To Bit

Sending your work out into the marketplace is not rocket science.

Buy a lot of envelopes and stamps.

Put a simple query letter and brief resume (with writing accomplishments and training clearly listed) on your computer. Write a one-paragraph description of the work you want to sell, and test that description with a disinterested friend or two. Beware making the claim that no one has ever told a story like this before. Your letter will take a short detour to the circular file beside the editor's desk.

The harder part is deciding whom to query. The days of querying one editor at a time are over. But sending a query about your novel to every publisher in the galaxy that says it does fiction is a waste of everyone's time. Invest your time in building a carefully considered list of appropriately chosen editors (not houses, but specific editors).

How? First, go to the bookstore and the library. Make a list of specific titles that are precisely in the category of your book. This may take several hours. You may have to read widely for a few months before you actually know which publishers are doing your kind of thing.

Second, list of titles in hand, go back to the library, this time to the reference desk, and ask for *Literary Marketplace* (the book is referred to as "LMP") and/or *Writer's Market* (both of these are annuals). In *LMP* find the section that categorizes publishers by the types of books they produce. Explore carefully. "Fiction" is too broad a category. Within "fiction" there is "adult fiction," "juvenile fiction," and probably other segments as well. Learn the publishers' lingo for the niche where your book belongs. If you're stumped, ask your local bookseller for help. Booksellers know the jargon; they use it to build their plans for inventory and marketing.

Keep it clear in your own mind that the term "editor" covers a lot of ground. *Copy editors* clean up and repair (and rescue) manuscripts. They do not buy, acquire or sponsor new books for the house. What you want is an *acquisitions* or *sponsoring* editor whose specific territory includes your type of work.

Third, with a narrowed, winnowed, focused list of publishers, look up those houses in *LMP* and note the names of editors whose job titles suggest they are the decision makers in your specific category. There's no point in sending your children's book manuscript to an adult science editor just because he or she has the title "editor." If the publisher's listing in *LMP* does not identify editors specifically enough for you to be sure you've found the right one, call the publisher, ask for the editorial director or his or her assistant, and ask for the correct name and title.

Some houses have all submissions, especially unsolicited manuscripts from authors (as opposed to agents), pass through an *editorial assistant's* or *managing editor's* hands, working as a kind of manuscript traffic cop. These houses may have a policy of protecting their acquisitions editors from distracting mail and phone calls from eager-beaver authors who, most of the time, are calling the wrong house for the wrong reason. Don't be put off if a house you think is right for your work has this policy. Work with it and respect it.

Send a clean photocopy of your manuscript, with dark, legible print, double-spaced and carefully spell-checked. Provide an annotated outline. Enclose a self-addressed stamped envelope (SASE).

Let the publisher know that you are also submitting the work elsewhere. Give the editor four weeks or thereabouts to read your work. Imagine the Leaning Tower of Pisa: this is the stack of unread manuscripts on the editor's desk—in a good week. Lava flowing off Vesuvius is more like it in a bad week. Then follow up with a phone call. If time drags on and there's no reply, ask for the manuscript to be returned. Keep a notebook and a file system so you'll know how each submission was treated.

Publishers and Editors

Literary Marketplace, R. R. Bowker, annual
Writer's Market: Where & How to Sell What You Write. Mark Garvey, ed.
Writer's Digest Books, annual.

Tools of the Trade

Computers

If you prefer paper and pen to write your drafts, or a manual typewriter, we are sympathetic. The quiet slide of the nib across the page, or even the clatter of mechanical keys, can be music to a writer's ears. Nonetheless, sooner or later, almost every writer these days, even poets, will need to produce an electronic manuscript, and that means making friends with a computer.

It's a rapidly changing and improving technology, and whatever advice on specific computer systems we might give in 1997 would be old hat by 1998. Find a computer salesperson, trainer or consultant who seems honest and who listens to your description of your needs. Beware of underbuying or overbuying. If manuscript work is your primary emphasis, you don't need a system comparable to the Pentagon's. Think backward from the results you want. Cleanly and rapidly printed copy (from a DeskJet or laser printer, probably; dot-matrix printers are on the way out). Lots of memory for storage of long files as your magnum opus grows, and then you write another one, and another. An easy-on-the-eyes monitor. If you must do research in the library or interviews in the field, probably you want a laptop computer (to which you can add a more comfortable keyboard and monitor for use at home).

Computers are either "PC" (for IBM-Personal Computer, or a clone of same), using an operating system called Windows; or they are "Mac" (for Macintosh, from Apple Computers; no clones here). Buy what pleases you. Most publishers can read files from either a PC or a Mac.

As for word-processing software, most publishers can read text files written in Microsoft Word or WordPerfect. Less popular or obscure programs lead to confusion later on.

If you're new to the game, take a basic course in word processing, and above all learn how to:

Build a system of directories and files (with appropriate names), the computer equivalent of setting up organized file cabinets and manila folders. As a project moves forward in an essentially paperless office, you must know how to store and recover correspondence, various drafts of manuscript, research notes, etc.

Save, back up and archive everything you write.

Spell-check.

Finally, do yourself and your publishers a favor: Get a system with a built-in modem and fax/modem software, and subscribe to an e-mail service (America Online and CompuServe are two popular starting points). The money you'll save on postage and the speed you'll pick up by transmitting memos and files (whole chapters, entire books) by e-mail and the Internet will be appreciated all around.

Electronic Submissions

Some publishers (more magazines than books) want authors to submit queries, samples and finished work electronically rather than on paper. They are in the minority as of 1997, and we suspect they will remain there, but if you set up a computer system as discussed above, you'll be ready should the need arise. Query the publisher for specific instructions.

Manuscripts Editors Will Love

Be kind to your editor's eyes. Double-space, leave 1.5-inch margins left and right, 1-inch top and bottom. Use 12-point type. No fancy fonts. Courier is good if you like a serif face; Arial is fine if you prefer a sans serif font. Number pages consecutively within chapters. Date each version of your manuscript (date on each page in a running head with the page number and an abbreviated chapter name). A fresh printout is the best thing to submit, but a clean, dark photocopy is okay, too, with initial queries.

About Word Count

The better word-processing programs will count words, characters, lines, paragraphs and pages for you (but not the hours you invested in the writing!). If the editor asks for 2,500 words, be sure that's what you supply. If you are sending more or fewer words, explain why. If you have a sense of how long your novel will be when done by extrapolating from the initial chapters, let the editor know in your query letter.

Photographs and Artwork

Remember how Mom used to label every piece of clothing before you went to camp? Follow her lead. Label and number everything.

Never submit your only copy of anything. Make duplicates or color photocopies and submit them, letting your editor know that you have the originals, which may be slightly better. Use professional-quality slide protector sheets or substantial-weight envelopes for photographs. Be prepared for damages in the mail or at the publishing house, or for total loss. If the photos and slides are linked to your manuscript, be sure that the manuscript shows clearly where each image goes. Most word-processing programs allow you to insert a blank box in which you can then indicate a picture number.

Shipping and Postage

The availability of overnight mail does not mean you have to use it. Somehow the world kept turning for several billion years before FedEx came along. Priority Mail at the post office, which as of late 1996 was $3.00 for up to 2 pounds and gets a bright "Priority" sticker on it, is usually sufficient even when time is important. "Priority" moves as fast as or faster than first class, and in most areas of the country that amounts to overnight or second-day delivery. There are exceptions, and it's not guaranteed. Nor can you track a Priority Mail package. Still, it's the best deal if guaranteed overnight delivery is not essential. UPS is next cheapest. FedEx, with the best services, is more expensive.

If you will be doing a lot of overnight mail, or if you need to track your packages' progress, set up a FedEx account (UPS is cheaper but your volume must be higher to qualify for convenient services), and ask for the "FedEx Ship" software for your computer (no charge): it fills out shipping labels for you and provides easy tracking via your modem.

Insurance

Insurance is usually not necessary for simple manuscript submissions. If illustrations are included, you may want to insure the contents, but dupes of slides are cheap and insurance is not. Invent a typical package and check out the costs, insured and uninsured (consider loss and the cost of replacement). The basic overnight and second-day services from FedEx and UPS include minimal insurance, which is usually sufficient. The post office's Express Mail does, too.

Cutting the Deal

Copyright

You establish copyright (legal ownership of your written work or photographs or artwork) by declaring it. On the manuscript, photograph or illustration, print the copyright symbol ©, the year, and your name. To make it really official, send a copy to yourself by certified mail. Do this before you send out your first submission. You do not have to send a copy to the Library of Congress or anywhere else to give your copyright legal standing.

Then, when you sell your work to a publisher, you assign the copyright to the company if that's part of the deal. Should it be is the question. It's possible to have your cake and eat it, too. If the publisher wants to hold the copyright (often there's a policy to this effect for all the publisher's titles or all the books in a series), you can retain appropriate control by having the contract say that the publisher may not reassign the copyright to anyone without your permission. On multiple-author books it may be simpler to let the publisher hold the copyright (and do the paperwork) as long as you retain some control over reassignment.

We discuss types of writer-publisher contracts below. Copyright is handled differently depending on the type of contract. On royalty-based contracts, authors may or may not hold copyright; it's usually negotiable. On work-for-hire projects, the author rarely holds the copyright. Whatever type of contract you have, be sure it clarifies whether or how soon as author you may sell a similar work (spun off from this one) in another market. And be sure you honor this part of the agreement, keeping your publisher informed about any subsequent sales of similar work you want to make on your own.

Writers' Contracts

We all know how easy it is to fall in love and how hard it is to get divorced. A good written contract or agreement for your writing project should cover both the romance (why you're doing it, what each party expects to get out of it) and what happens if things turn sour (the "termination" clause).

Don't be naive. Oral agreements and handshakes are a necessary part of any deal, but what really binds publisher and writer together is the written agreement or contract. At least get a letter detailing what's expected, when it's due, in what format, and what the pay will be and when it will arrive, assuming you do your job. Better yet, get a real contract.

These come in essentially two forms.

Work-for-Hire and Royalty-Based Contracts

One is *work for hire,* under which the writer is paid a fee (and sometimes expenses) to produce the work but has no copyright ownership in it and does not (usually) share in revenue beyond the initial fee.

The other is a *royalty-based contract,* under which the publisher and author share the risk of unpredictable revenue. The publisher makes an "advance against anticipated royalties" to get the project started (on most books the advance is paid out in thirds—on signing, halfway through, and on publication). Then, after the book's actual sales have "earned out" or recovered the advance, additional royalties accrue and are paid twice yearly.

Which type of contract is better? No simple answer applies. There are too many variables. Several of the Writers' Conferences described in this book have business workshops or seminars within them, and contracts are often one of the topics. These are well worth attending if you're new to the game.

Typically, when the publisher initiates the project (idea, outline, plan, resources), a work-for-hire contract is offered, and there's little to negotiate. In the magazine world, whether the publisher or the author initiates the article, the deal is almost always work for hire, a simple fee. If the author initiates a book and shops it around to various publishers, he or she is in effect conducting an auction, and the highest bidder wins. But bear in mind that "highest bidder" does not necessarily mean "biggest advance against royalties." The royalty rate, the escalator clauses making the royalty increase as sales grow, and numerous other factors can sweeten or sour a deal. Among those other factors are what publishers call "rights" or "subsidiary rights" (subsidiary to the main work).

Rights

Your book has been accepted for publication. Hooray! But before it comes out as a book, a chapter is sold to a magazine. Who gets the money? After the book is out, another magazine wants an excerpt. How is the income shared between the publisher (who solicited this sale) and author (who holds the copyright)? You wrote an auto repair manual and woke up one day to find that the publisher has sold the rights to electronic publication of your work to a CD-ROM producer. Who gets what in this deal? It goes on, and on. A good contract anticipates everything that might someday happen to your original publication.

The revenue splits can be fifty-fifty with the publisher or any other division. Read the fine print, discuss precedents and industry standards with colleagues at writers' conferences, and do not assume that the first draft of the contract is what you have to accept.

Should you see a lawyer? It's expensive, and few lawyers know publishing contracts specifically. In larger cities you may be able to find a publishing lawyer, sometimes through a literary agency. The first time out, the investment may be worthwhile, but if you or your publisher use the same contract repeatedly, you can review it yourself. As circumstances change (different methods of payment or more complex obligations for secondary authors or illustrations), you can consult your attorney on these details.

The Price Tag on Your Work

HOW MUCH IS YOUR WORK WORTH? Should you estimate its value on the basis of the amount of time invested in writing it, and if so, what hourly rate makes sense? Should you surrender to your sense of the absurd and accept whatever the market tells you your work is worth? Is there any way to be reasonable about all this? You guessed it: the answer is yes, and no.

Publishers and authors everywhere work from precedents, the "going rate." Nobody claims this is reasonable, but what else is there to do? There is no official pay scale for freelance writers or book authors, although the National Writers' Union offers guidelines. Inside the film or TV industry, where writers are organized in a union that bargains collectively for them, yes, there are pay scales.

But for most writers each project raises the same old question: how much is my work worth, and how can I negotiate for the highest payment? First, study the precedents. Use *Writer's Market* as a good starting point. Attend a conference or two where the emphasis is on the business side of publishing, and don't be shy about asking for real numbers. Second, play poker. Whoever bids first in the negotiation is at a disadvantage. The next guy is bound to make a move to his advantage based on the first bid ("Sorry, you're too high, or too low"). Rehearse with another successful writer. Set some limits ("I'll do it for no less than $X"), and stick to them.

Working for unreasonable pay helps no one, and usually a writer will do a shoddy job under these circumstances, and the publisher will complain, and the ripple effect through the business is bad news. An agent can be very helpful here, but as noted above few agents will help writers sell anything that nets the agent just a few hundred dollars. Learn to be your own agent.

As *Writer's Market* helpfully points out, a simple formula will keep you sober and may help you to avoid underselling your ideas and skills.

Set a gross income target. Calculate the number of billable hours per year for which you expect payment. Divide the gross income by the billable hours to get an hourly base rate. Add 33 percent to the base rate for fringe benefits and taxes you must pay for yourself as a self-employed writer. Assume about $5,000 for overhead costs (office rent, computer equipment, postage and phone, etc.). Divide the overhead by the billable hours and add that to the base rate. Add 10 percent profit to the base rate. The result is what you need to be paid per hour to hit the gross income target. Discuss your arithmetic with colleagues. If the precedents in your category of writing support your figures, don't be shy about asking for this kind of pay. You'll be well armed to discuss it with an employer if you know the market and can explain your own arithmetic.

Starting a Writing Business

Sole Proprietorship

It may be tempting to think of your freelance writing enterprise as "Joe's Intergalactic Writing Service," capable of and ready for any assignment. In fact, in terms of the legal form your writing business might take, the simpler the better. Almost all writers operate as "sole proprietors," meaning that they are the sole owners of their business and of their work (until each piece of work is sold or licensed to a publisher).

While the status of sole proprietorship has no tax advantages and offers no protection from business losses, it does have one advantage: it costs almost nothing to start. Go the bank and open a checking account in your business name. Have some business cards and letterhead printed. Hang out your shingle. Presto, you are a sole proprietor, disguised as a mild-mannered writer.

Incorporation

Why would a writer incorporate? Not many need to. But if, for example, you are the head writer on a team that's producing a series of textbooks for a publisher, and if you in turn will be hiring several other writers or designers or editors and paying them a salary, and if, perhaps, there are liability issues in the work (maybe it's a series of medical textbooks or aircraft engine maintenance manuals or profiles of businesses with dubious environmental protection records)—then, maybe, you might want some extra protection. That's what incorporation can bring: protection against certain losses and liabilities. Incorporation also brings fees and additional taxes and more complex bookkeeping and accounting.

What to do? Don't guess at it. See your lawyer and accountant, and look for a writers' conference featuring seminars on legal issues.

Taxes

If there is a more tedious subject, we don't know it. However, if you're serious about a writing career or if you think your freelance supplemental income may rise to the point where you can't avoid reporting it to

Uncle Sam, then think of the costs of setting up a bookkeeping system and of laying a plan for minimizing your taxes as a basic business expense. Find a bookkeeper who is savvy about self-employment; learn to use a software program like Quicken (from Intuit) to put your checkbook register on the computer; and save/record those receipts as only a tax-hating maniac would. Every penny counts at the end of the year. Find also an accountant who knows the ropes concerning deductions allowable for writers who have home offices, unreimbursed travel and research expenses, equipment investments that can be amortized, etc. An accountant with only general experience, rather than with at least some taste of the publishing world, may miss tax-deduction opportunities for you. It's worth paying these number-crunching folks a few hundred bucks to set you up with easy-to-follow systems that will repeat year after year. If you work with appropriate professionals (whose fees are themselves deductible business expenses), you'll most likely cut your tax bill more effectively than if you muddle through on your own.

Several writers' guides we have seen recommend that you call the IRS to request this booklet or that. Our experience with the IRS is that it's hard to get anyone to answer the phone and harder still to get help. Start with your accountant.

Investing for Your Future

As a full-time nonsalaried writer, in no matter what genre, you'll need a plan for the long term just as would any salaried employee in a corporation. Health insurance is one issue. A retirement-plan is another. Systematic savings (for a rainy day or an emergency) should be a third.

Certain writers' organizations, such as the National Writers' Union (see Part Two, "Associations and Organizations"), provide access to what they consider affordable health insurance. There is strength in numbers, and you may be able to get a better deal through an organization than on your own. In 1996 Congress passed health insurance reform legislation permitting individuals to set up tax-free health-care savings accounts, potentially a good idea for self-employed people. Research carefully.

The IRS allows various retirement-plan payments (into specific accounts such as IRAs, SEP-IRAs, and Keogh plans) for nonsalaried workers, providing tax deductions in the year when the contributions are made. See your accountant to discuss which plan is best for you.

For young people the news is good: even a small monthly investment will accumulate nicely by the time you hit 65 or so. Those who are more advanced in age must invest more aggressively, and an investment adviser is likely to be a key player on your professional services team. For nonsalaried writers the key in all of these decisions is discipline. From every check received, you'll have to set aside tax dollars (for estimated quarterly payments), and you should set aside savings/investment dollars, too. If you establish a plan, set up the accounts, keep the paperwork simple, and adhere to the discipline, the system will flourish.

Now all you have to do is write and get published!

Bibliography

Financial Aid for Writers—Contests, Grants, Awards

At bookstores or via mail order:

Awards for Writers, P.O. Box 4437, Ithaca, NY 14851.

AWP Chronicle. See Associated Writing Programs listing under *Associations.*

Grants and Awards Available to American Writers, 19th ed. 1996–97, PEN American Center, 568 Broadway, New York, NY 10012; 212-334-1660.

Poets & Writers Magazine. See Poets & Writers listing under *Associations.*

At libraries:

Annual Register of Grant Support, National Register Publishing Co., 3004 Glenview Rd., Wilmette, IL 60091.

Foundations and Grants to Individuals, Foundation Center, 79 Fifth Ave., New York, NY 10003.

The Business of Writing

ASJA Handbook: A Writer's Guide to Ethical and Economic Issues, American Society of Journalists and Authors, 1501 Broadway, Suite 302, New York, NY 10036; 212-997-0947.

Business and Legal Forms for Authors and Self-Publishers, by Tad Crawford, Allworth Press, 1990. Available from Volunteer Lawyers for the Arts, 1 East 53rd St., 6th Floor, New York, NY 10022; 212-319-2787.

Directory of Literary Magazines, Council of Literary Magazines & Presses, 154 Christopher St., New York, NY 10014; 212-741-9110.

From Printout to Published, by Michael Seidman, Carroll & Graf, 1992.

International Directory of Little Magazines and Small Presses, Dustbooks, P.O. Box 100, Paradise, CA 95969; 800-477-6110. (Also from Dustbooks: *Directory of Poetry Publishers, Directory of Small Magazine Editors,* and *The Small Press Information Library, 1996–97.*)

Into Print: Guides to the Writing Life, Poets & Writers, Inc., 72 Spring St., New York, NY 10012; 212-226-3586.

LMP (Literary Marketplace), R.R. Bowker, 121 Chanlon Rd., New Providence, NJ 07974; 800-521-8110.

The NWU Guide to Freelance Rates and Standard Practice, National Writers Union, 113 University Place, 6th floor, New York, NY 10003; 212-254-0279.

The Writer's Legal Companion, by Brad Bunnin and Peter Beren, Addison-Wesley, 1993. Available in bookstores or by mail from Volunteer Lawyers for the Arts, 1 East 53rd St., 6th floor, New York, NY 10022; 212-319-2787.

Writers' Market, Writer's Digest Books, 1507 Dana Ave., Cincinnati, OH 45207; 800-289-0963. (Also from Writer's Digest Books: *Novel & Short Story Writer's Market* and *Poet's Market.*)

On copyright:

Queries to the U.S. Copyright Office in Washington, DC: 202-707-3000 for questions; 202-707-9100 for forms.

A Writer's Guide to Copyright, Poets & Writers, Inc., 72 Spring St., New York, NY 10012; 212-226-3586.

The Copyright Handbook: How to Protect and Use Written Works, by Stephen Fishman, Nolo Press, 1994.

Every Writer's Guide to Copyright & Publishing Law, by Ellen Kozak, Henry Holt, 1990.

On literary agents:

Guide to Literary Agents, Writer's Digest Books, 1507 Dana Ave., Cincinnati, OH 45207; 800-289-0963.

Literary Agents: A Writer's Guide, by Adam Begley, Penguin Books, 1993.

Literary Agents of North America, Author Aid Associates, 340 East 52 St., New York, NY 10022; 212-758-4213.

General Resources

Artists and Writers Colonies: Retreats, Residencies, and Respites for the Creative Mind, by Gail Hellund Bowler, Blue Heron Publishing, 24450 Northwest Hansen Rd., Hillsboro, OR 97124; 503-621-3911.

The AWP Official Guide to Writing Programs, 7th ed. 1994–1995, Associated Writing Programs, George Mason University, Tallwood House, Fairfax, VA 22030; 703-993-4301.

The Complete Guide to Writers' Conferences and Workshops, by William Noble, Paul S. Eriksson, P.O. Box 62, Forest Dale, VT 05745.

Dramatists Sourcebook 1996–97, Theatre Communications Group, 335 Lexington Ave., New York, NY 10017.

Go Wild! focus Report #1: Artist-in-Residence Programs in the National Parks, Lucky Dog Multi•Media, Studio #11, P.O. Box 65552, St. Paul, MN 55165; 800-377-6650.

The Guide to Writers Conferences, ShawGuides, Inc., 625 Biltmore Way, Suite 1406, Coral Gables, FL 33134; 800-247-6553.

Working Writers, Poets & Writers, Inc., 72 Spring St., New York, NY 10012; 212-226-3586.

Writers Conferences: An Annual Guide to Literary Conferences, Poets & Writers, Inc., 72 Spring St., New York, NY 10012; 212-226-3586.

We are indebted to our sources for this list. We consulted friendly librarians and booksellers, Poets & Writers, *Writer's Market,* Volunteer Lawyers for the Arts, and a variety of individuals and organizations.

Index

General Index

Writing Programs

⌂ Residential Programs

 **Workshops**

Conferences

🏠 Academic Programs

Financial Aid

About the Authors

DAVID EMBLIDGE CUT HIS TEETH as an editor in New York City at Cambridge University Press and at Continuum. Now he is a book packager specializing in reference and outdoor recreation books. In 1996 he edited and packaged *The Appalachian Trail Reader* (Oxford University Press); previously Emblidge edited *"My Day"—Eleanor Roosevelt's Acclaimed Columns* (Pharos Books). His writing has appeared in *The New Republic, Saturday Review, MD,* the *Boston Globe,* the *New York Times* and other publications. Emblidge is a former college literature and writing professor (University of Minnesota, Simon's Rock of Bard College and University of Toulouse). Barbara Zheutlin has worked as a freelance writer, publicist, filmmaker, story editor, fund raiser and psychotherapist. She co-authored *Creative Differences: Profiles of Hollywood Dissidents* (South End Press). Both authors work in Great Barrington, Massachusetts.

About Getting Your Act Together™

The Watson-Guptill Resource Guides to:
• Workshops • Conferences • Artists' Colonies • Academic Programs

WITH ATTENDANCE SOARING at workshops, seminars, conferences and other opportunities for continuing education, this particularly timely series presents dependable, candid resource guides tailored to meet the needs of adult artists in several specific categories.

Taking the frustration and guesswork out of the process of finding the right venue for further training, each guide offers a comprehensive and critical review of arts programs, organized alphabetically by state, covering workshops, conferences, artists' colonies and academic programs.

Each program entry provides such key information as contact name and address (plus phone and fax numbers, e-mail and Web site addresses), application requirements, financial aid opportunities, and size of program. The books also cover general information on relevant associations, organizations and unions, as well as the business side of each discipline.